CW00402722

Close-Ups

Conversations with
Our TV Favorites

by Eddie Lucas

Close-Ups: Conversations with our TV Favorites
© 2007 Eddie Lucas. All Rights Reserved.

All illustrations are copyright of their respective owners, and are also reproduced here in the spirit of publicity. Whilst we have made every effort to acknowledge specific credits whenever possible, we apologize for any omissions, and will undertake every effort to make any appropriate changes in future editions of this book if necessary.

No part of this book may be reproduced in any form or by any means, electronic, mechanical, digital, photocopying or recording, except for the inclusion in a review, without permission in writing from the publisher.

Published in the USA by:
BearManor Media
P O Box 71426
Albany, Georgia 31708
www.bearmanormedia.com

ISBN 1-59393-120-4

Printed in the United States of America.

Book design by Darlene Swanson of Van-garde Imagery, Inc.
Cover design by Dan Swanson of Van-garde Imagery, Inc.

Contents

Dedication & Thanks

This book is dedicated to the memory of my father, William Edgar Lucas (1928-1995), and to my mother, Dorothy Curry Lucas (my Ward and June Cleaver), for their years of unconditional love and guidance. And to my sister, Mary Kay Kahler, for not caring if I controlled the TV channels all those years ago when we were growing up in Altoona.

Thank you to Wesley Hyatt, for his inspiration and ideas in getting this project to come to fruition. A very special thanks to Ken Fagan for his invaluable ideas, input, and friendship. And to Donna Campbell and April Johnson (my work wives) and Donna Brashier for their encouragement and support throughout this project.

Special thanks to Laurie Jacobsen of Living Legends, Inc. for her gracious assistance in locating many of the subjects that were interviewed for this book. She opened many doors and I am most appreciative.

This book could not have been, if not for the kindness of those interviewed. I will always be grateful for the time and stories they shared with me. My heartfelt thanks to: Kaye Ballard, Barbara Billingsley Mortensen, Lynn Borden, Peter Breck, Elinor Donahue, Tony Dow, Ray Fulmer, Alice Ghostley, Marla Gibbs, Dwayne Hickman, Peter Lupus, Haywood Nelson, Jon Provost, Stan Livingston, Keith Thibodeaux, Ernest Thomas, and Jon Walmsley. Special kudos to Diane Breck, Lauren Dow, Joan Roberts, and Laurie Jacobson for scheduling a convenient time for me to talk with their TV husbands.

And last, but not least, my biggest thanks to Ben Ohmart, of BearManor Media, who took a chance on an unpublished author and gave him the chance to fulfill one of his lifelong dreams.

Eddie Lucas
November 2006

(The photographs used in this book are from the author's private collection or were kindly supplied by the celebrities themselves.)

Introduction

Ever since television entered our lives it has enthralled and entertained us. It has taken us places we would have never been able to visit. It has transported us into space, sent us back in time, and propelled us into the future.

We welcomed its characters into our living rooms with open arms. We convulsed with laughter at the riotous antics of the Ricardos and the Mertzes. We imagined the fun of being stranded with the gang on *Gilligan's Island*, and Wally and the Beaver became our pals when there was no one to play with after school. These fictional, yet *real* people became part of our families and our memories.

I wanted to know how these old friends were doing, who they kept in touch with, and what life was like on the set. I wanted to go beyond what I was reading in articles and books to find the answers to questions that casual, as well as die-hard fans wanted to ask. And, most importantly, I wanted to hear what they had to say in their own words.

That's why I began *Close Ups*. I wanted the chance to reminisce with these old friends we grew up with. So I did. And our conversations exceeded my expectations.

Apart from the historical significance of their time on some of the most beloved shows on television, this book is also full of amusing anecdotes and fond remembrances. I hope you will enjoy, as I have, this entertaining glimpse into our TV favorites, as seen through the eyes of the people who were there, thus allowing us the privilege of being right there with them.

Alice Ghostley

Bewitched: Esmeralda 1969-72;
Designing Women: Bernice Clifton 1987-92

A lice Ghostley's distinctive voice and quirky mannerisms have made her one of the funniest character actresses the world of entertainment has ever known.

A Tony Award-winning actress for her role in the 1965 production of *The Sign in Sidney Brustein's Window*, Ghostley has also appeared in numerous films, including the role of Aunt Stephanie in the 1962 classic *To Kill a Mockingbird* with Gregory Peck.

Even with such distinguished accolades, she is perhaps best known for her roles on the small screen as nervous nanny Esmeralda on Elizabeth Montgomery's *Bewitched*, and later as the daffy but loveable Bernice Clifton on *Designing Women*.

During my initial request for an interview, Ghostley, now eighty, shared with me that at the time, she was not in the best of health. Feeling badly, I promptly apologized that I had approached her, albeit unknowingly, at such a rough time. But Alice being Alice, kindly insisted that we schedule a time, so she could answer my questions about two of her most famous TV roles. That makes this particular interview all the more special.

Alice, you've appeared in some wonderful movies, Broadway shows, and made countless television appearances. What does the majority of your fan mail mention?

Oh, definitely *Bewitched* and *Designing Women*.

Do you remember your first time on *Bewitched*?
Yes. I was playing a maid that couldn't do anything right. ["Maid to Order"]

Yes. Naomi Hogan, a maid that Darren hired to help out when Samantha was pregnant.
That's right, and I was a terrible maid! I burned the roast and broke the dishes. By the end of the show, they decided I would be a much better accountant, because I could add up the cost of everything I had broken so fast.

And Darrin ended up getting you a job at McMann and Tate.
(*Chuckles.*) That's right.

Could you tell me a little about Elizabeth Montgomery? What was she like?
She was just like you see her. She was so sweet. She really was. She was one of my favorites.

So she was a pleasure to work with.
Oh, she was wonderful. And so was her husband, at the time, William Asher. The whole cast was good.

Did you keep in touch with Elizabeth through the years?
Yes. My husband and I, and she and Bob Foxworth, after they got together, went out to dinner a lot. We'd go to dinner quite a bit. Elizabeth was very much into going out to restaurants. She liked that.

Her death came as quite a shock. Had you known she was ill, or were you surprised to hear that she had passed away?
I was totally surprised. I didn't know about it at all. I wasn't working with her then. She was doing those movies, and I didn't get to see much of her.

What do you remember about Dick York?
I only did one show with him, but I remember that he was kind of solemn. I suppose it was because he was in such pain with his back.

Ghostley, as nervous nanny Esmeralda, from Bewitched.

And Agnes Moorehead?

She was fine. (*And then a pause. She chuckles.*)

Why are you chuckling?

Oh, she and David White [Larry Tate] would get into *terrible* arguments. She was a fundamentalist. Her father was a Baptist minister, I think, and she and David were, of course, on opposite ends of the spectrum [on religion], so they would constantly argue. But it was fun to listen to them. (*She chuckles again.*)

Did they not get along?

Oh, no. They got along, except when they were discussing religion. They were friendly to each other. Everyone seemed to get along.

A 1960s publicity shot.

Since the producers of *Bewitched* were familiar with your work, did you have to audition for the role of Esmeralda, or did they write it with you in mind?
They must've written it with me in mind, because I didn't have to audition.

Well, that was a nice compliment on your work.
Yes.

What do you remember about the special effects on *Bewitched*? Let's say, if you were in a scene and someone "popped out," how did they do that?
I would have to freeze, and try to stay that way. It really depended. My character kept fading in and out, so when they wanted someone to disappear like that, they had to have the blue screen behind them, and you had to be dressed in blue. And you just faded into it. That was the hardest part. When we had to do certain things, they just turned the camera off.

That was one of my next questions. I wondered if they stopped the camera or kept it going, and then edited out the part when someone walked in or out of the scene.
They would stop the camera.

I'm sure it was a lot of work, but did you have fun on the set?
Yes, I did. It was a very friendly set. Very warm.

Did you keep any of your scripts from the show?
None of the scripts, but I kept everything else.

Oh, like what?
Oh, I have all the memorabilia, the write-ups, and the pictures. Things like that.

A lot of people remember the episode called "The Not So Leaning Tower of Pisa," where Esmeralda mistakenly straightens the Leaning Tower of Pisa.
Yes, that was my favorite.

Esmeralda was a popular character.
Oh, yes. People write and ask me all the time if I have any pictures as Esmeralda from the show. Unfortunately, I don't. As a matter of fact, I don't think I ever did! (*Laughs.*)

You were in an episode of *The Mothers-In-Law*, with Eve Arden and Kaye Ballard. You played the head nurse in the episode where Susie had the twins.
Oh, yes.

Kaye and Eve tried to get past you by dressing up like nuns and doctors, so they could see Susie. That was a funny episode.
(*Laughs.*) I had forgotten about that! That was a long time ago. [1969]

You did an episode of *The Golden Girls* ["Mother's Day"]
Yes. I played Stanley's mother.

The one where Dorothy and Stan came to borrow money.
Yes.

What was your experience like on that show?
I enjoyed that. It was fun to work with Bea [Arthur]. A lot of people didn't like working with her, but I did.

Why was that?
Well, she could be a little hard-headed. (*Chuckles.*)

(*Laughing.*) Oh, is she?
But we had a good time.

Designing Women was taped before a live audience with three cameras and *Bewitched* was filmed with no audience and one camera.
That's right.

*For Eddie —
with many
Thanks &
lots of love
from
Alice Ghostley*

DESIGNING
Women

ECCENTRIC - Alice Ghostley stars as Bernice Clifton in "Designing Women," a
Bloodworth/Thomason Mozark Production in association with Columbia Pictures Television,
airing Mondays on the CBS Television Network.

An autographed photo of "Bernice."

Do you have a preference?
Yes. I like the audience. You get immediate reactions from an audience.

How did you get the role of Bernice Clifton on *Designing Women*?
I didn't have to audition. They just called me.

The first show you did was a Thanksgiving episode ["Perky's Visit"] during the first season. Bernice comes to Thanksgiving dinner with Julia and Suzanne's mother, Perky [Louise Latham].
That's right. And she described me to the girls as having "an arterial flow problem above the neck."

Right! (*Laughing*) That line was a classic! Was your appearance originally supposed to be just a one time guest shot?
I think it might have been a one time thing.

But you went over so well!
Yes. And when I came on, the audience really applauded, and the producers were very surprised at that. I don't think the Thomasons even knew who I was.

(*Astonished*.) Seriously?
I really don't, because they were so surprised when I got the applause. They said, "You must have a lot of fans!" I said, "Yes, I do!"

You sure do!
Thankfully!

How was the feel of the set on that show? Did you feel comfortable on it?
Sometimes. I didn't feel comfortable all of the time, but most of the time I did. Sometimes I felt kind of like an outsider.

Why did you feel that way?
I think it was because I came in last. I wasn't one of the main characters, so I

felt kind of like an outsider. I never did feel as much at home there as I did on *Bewitched*. But I had more fun on *Designing Women*.

Were the producers nice to you?
Oh yes. They were very nice.

Did you ever get to give input on any of the storylines for your character?
Only in the way I read the lines. They didn't *ever* tell me how to read a line.

Did you work a five-day week on *Designing Women*?
Sometimes, if she [Linda Bloodworth Thomason] got the scripts ready in time. But sometimes we were up to the fourth day and hadn't really blocked it yet.

Wow!
She works under pressure.

Some people work better that way.
I think she does.

On what day would they do the taping?
It was always on a Friday.

Some shows do a dress rehearsal and tape that also. Was *Designing Women* taped twice?
No. I think we only did it once. I really don't remember doing it twice.

Were cue cards ever used on the show?
Oh, no.

The reason I asked was because whenever Julia [Dixie Carter] got fired up about something, she would have all those long speeches to give. So she had to memorize all that dialogue?
Oh, yes. We *never* had cue cards.

Did you feel that it hurt the show when Delta Burke left?
Absolutely! They never should have let her go.

Do you think people thought she was just being difficult, or do you think they realized that she was really going through something at the time?
(*She pauses.*) I don't know.

What did *you* think?
I thought that she *was* going through something. She really was with that weight thing and all.

Anthony and Bernice had great chemistry! What was Meshach Taylor like?
He was great! In fact, I thought that when Delta left, they should have worked more of the shows around us. (*Chuckles.*)

That would have been a great idea. Your characters were very popular.
I think it would have been good too. (*Laughs.*)

The "Black Man! Black Man!" song became one of Bernice's classic trademarks. How did that come about?
Well, it was actually written into the script. It said, "Sing *Black Man.*" And, supposedly, there really is a song called "Black Man," which I had never heard. So I looked around and said, "How does it go?" And no one knew, so I just had to make it up as I went along.

(*Laughing*) Is that right?
(*Chuckles*) Which I've never done on a show before. But I loved doing it.

Yes. You even sang "Black Man" in the final scene of the last episode of the series, as Anthony was carrying you up the staircase in that *Gone with the Wind* take-off.
Oh, yes! That was fun! He was wonderful.

Were you sad to see the show end, or do you think it had run its course?
I feel that if Delta had stayed on, it could have run its course. But I don't think it did. I think it could have run at least another two seasons. But I don't know, with those new girls. They really didn't fit in.

Jan Hooks' character was funny, but Julia Duffy [*Newhart*] must have had a hard time because most fans didn't care for her character.
I don't think so either.

I think it was because of the way she was written. She played the heavy, but she really didn't have much of a chance to be liked.
That's right.

Do you have a favorite episode?
(*Chuckles.*) Any one where I sang the "Black Man" song.

One of my favorites is when Charlene has the baby on New Year's Eve, and Mary Jo gives you a Christmas tree skirt as a Christmas present, and you actually end up wearing it as a skirt to the hospital!
Oh, yes. (*Laughs.*) I liked that one, too. That was a great sketch.

Have any of the cast kept in touch with you?
Do you know I haven't seen a single one since the show was over?

Really?
I'm kind of surprised, because people knew that I was in the hospital for a while.

I guess everyone gets so busy with their own lives. It's hard sometimes.
Yes. That's true.

You mentioned that you were in the hospital. Was that when you had the stroke?
Yes. It affected one leg, so I limp. I can't walk unless someone is with me, so

that limits my work. But if it ever gets well, I'd like to get back out there. I take physical therapy twice a week, and I think that'll help.

Did you enjoy doing the *Designing Women Reunion*? [Lifetime, 2003]
Well... (*As she begins to speak, her voice begins to quiver. Then a long pause.*)

Alice? Is everything all right?
(*A slight pause.*) I'm okay. It's just that we did that reunion show two days after my husband's funeral.

Oh, I'm sorry to hear that.
But he really wanted me to do it. We were married for fifty years.

I didn't know. I'm sorry.
That's quite all right. You know, it's just that you get so used to a person for that long of a time. It's not easy.

I can imagine how hard that must be.
Yes, it is.

You were in one of my all-time favorite movies, *To Kill a Mockingbird*.
Oh, yes.

What was that experience like?
I tell you, it was good. But a lot of the things I had done were cut out of the film.

Really?
Yes, because the film ran so long. I had some scenes with Gregory Peck and they had to cut them. When I was doing it, it seemed just like any other movie, but it was a good experience.

What was Gregory Peck like to work with?
Oh, he was very nice. A real gentleman.

Another of your movie credits is *The Graduate*.

Yes, but that was just a small part. I was in a scene with... (*a pause*) another lady from *Bewitched*. I just lost her name... The one that had all the doorknobs...

Oh, Marion Lorne! [Aunt Clara]

Yes! Marion Lorne. She and I were together in this scene where we got into the wrong room in a hotel and got in on the reception for somebody. We just had a couple of lines, but it was funny.

Of all the roles that you've done in films, theatre, and television, which is your all-time favorite?

My favorite show was a live show that I did in New York called *The Sign in Sidney Brustein's Window*.

That was the one that you won a Tony Award for on Broadway, correct?

That's right.

What was it about?

It was about protests, and people that couldn't live on certain streets because of their ethnicity.

What part did you play?

I played Mavis Bryson, the sister of Gabe Dell [Sidney Brustein].

That's certainly one to be proud of.

Thank you.

This has been an enjoyable experience for me, speaking with you. You're one of my all-time favorites and I appreciate it. Thank you, Alice.

You're very welcome, my dear. Thank you for remembering me.

   [Alice Ghostley is semi-retired, and lives in North Hollywood. Despite her stroke, she still enjoys life. "I go and do what I want to with the help of my girls who are with me around the clock." She enjoys reading and answering fan mail, the bulk of which comes from fans of *Bewitched* and *Designing Women*.]

Peter Breck

The Big Valley: Nick Barkley 1965-69

Peter Breck wasn't always a television cowboy. In fact, growing up in Boston and New York is about as far as you can get from the open range. After finishing high school and a stint in the Navy, Breck decided to enter college. While pursuing an English and Drama degree at the University of Houston, it was there he began his acting career in the college drama department.

The ruggedly handsome, six-foot-two actor was spotted one night by Robert Mitchum in a theater production of G.B. Shaw's *Man of Destiny*. This led to more work in the theatre and eventually to roles in such films as *I Want to Live!* with Susan Hayward.

It was his work on the opening night of *A Thousand Clowns* that nabbed him the role of Nick Barkley, the eldest son of widowed and wealthy Victoria Barkley [Barbara Stanwyck], in *The Big Valley*. Three producers by the names of Gardner, Levy, and Laven were sitting in the audience and looking for a male lead in the forthcoming series. This role would eventually make him one of the best-known and well-loved cowboys of the small screen.

Peter, I understand that you had never trained with horses before you got into television.
That's right.

So riding came naturally?
Yes. I never, ever, had a lesson in my life. In fact, one of the greatest compliments

Peter as Nick Barkley with Coco.

I've ever received was from Ben Johnson. He was a famous horse wrangler and stunt double for John Wayne, Gary Cooper, and Jimmy Stewart. He once told me, "There are three cowboys that can sit *in* a horse in Hollywood and *only* three... You, me, and Glenn Ford." I said, "You're kidding me." "No," he said. "You sit *in* a horse. You sit not *on* the saddle, but *in* the saddle. You become a part of that horse. So the horse and you become one."

That *is* very impressive.
Thank you.

How would you describe Nick Barkley?
Nick was what we'd all like to be. He thought he could do almost anything. At the same time he's embarrassing, but he doesn't consider himself an embarrassment, because that's who he is. He believes in his truth.

Where was the series filmed?
At Four Star Studios. They took over Republic. Do you know who the *Four Stars* were?

No, I don't.
Ida Lupino, David Niven, Charles Boyer, and Dick Powell.

Wow! What a line-up!
Yes.

Where were the exteriors for the Barkley home and ranch shot?
The exterior for the house was out in the Four Star back lot and it was originally built for *Gone with the Wind*. It was Ashley's mansion in the movie. That's a good bit of trivia to know. You could get a beer for that. (*We laugh.*)

Do you know if it's still there?
I believe it is. I've seen it used a lot over the years. In fact, they used to use it for Conrad's series [*The Wild Wild West*]. They just redressed it. We had a darn good back lot. In fact, *Gilligan's Island* was done on the same lot.

Did you do your own stunts?
I sure did.

Did you ever get hurt?
Yeah, I got hurt! (*Laughing.*) One time was with Martin Landau. And Marty will remember this, because whenever we see each other, he just shakes his head and laughs. He was in one of the segments as a bad guy. He was behind the rocks up in Vasquez Rocks, where we did some of our locations. That's a place that

every Western eventually uses. If you're in any kind of a Western, eventually, you *will* end up in Vasquez Rocks. (*Laughing.*) So Marty was behind the rocks, and I was riding Coco in with Lee [Majors] on my left side. In the scene, there was gonna be a shot fired and it was gonna go right underneath the horse. So they laid down the explosion, and I'd ride up to where the explosion was gonna go off, which was about four feet in front of the horse. We're going along just fine, and had done about four or five rehearsals, and every time we were right on the money. So then the director says, "This will be live action, and this will be the shot." So I was leading the pack, and Marty is over behind the rock with a gun, and he's supposedly put dynamite where the explosion is gonna go off. So now I come riding up with the guys and I suddenly had this horrible sensation that said, "I think I'm over my mark."

Uh-oh.

It had just hit me that I was over, and BOOM!!! It went off right under the horse. Well, needless to say, I had the wildest eleven-second ride of my life!! Coco was panicked, but I had him in my lap. I had his head back holding him. I was trying to figure out when to go and drop the reins, and look for a soft spot to bail out. So by this time Coco was haulin' buns, and we're going full gallop. So I laid out off of the saddle, pushed the horse over, and took what I *thought* was going to be a slide. Well, I hit it too hard. I went off the horse, hit the ground, and like a slate rock skimmin' across a swamp, I went bump, bump, bump across the ground. And I look up and I see a post. And around the post is barbed wire.

Oh no!!

Unfortunately, *yes*! So I threw my head back and BAM! I hit it right under my chin. I had a black and blue mark you wouldn't believe. Interestingly, they painted it black for the next day's work because it was a little swollen, but I didn't miss a day! The special effects guy felt terrible and was apologizing all over the place, but you can't control dynamite. There's no way. Fortunately, God was looking out for me.

Did you have Coco for the entire run of the series?

Yes. He was a Strawberry Roan Appaloosa, which I didn't really like because they are skittish. People would say, "Be careful with those horses. They'll panic at a gum wrapper!" And they were right!

Had you previously worked with any of the cast?

I worked with Richard Long. He's passed on now.

Yes. I believe he was only forty-seven at the time.

Yes. He had a series of about five heart attacks while working at Warners.

Did you keep in touch with him after the series ended?

Oh yes. Dick and I were very good friends and our wives got along great too. I worked along with him at Warner Bros. on *Cheyenne, Sugarfoot,* and all of those Warner Bros. shows. Do you remember *77 Sunset Strip?*

I sure do.

Well, my wife, Diane, did that one with me. My wife is a dancer and a good one. She worked with Wayne & Shuster. They were a Canadian comedy team. They had a show on every week, something like Carol Burnett, the same kind of thing, and she was in the dance trio. That's where I knew her, and later on we found each other again and got married.

Tell me about the rest of the cast.

All of the people on the show were very, very warm toward each other. We never had a problem!

That's unusual, but it's nice to hear.

Yes, and that's what I told the rag magazines. They'd be doing articles on us, and I'd say, "Well, we're not controversial. We get along!" And they don't want to hear that because it doesn't sell magazines.

What was Barbara Stanwyck like? What are your memories of her?
She was a great gal. A very, very dear friend, and a wonderful person to work with. She was the ultimate professional. Not that it got in the way, or became stodgy, like, "We'll do it this way." No, no, no! She was very easy-going about everything. And if she liked the way you played a scene, she'd let you know. Barbara and I had many, many scenes together. She was such a lovely lady, and so gentle. And she loved to be led. And [*a slight pause*] Nick was her *favorite* son.

(*Laughs*) So she didn't pull the big movie star, "Call me Miss Stanwyck," thing?
Oh, no. None of that. You can put really big, fat underlines under that! She was dead-on straight with you. She never, *ever* pulled any temper tantrums. Never! She was a great gal, and a wonderful actress. It's not always as cut-throat in Hollywood as they lead you to believe.

When you would get the script for the initial reading, would there be much rewriting?
Oh, yes! There'd be a lot, if indeed, it was a weak script. And rewrites were not difficult because everybody was seasoned to do that. It was no problem.

Who was the most vocal if the scripts weren't up to par?
Me!

(*Surprised*.) Really?
(*Laughing*.) I'm kidding. Barbara was. We'd go to her and say, "Look, this is not good." And she'd say, "Okay. I'll call 'em in." So the producers would come in. Gardner, Levy, and Laven. We called 'em *The Pep Boys*.

I've seen their names for years on the credits. Did you have much interaction with them?
Oh yeah, we did. We had a very good crew, and very good producers. They were excellent. Sometimes we had battles, but it always boiled down to the fact that we all wanted the same thing in the end. And it was wonderful to work with Barbara, and Lee, and Linda [Evans].

Tell me about Lee and Linda. What were they like?

Linda was very, very easy to work with, because Linda was only concerned about what she looked like.

(*Laughing.*) Oh, really?

I'm not telling any tales out of school. That's just the truth. And Lee was new in the game with *Big Valley*. But he did a beautiful job. He did excellent work, and was really growing as an actor. I certainly had it very easy and a very good time working with him. He's a good man, and a good actor. But he's not as good as I am!

(*Laughs.*) Well, I know you're kidding, but you're very good. I've watched you in many scenes and you're believable. Some people aren't. You watch them and think, "These people are not very good. You can tell they're acting." But you're a natural. You've got it!

Well, thank you. You can underline that part for me too if you will! (*Laughing.*) Eddie, actors are truth seekers. We seek the truth and once we find the truth, then we play that truth, because we believe it. Then the audience believes that we believe it, so they believe the character. You have to find that truth that you're comfortable with it, and then you've got a truthful work. And people will believe it.

That's good advice. Have you ever taught acting?

As a matter of fact, yes. Diane and I had *The Breck Academy for the Performing Arts* in downtown Vancouver for ten years. We had a good roster of people. It went very well and we were happy with it.

Recently, I've been watching some episodes of *The Big Valley* on DVD. I noticed in the first season that there was a younger brother named Eugene. He was only on the first season, and then he disappeared. What happened to him?

Oh, Charles Briles. He was a good, young actor. It was just a simple thing they did. They signed Charles for the younger brother, and as they were getting more into the show, they felt that Lee could do the scripts that Charlie was doing. So, they saved money by writing him out and going with Lee.

How did they write him out?
They sent him off to college. Lee wasn't that much older than Charlie, and naturally was upset at the time, but Charlie is a good actor. And afterwards, he continued to work.

Speaking of DVDs, do you, the actors, get anything from the DVD sales?
Yes! Yes! The Screen Actors Guild is really going for the biggie on that one.

Well, good, because sometimes you hear that the contracts that were signed back then only paid for five or six reruns after the show was over and that was it.
Yes, that *was* it. But finally the Screen Actors Guild said, "No more of that!" Their bone of contention is that when the lead characters of a show signed away their revenue, DVDs didn't even exist. So there was nothing in the contract about them. The studios couldn't go back and say, "We have it on paper. You can't get paid for them."

Well, fair is fair. That's how it should be.
Exactly! Another good thing about DVDs is that it keeps your visibility going, and you never stop working! I get a lot of personal appearances that way, and I love doing 'em.

Are there any plans for any of the cast members to do any commentaries on any future DVD releases?
We have tried to talk FOX into that.

That would be a great plus for sales, not to mention for fans of the show.
FOX doesn't think so. They just don't realize it. I said to them, "If you'd gotten my e-mails, and there are stacks of them, you'd know what we're talking about." The fans don't hold any punches back. They want commentary! They tell it like it is. They let you know what they think of Heath, and Linda Evans, and Nick. Nick, by the way gets great reviews, which is all right with me. (*Laughs.*)

Of course! Nick is, pardon the expression, a bad-ass. But he's a likeable one.
(*Laughs.*) Yeah, and it's fun to play it that way!

When the show came to an end, did you feel that it was time, or did you want to continue?

I thought it was the time for it to end. I really felt that we had done our job, and done a good one.

Did you keep any of your scripts from the show?

I've got some of them. Not a lot.

Do you have any favorite episodes?

"Night of the Wolf." [Season One]

That's one of my favorites, when Nick gets bitten by a rabid wolf.

Yes. Ronny Howard was in that one.

Right. He played your ex-girlfriend's son.

Yes.

Can you remember any funny stories that happened on the set?

You say you liked "Night of the Wolf"?

Absolutely.

Well, I'll tell you a story about *that one*. In the episode, Heath and I are out at night somewhere, and the problem starts when Lee says something like, "There's a sound I've never heard before." Which, of course, is this rabid wolf. Well, we get up, and sure enough there's a wolf up on the rock. But it's tied up, you know, because they can take your head off with one bite. So, of course, they used a double, when it's supposed to jump on me. In this case, it was a German shepherd that had the sort of same grey-looking fur. It was almost a silver color, which was almost haunting.

So we rehearsed over and over again, and I worked with the shepherd, so that the shepherd got to know me very well. So when the shepherd, supposedly the wolf, jumps on me, the handler would catch him. So from the angle of the camera, you just see the back of the shepherd jumping on me thinking it's the wolf.

The problem was that the shepherd was a pussycat. He liked me, 'cause I would pet him while they were setting up. So by the time they started to get the shot, every time the shepherd would jump on me, he would wag his tail! He knew he was "coming to Daddy!" And he liked Daddy! (*Laughing.*) So it kept ruining the shot. Finally, somebody got the idea to wire his tail down to his right leg so it wouldn't wag.

Smart thinking!
Yes, and it didn't hurt him or anything. The ASPCA was there. Make sure people know that! (*Laughs.*)

I was looking at your credits and saw that you were in *I Want to Live!* with Susan Hayward.
That's right.

That was some of her best work.
Susan read with me when I auditioned, which I thought was a beautiful thing. And by this time, of course, Susan Hayward had some very good work under her belt. So, I go on the set and there she is sitting in her chair. Robert Wise was directing. So, I'm reading, and I'm as nervous as a cat. This was the first time I was working with a big star or a big director. So I'd make a mistake and she'd say, "Bobby, that was my fault. I did that. I gave him the wrong cue." Well, she *didn't* give me the wrong cue! She just didn't want me to get any more nervous than I was. I've never forgotten her for that.

I have to ask you about this. I read something about you, James Dean, and a motorcycle?
Oh yes. (*Laughs.*) That was at Sheraton Square in New York.

How did you meet?
I met him at Patsy and Carl's Bar. It was just down the street from where all the theaters were. We became friends, and he was really into motorcycles at the time. He told me he had a Harley. So we go out to look at it, and he says, "Why don't we take a ride and go get some coffee?" I said, "Okay." That was the time

Peter today.

when there were coffee houses everywhere. Every city had a coffee house where they had people come in the evening or the middle of the night and read poetry. So I climbed on the back and he took me all the way down to Greenwich Village. So we came to this particular coffee house, and there were about fifteen steps going up from the sidewalk into the place, and the door was open. I was on the back of the bike and Jimmy was drivin', so he just drove up the steps and we went right in. I said, "What are you doin'?" He said, "You wanted coffee, didn't ya?" (Laughs.) We went up two flights of stairs, through the coffee house door, and parked it right beside a table.

That's a story you won't forget! He sounded fun. Very adventurous.
He was. He used to go out and direct traffic in the middle of the streets of New York and wave a piece of cloth like he was a bullfighter in a bullfight. He would go out and do that to the cars right on Broadway. We had a lot of fun together. We went everywhere and had a ball. And I've never understood all this talk about everybody saying he was weird. I didn't think he was weird!

Well, I have to admit that I've heard that about him - that he was real strange.
He was *not* real strange. He was just a little bit loose in the head. Every once in a while, he'd shake it and see if the nuts were still rattling. (*Laughing.*) He just liked to have a good time.

Well, anyone that reads this interview will see that you do as well. You have a terrific sense of humor, quite unlike old Nick Barkley.
Shhh. Don't tell anybody.

Deal. I've really enjoyed this, Peter. I know your fans will too.
Thank you. Write when you get work!

[Peter Breck lives in British Columbia with Diane, his wife of forty-seven years. He has been keeping a busy schedule working in such recent projects as *Whispers of the Innocent*, *Calvin's Dream*, and *The Last Man's Club*. Still making personal appearances as far around the globe as Australia, Breck has also recorded a CD called *Kickin' Back*. He enjoys reading and answering questions from fans on his website **www.peterbreck.com**.]

Elinor Donahue

Father Knows Best: Betty Anderson 1954-60;
The Andy Griffith Show: Ellie Walker 1960-61

Elinor Donahue's career has literally lasted a lifetime. From her debut in movies as a very little girl at MGM, to her TV appearances as both a guest star and a series regular throughout the years, Donahue, perhaps, will most likely be remembered as pony-tailed Betty Anderson in the 1950s idealistic family comedy *Father Knows Best*.

After *Father Knows Best*, Donahue moved straight to Mayberry as new lady druggist, Ellie Walker, in the premiere season of *The Andy Griffith Show*. Countless TV appearances would follow in an array of shows such as *Star Trek* and *The Flying Nun*. In 1972, Donahue began a two-and-a-half-year run as Tony Randall's girlfriend on the ABC comedy *The Odd Couple*.

Before she began a recurring role as Jane Seymour's eldest sister on *Dr. Quinn, Medicine Woman*, Donahue would spend time with *Ellen, The Golden Girls*, and *Friends*.

Donahue continues to make guest appearances on television and film when it fits into her busy schedule.

I caught up with the delightful and expressive actress one Tuesday afternoon by phone at her home in Palm Desert, California. Interestingly, her voice still contains the same lilt and buoyancy as the teenaged Betty Anderson.

Elinor, was there a lot of competition when you auditioned for the role of Betty on *Father Knows Best*?
My suspicion is that there must have been. There were still a lot of people there

for the audition and after knowing Gene Rodney, the executive producer, for those subsequent years, he was a notorious auditioner. He saw *hundreds* of people for every role.

I did go three times to see him. The first time I had just washed my hair, and my agent called and said, "Get over to Sunset Boulevard right away!" I said, "I can't. I just washed my hair." But she wouldn't take no for an answer, so I went with frizzy hair and clothes that were not too great. I was told later that he said he liked me, but that I was too much of a little girl. So then she got me another audition and dolled me all up, had my hair professionally done, and bought me a suit and high heels. So I went up again, and he said, "I like her a lot, but she's too sophisticated and too much of a starlet for the role." So she kept pestering him to test me on film and he finally did, and that clinched it. Although, I think that I was not Mr. Rodney's first choice. I always got the feeling that he really didn't like me very much. And it wasn't until many years after *Father Knows Best* that he began to respect me and would tell me that he was proud of me. Early on, he just didn't like me very much, but Robert Young did. I think it was Robert Young who was instrumental in hiring me. They were co-executive producers of the show, and Mr. Young had equal say in many things. There was just some kind of connection between the two of us.

At the audition, I had gotten all teary. I had forgotten my lines and got embarrassed and started to cry. I think that the fellow who was directing the test just wanted to say, "Thank you very much and goodbye," but Mr. Young said, "Let's give her a few minutes to collect herself." He asked me if I wanted a Coca-Cola or something cool to drink, and I said, "Yes, thank you." So we went over to the side while another girl did her scene, and, of course, she did it bing, bang, boom, and was perfect. And it turned out that she was the girl that was playing the role of Kathy in the *radio* version of *Father Knows Best*! I was sure that she was going to get the part because they all knew who she was and they knew her work. She and Robert Young had worked together on the radio show every week, so I thought, "Well, that's the end of that." But after she finished, we did my scene and it was just one take and it went fine. I didn't make any mistakes. When we left, they said they'd call my agent and let me know. I just wanted to get out of there because I was just mortified by having broken down and cried. I was so embarrassed and grateful that we had gotten through it. So I came out of the office and saw my mother, and we had to walk about a block and a half to the bus stop and I hadn't said a word. We walked down to the corner and she finally asked, "Well, how did it go?" And I turned to her and said, "Mother, I don't want to talk about it ever, ever again." And she said, "Okay, that's fine." So she knew something had happened, but she never did ask me another thing about it. And it was about a month later, that I got a phone call from my agent who was screaming over the phone, "You got it!! You got the part!!" And I said, "What part?!"

You'd written that one off, hadn't you? (*Laughing.*)
I guess! I just forgot about it. It was just never gonna happen!

But it did.
Yes, and recently, I've found out some other things from talking with Jane Wyatt. To her great amusement, Jane told me that she and Mr. Young used to sit around the set and chat about us kids.

Really? How so?
Well, they really felt that Lauren had a terrific chance at stardom. They just thought she was the best, and Billy, for sure, was going to go on and have a marvelous career as a young leading man. And then there was "Poor Elinor. We hope that she gets married, has children and has a happy life, but she just doesn't have a chance." And both of them agreed! (*Laughs.*) They were surprised that I never did anything else!

I noticed that you refer to Robert Young as "Mr. Young." Did you always call him that?
Yes. I never did call him Bob. I know that Lauren, by the time she was ten, was calling him Bob. And Billy certainly did. And he certainly didn't expect me to call him Mr. Young, but I just did. It was a sign of respect, and I suspect he kind of liked it.

Father and Princess have a heart-to-heart.

Tell us about Robert Young.

Robert Young was very, very much like the character he played on the show. His personality was very warm and terribly sweet. I absolutely adored him. He would never say a cross word. There were different times when we must have tried his patience, and we would always know when we did, because it would frequently happen as we were all seated around the reading table and we'd just get fidgety, or start to pester one another. "She's kicking me." Or "Stop that!" Bickering like brothers and sisters. And if he would get upset, he'd take his glasses off, he'd put them on the table, he'd move the chair back, and he'd stand up and silently walk off the set. He never did it in a dramatic or angry way, he just quietly left. Then we knew we had crossed the line, and we'd go, "Oh, we'd better straighten up." So we'd get our act together. Then he'd come back and he'd never say a word. He'd just smile around the table and he'd continue on from where we were supposed to be. He was wonderful.

And Jane Wyatt?

(*Laughing.*) Jane Wyatt would be more apt to say, "Now, children, stop it right now! Look what you're doing!" Her personality was quite different from Margaret's. Margaret Anderson was a housewife and Jane Wyatt came from quite a privileged background. Her mother's family was the Van Rensselaers. She didn't cook, and she didn't iron in real life. Her husband, Edgar Ward, was an investment broker, and came from the same type of background. Both of their families were in the New York Social Register. They had two sons, and they lived in a beautiful home with servants. So Margaret Anderson was something entirely different.

So that really was a good acting job when she would be cooking or cleaning the house as Margaret Anderson.

Right! Jane was also a warm and wonderful woman, very well educated, and would correct us on our grammar. And she is still apt to correct my grammar when we talk on the phone. (*Laughs.*)

How is she doing?

She's doing pretty well. She's going to be ninety-six this summer. She's had some physical problems, but her mental capacities are fantastic. She's as bright as a penny. We saw her about three weeks ago. We were going somewhere and we had to pass through Bel-Air, so we stopped by and took her a book. She still reads her books, and goes to Mass every Sunday, and has wonderful people there in her beautiful home that she's had for many years. Her husband passed away about ten years ago. But she's very grateful that she's able to still live at home, and she's doing well. [This interview was completed two months before Jane Wyatt died peacefully in her sleep at her home in Bel-Air. She was 96.]

I read Lauren Chapin's book, and she writes about having quite a rough childhood. Were you aware that she was having such a hard time when you were doing the show?
Well, like most teenagers, I was a bit self-absorbed, and learning lines and all, so I didn't notice a whole lot. But I knew that her Mother could be a problem because she had a drinking problem, and it was pretty apparent that Lauren was unhappy at times, but that was all I really knew.

Tell me about your work schedule.
In the beginning we worked a six-day week.

Six days?
Yes. They didn't do the five-day-a-week thing until probably 1955 or '56. I know for at least a good year we worked six days a week, and we would rehearse at least two days in the beginning few years. We'd rehearse and block, and then have four days shooting. Then when they went to five days, we still had one day of rehearsal, but when Peter Tewksbury took over as director, the shooting times got longer and longer because he was a little more creative than Bill Russell. Bill Russell was fun, and Bill Russell was Lauren's favorite director, and I loved him too, but he was more of the "old school." He made the work quite jolly. He was a fun, fun person. But that real old-school way was, "Okay. Let's rehearse it. Let's shoot it. Okay, got it!" that kind of thing. When Mr. Tewksbury became our director, he wanted perfection, and he would niggle at it and work at it for many, many takes, and get lots and lots of coverage.

And this was a one-camera show and not filmed in sequence, correct?
Yes.

Any rewrites?
Oh, no. When we got the script it was *gold*. That was the Bible. Even Mr. Young wasn't allowed to change a *word* without going to the phone and asking Gene if he could.

Were you required to learn the lines verbatim, or could you rephrase things as long as the same idea was there?
They were real sticklers about that. Absolutely. We couldn't change one *word*. Never, never on *Father Knows Best*. Gene Rodney went over those scripts with a fine-toothed comb. And unlike sitcoms today, we only had two male writers and one female writer and each one person was responsible for a week's script. In other words, it wasn't at all done by committee, where they all have ten and twelve writers in a group as in sitcoms today. Mr. Rodney would work on a draft with a writer until it was perfect. We only had the three writers the whole six years we were on.

Why have I read that the show was on for seven seasons?
That was because we had shot so many shows that we had enough in the can to make a whole extra year's worth. By that time, they had made the seasons shorter. We used to do a season of thirty-nine, and then it went to twenty-eight. But we had plenty in the can to eke out another year. That's why we were on network for seven.

And these shows were new, never shown before?
Yes. They were all new.

That would be unheard of today.
Yes. Today it's sometimes only thirteen episodes. And they'll do reruns, and then do another thirteen.

Were you allowed any input into storylines for your character?
Heavens, no. I don't think anyone did. I doubt even Miss Wyatt did.

What did you like about the character of Betty?
I thought that she was strong and very bright.

Would you describe her as a typical teenager?
I don't know, because I didn't know any typical teenagers. I was a working kid, and I was in show business. As a matter of fact, I went to Beverly Hills High School for three months before I started filming *Father Knows Best* because I wanted to find out what being a teenager was like. I had never gone to a dance. I had never gone to a football game. I had never sat in a classroom with a bunch of other kids my own age. So I had fun those three months. I enjoyed it! I think I got way younger real fast from that experience! I giggled, and flirted with boys, and did all the things that teenagers do. I had a real good time.

But Betty's character was so much different than mine. Mine being, if not shy, hesitant, not so confident. And Betty was the *epitome* of confidence. (*Laughs.*) So I kind of lived vicariously through her.

How are you at learning lines? Are you a quick study?
I always feel that I'm not, but I probably am. But I have found that when you're on a series, with each succeeding episode that you do, you find the lines easier to learn because the writers have picked up on your natural way of speaking. They will tend to write in your rhythms, and or, you become more comfortable and know the character that you're playing better. You are beginning to think like the character, so I think those two things begin to come together and that makes learning your lines a lot simpler. Any series I've worked on was like that. I didn't ever have to work terribly hard at learning lines. And if I had trouble with something, I found that if I studied right before I'd go to sleep at night, by the time I got up the next morning, it was in there pretty solid.

So no horror stories of freezing up before the camera?
I do remember this one time that was a bad experience. It was one of those times when I just had too much emotionally on my plate and I didn't realize it. I had a long, almost two-page monologue about a dream that I had had, and I was supposed to tell Mr. Young about it. We were on the kitchen set. And, boy,

Father not only knows best, here he's the center of attention. From L to R: Bill Gray (Bud), Elinor Donahue (Betty/"Princess"), Robert Young (Jim), Jane Wyatt (Margaret) and Lauren Chapin (Kathy/"Kitten.")

do I remember that! I couldn't learn it! I'd have the script, and every day I'd work on this speech and I just couldn't get it. I thought, "Well, there's nothing to it. I'll just go home tonight, and have my little bowl of cereal and get in bed with a cup of tea and I'll work on this until I go to sleep." And I did. So I woke up in the morning absolutely certain that I knew it. So I got on the set, and do you think I could do it?

My guess would be no... (*Laughing.*)
It went multi-takes! Gene Rodney was absolutely furious! But Mr. Young and Mr. Tewksbury were very supportive. They knew that there was something else going on that was causing me to have this problem. Anyway, luckily it was only one day out of hundreds.

And there was no such thing as cue-cards back then.
Absolutely not!

Where was the series filmed?
At Columbia Studios on Stage 11.

Is the exterior of the house still around?
Yes. The exterior is at what used to be called the Columbia Ranch. I'm not sure what they call it now. And the ranch wasn't just exteriors. They actually built a couple of soundstages there as well. In fact, that's where we shot most of the first Christmas episode we did, right there on a stage. You know, the one where we're at the cabin when we got snowed in looking for a Christmas tree ["The Christmas Story"].

Yes. That's one of my favorites.
There's also a lake there. There was an episode where I get stuck on a boat and I was holding onto the boat and standing on the shore and the boat begins to drift away. It was a kind of comedic scene for Betty, stretching out trying to hold onto the boat.

I read where you left the show for a while, and didn't think you'd be coming back, so you cut off your trademark ponytail, and then you found out you would be returning.
Yes! That was when I ran away and got married at nineteen. Mr. Rodney, once again, was furious with me and didn't want to have me back on the show. I think I missed two episodes. It was rumored that I would not be coming back, and they'd have Betty leaving for college and writing letters home once in a while. So I decided I wanted to cut my hair. I had gotten pregnant a couple of months after the marriage, and I didn't want to be dealing with long hair, so I cut my hair off. Then a few weeks later, my agent called and said, "They've agreed to have you back on the show." And the first thing I said was, "Oh no! I just cut my hair!" And she said, "Don't tell them! Just show up!"

So once again, Mr. Rodney was furious with me. So there were three or four shows where I had short hair, but I think he thought I looked too grown up, so they got a false ponytail and pinned it on. I found that was much easier than having to grow my own. It was easier for hairdressing actually. All we had to do was the front of my hair, and groom the ponytail when I wasn't there. When the show was over, they gave it to me! (*Laughing.*)

Do you still have it?
No. I donated it to a girl's school. They were having "Betty Anderson Day," so I gave it to them. (*Laughs.*)

Was your pregnancy showing when you came back to the show?
Yes.

How was that handled?
They had to do various silly things like having me carry a laundry basket or stand behind a chair, things like that. That's how they got around it.

You kept your ponytail for a while. Did you keep any of your scripts?
(*Laughs.*) Not a one... I didn't have the foresight then. By the time we did them, though, they were pretty beat up. And if I didn't have a big part, and I still do this today, once I've read the script and we've done a table reading and you've got all the changes in, I'd just take my pages out and not have to lug around this big old thing.

Do you have any favorite episodes of *Father Knows Best*?
That's hard to say... (*Thinking.*)

Do they kind of run together for you?
Yeah. They kind of do. But I liked the high school graduation one ["Betty's Graduation"]. And I don't remember the premise now, but there's one where I tap danced. That was fun ["Betty Makes a Choice"].

Were you aware that the sixth season would be the end of the series?
No. As a matter of fact, we stopped filming in February because there was a writers strike and when there's a writers strike, you had to stop. So we shut

down production, and we just never came back. All of us thought that we would be coming back. So there was never a goodbye party, we never got to say goodbye, there was never an *anything*. I mean, boom, we just didn't see each other for the longest time, and the next time we actually saw each other was when we did the first reunion.

Are there any plans for the series to be released on DVD?
Nope. And I say that because I don't think they can. I believe Universal owns the rights. As far as I know, they were the last to own it because my late husband, Harry Ackerman, had an idea of doing an update of *Father Knows Best* as a new series. The premise was Betty was grown up, married to the pilot, and had her children. Bill and Lauren would make guest appearances, and Mr. Young and Miss Wyatt, to their liking, could be a voice on the phone, or read a letter or make an appearance or something. And I believe we were negotiating with the Family Channel at the time, and they were very excited about it! So they needed a co-production deal, and Universal got all excited about it as well. So a representative from their channel came out to Universal and, eventually, in relation to the network, got greedy and asked for something they weren't about to get, and they lost it completely. That's why I think Universal still owns the rights.

How many *Father Knows Best* reunion shows were there?
We did two. The premise of the first one was that we were coming back for Jim and Margaret's thirty-fifth wedding anniversary, and the second one was a Christmas show. They've shown the Christmas one, but I don't know why they never show the first one. I think that one is better.

How did you feel about going back and doing the reunion shows?
Well, Billy and I had mixed feelings about it. We didn't really want to go backward in time. We were very nervous about it, and as it turned out, Mr. Young was nervous about it too, because on the first day of production, he went into the men's room and didn't seem to want to come out! We kept waiting for him, and waiting for him, and finally he came out. So after we did the first read-through, there was this collective sigh of relief. It was as though time had

stopped and it was like it was the next day. And instead of everybody going backward, we had brought who we were then to who the characters were now, with a kind of maturity. It was really quite good. And because it turned out so well, the network hurriedly wanted a Christmas one. That one was rushed.

I have both of those in my collection, and I think you're right about the first one. It was better. But I enjoy watching the Christmas one every year during the holidays.

If you notice, I'm not really in that one until the last fifteen minutes or so.

Why was that?

I was shooting a new show for NBC called *Mulligan's Stew* and they wouldn't let me off. They couldn't let me off because I was one of the stars. So my first day on the set was my last day on the set. I just shot it in one day. And when I got there, Robert Young said, "Boy, you'd better be good. We've been talking about you for forty-five minutes!" (*Laughs.*)

Were you happy with the way Betty turned out?

Yes. I really was. I think that's why I encouraged Harry to contact The Family Channel when he had the new series idea, because I really thought that she was a nice, strong womanly character. I really liked Betty.

I know that you mentioned that you have seen Jane Wyatt recently. Do you keep in touch with Bill and Lauren?

Not so much with Lauren because she's in Florida. It doesn't occur to me to pick up the phone and call Florida that much, but I will talk to Bill. He's here in California in Malibu.

Let's talk about Miss Ellie, Mayberry's lady druggist.

Sure.

How did you get the part on *The Andy Griffith Show*?

I was asked to come into a meeting with Sheldon Leonard, and the line producer. I had brought my little boy Brian, and he was out in the room with the secretary, and I was sort of half listening to him to make sure he was behaving well. And I'd hear him giggle, and I'd hear her talk, and I was paying practically no attention to what they were saying. And it was summer, and I was tired, and I could hardly keep my eyes open, and they were talking, talking, talking. Then finally it was over. But by the time I got home, I found out that I had the part.

So you never really auditioned for the role.
No. I had done all those years on *Father Knows Best* so they knew my work. But that doesn't work anymore. The business has changed greatly. In today's world, even with all those years on *Father Knows Best*, I would have had to have done an audition and a test, and meet the network, the whole magilla. But that was it then. No audition. I sort of knew that I was going to be a lady druggist who comes to the South.

And made big waves the first episode, making poor Emma Brand so upset she had to take to her bed! (*Laughing.*)
(*Giggling.*) Yes. She was adorable. She was a wonderful character actress that had a great career. [Cheerio Meredith]. She worked in a lot of Westerns. If you ever watch any old Westerns, you'll see her.

Was Andy Griffith at the meeting?
No, he wasn't.

How long after you met with the producers did you begin filming?
It was two or three months later that we did the first episode I was in. I think I was in the fourth show. I only did eleven shows that first season.

Was that the first time you met Andy?
Yes.

What is he like?
He's wonderful. He's a terrific person. He certainly knew what he wanted out of the show, and if he didn't know on that first day, he'd figure it out as he went.

Frances Bavier (Aunt Bee) and Donahue relax between takes.

He had a great vision for what the show should be. He was able to see that Don [Knotts] was going to be the other dominant character, and in the very beginning, a lot of lines that were Miss Ellie's were changed and given to Don. And they worked better that way.

I read that you and Frances Bavier [Aunt Bee] were pretty close during your time on the show.
Yes. She was darling. People would say that she had a sharp tongue and could be gruff, but she certainly wasn't with me. She was just a dear. I wasn't that aware of her long career at the time, but my mother was. So Mother would occasionally bring my little boy Brian down to the set. They would visit and Frances just loved Brian. And she loved Ronny [Howard]. Whenever we were waiting to do scenes, we'd talk about recipes and knitting. Something girly. I liked her a lot.

What do you remember about Don Knotts?
I used to give Don a ride into Westwood. I used to live in Woodland Hills, and he would go to a doctor in Westwood, and I would drive him. And I guess his lady friend would pick him up after his appointment there. So we spent more "real time" together. I was in the hospital one time with a very serious pneumonia, and he was the only one from the show that called me.

I heard he was shy.
Yes. Yes. Not bashful kind of shy, but very quiet and unassuming. Very sweet. And what I didn't learn until many years later, from his good friend Tom Poston, was that he was *quite* the ladies man, and that he had lots of girls, and was hitting on people all the time. And I said, "Well, my feelings are hurt, because he never hit on me!" (*Laughing.*)

Do fans mention any particular *Andy* episodes that you were in?
Yes. The Christmas one ["The Christmas Story"]. And if I had to pick a favorite episode of mine, I think it'd have to be that one. I certainly try to watch it every year. I get a big kick out of seeing that one around Christmas time. They usually play it on Christmas Eve day, or Christmas morning. It's fun. My husband loves to watch it too.

You sang "Away in a Manger" in that episode. Was that pre-recorded?
Oh yes. I wasn't particularly thrilled about them having me sing, but my mother said, "Why not? You've sung that song your whole life!" So I went to the record-

ing studio after work one night and Andy was there with the line producer. Andy said, "Let's try to find a key." But I was very nervous, and my voice kept breaking, and I was just a nervous wreck. And he said, "We've got all the time in the world. We don't have to hurry. I'm just gonna play a few chords here and see if this key is comfortable for you. Let's try it. Sit down here on the floor." So he threw some pillows down and we sat on the floor and he's playing the chords and he starts to hum the first few bars of the introduction, and he nods at me, and he whispers, "Go ahead and try it." So I start singing and, somehow, we got through the whole thing. And then he stands up and looks around, and says, "Well, is that all right?" Some voice in the back said, "Yeah. That was fine." Not quite having caught on yet, I said, "Well, aren't we gonna record it?" And he looked at me and smiled and said, "We already did." So he fooled me! But it worked. If they had said, "Okay, take one," I would have tightened up and it would have probably taken forever.

So that was Andy actually playing the guitar when you sang?
Oh yes. And then when we shot it, they apparently did a tracking shot, which means that they did it all in one take. It was all a single tracking shot with no cuts or close-ups. It came out well. People really like that episode.

I'm sure you get asked this question more than any other, but why were you only on the show for one season?
Andy has said since that they didn't know how to write for me. I don't believe that. They knew how to write for me. They wrote for me just perfectly fine. I was just going through evermore turmoil than I had been on *Father Knows Best* in my personal life, and in all honesty, I don't remember a lot of what happened then. I was just emotionally and physically drained.

So it was your decision to leave?
Yes. I asked to be let out of my contract. They agreed, but I think it hurt my feelings because they did it without a *hint* of an argument! (*Laughing.*)

How long was your original contract?
Three years.

Miss Ellie and Andy under the mistletoe.

So you could have stayed on for two more seasons if you wanted?
Oh sure. As a matter of fact, Earle Hagen, who wrote the theme song, was so upset that I left the show because he had written "Ellie's Theme." It was what was going to play under my scenes. They used theme music for each character and they had already recorded it. It was to be released on LP when the new season came out. He was just sick because he said it was the favorite piece of music that he had written up to that point. He just loved it. It was a beautiful piece of music. It's out there somewhere. I'd love for you to hear it. It was just gorgeous.

So they had high plans for my character, but I made the decision to leave. I was going through an anorexic period. I was determined that I was overweight, and I wasn't eating. I was just a mess.

Last year, I went to one of the *Andy Griffith* reunions up in Mt. Airy, and they do a Q&A thing. And they showed bits of episodes and they showed one I was in and I was s-o-o-o b-a-a-d!

You really think so?
Oh, I *know* so. The fans all applauded, and said they liked it, but it was bad. I was way too thin, and you could just see that this person was just falling apart. That happened to be the last episode before I said, "Let me go."

Have you ever regretted leaving?
At that time, it was the right decision for me. In retrospect, I'm not particularly sorry. It isn't like I stepped away from the business and never worked again. I worked as pretty much as I wanted to, and I married Harry Ackerman, and I was very happy.

Yes. How many times have I seen his name on the credits of a TV show?
Yes. (*Laughs.*)

Among the many shows he produced, *The Flying Nun* was always a favorite of mine. You were on a few episodes.
Yes. I played Sally Field's older sister, [Dr. Jennifer Ethrington] a doctor.

What do you remember about your time on the show?

Well, we knew Sally because Harry produced the show, and she was adorable. Very, very bright, and quick and funny. She was just a delight. The reason I did the first episode was that she had broken her leg skiing or something, and she had to be filmed in bed. I know the episode was called "My Sister the Doctor." And I came down to Puerto Rico to visit her. That was the first episode. Then later on, I did a couple more.

For those of us who only know him as a familiar name rolling by in the credits, tell us what the real Harry Ackerman was like.

He was a very brilliant creator, a creative genius certainly for his time. He was fun, bright, very erudite, but he could also be silly. He was a wonderful father. He was always fair. He didn't fly off the handle. As a matter of fact, he had ulcers because he internalized everything.

During one of the seasons, he had a show on network TV every night of the week except for the weekends. I was very happy to have had the almost thirty years that we had together.

I read that you and Harry were very good friends with Elizabeth Montgomery and William Asher.

Yes. They were terrific. She was like a sister to me during that time *Bewitched* was on the air. Elizabeth was very much like her character. Very fun, very fun loving. Just a delight. We spent practically every weekend together. They'd be at our house one weekend, and we'd go to theirs the next. Elizabeth was very sports-oriented, as I was not. She was a very good athlete. We'd play touch football sometimes on the weekends, and once she, or Harry, accidentally hit me in the Adam's apple, so that was the end of my touch football days. (*Laughing.*)

Trekkers will never forgive me if I don't ask you about the episode you did on the original *Star Trek* [Episode 31: "Metamorphosis"].

(*Laughs.*) I was called on the phone by Gene Roddenberry, and he described the show to me, which at the time meant next to nothing, but he asked, "Would you like to be part of it?" And I said, "Oh, absolutely!" So they sent me the script and I played two parts, Commander Hedford, and a creature. So that was that. I never had to go in and meet or anything. So we shot for several days and when we had finished on this particular set, they tore it down. Then they built all new sets, and I was supposed to come back in a few days and shoot the rest of my stuff. But they called me back one day and said something had happened to the film in the lab and they were going to have to re-shoot *everything*. So they had to shut down production, and rebuild this entire elaborate set. Meanwhile, I had come down with quite a bad case of pneumonia and by the time I was called back to the set, I had lost about ten pounds, so that outfit that I was wearing in the very beginning of the show was just *hanging* on me. So they took this big, beautiful, green piece of fabric and draped it over my shoulders so my bony chest couldn't be seen. (*Laughs.*) And it actually became part of the scene. They used the scarf as part of the scrim over the lens. It turned out well. That was Harry's favorite thing that I ever did.

Tell me about your time on *The Odd Couple*.
I played Tony Randall's girlfriend and if you saw the play, my character, Miriam Welby, was actually The Pigeon Sisters rolled into one.

Your character's last name was Welby, which reminds me of the famous Dr. Welby, who played your father on a previous series. Was that just a coincidence? (*Smiling.*)
No. (*Laughs.*) That was actually Tony's idea, because by that time Robert Young was famous for playing Dr. Welby. So he wanted my character named Miriam Welby.

I understand that he had a very hot temper and you got a taste of it when you were first on the show.
Oh yes. Tony had a tendency to lose patience very easily. I got very nervous at the dress rehearsal and couldn't remember my lines. He started hitting the table and literally screaming at me, "Say your lines! Pick up your cue! Pick up your cue!" all the while continually banging on this table. By that point I couldn't have remembered my own name, much less my lines!

Was he usually like that?

Yes! That was the real him. When he'd lose his temper, he would just blow! So the script girl came in and gave me my line, and Jack Klugman was saying, "Tony, calm down! You're scaring her!" But somehow, we finally got through the scene and I went home for sure thinking that I was going to get a phone call that said, "Don't come back." But I didn't. And the next day I went in, and in my dressing room was a bouquet of flowers and a card from Tony saying, "Please forgive me for yelling at you. You're beautiful and you're good. Welcome to the show."

So after that, I became a sort of semi-regular fixture and I had a lot of fun times. And Tony and I got along like a house a fire. I saw him lose his temper with other people, but he never did it again with me. He took a great liking to me after that, and I was honored. It was a close, close, very fun experience.

Did you work with Penny Marshall?

Oh yes. And the character she played [Myrna Turner] was very much like Penny. Her brother, Garry Marshall, who was the executive producer, would come to our dressing room to give us notes and he'd say, "From you girls I want perk and bubble, perk and bubble. That's all I want, perk and bubble." And in that Penny Marshall voice of hers, she'd say, "G-a-r-r-y, I don't do p-e-r-k and b-u-b-b-l-e." So it was left to me to do perk and bubble. (*Laughs.*)

You did an episode of *The Golden Girls* ["Stan Takes a Wife"], where you were going to marry Dorothy's ex-husband, Stanley. You had a long scene with Bea Arthur sitting at a hotel bar. Did you enjoy working with her?

Yes. It was a lot of fun. Bea Arthur is very shy and quiet. She doesn't chit-chat on the set, which is fine with me because I'm not a chit-chatter either. I had known most of the other ladies. I had worked with Rue McClanahan in the theatre. We had done a play together. And I had known Betty White for a long, long time. Our paths had crossed, and from her involvement in Actors and Others for Animals. I frequently did their annual fashion shows, so we'd frequently run into each other all of the time, so it was a lot of fun. I don't think I had to audition for it, I think the part was just offered to me. We did the taping and it was over, and Bea Arthur was very sweet to me. She had been kind of distant, and I had

Playtime on the set of The Odd Couple with Tony Randall and Jack Klugman.

been told not to take any mind of that because she was a private person, but when we finished the scene and they were breaking the set, she said [*in a very low-voiced Bea Arthur imitation*], "You know... you're very good." (*Laughs.*) They're all wonderful women. They all got along so well. It was a very happy set.

What was your experience like on *Friends*? ["The One Where Nana Dies Twice."]

I went in and read for that one. But I read for it about a week or so after my own mother had died. Her name was Doris, but we called her Nana. And it really hit home. So after I did the reading, I left the office and went out in the hallway, and I had not really cried, because when Mother died, I had just landed in New York to help my son James and his wife take care of their new baby. I couldn't turn around and come home, because there was nothing to turn around and come home for, because she had left specific instructions that there was to be no service, no funeral, and what not. So I had never really broken down, so when I left this office, I just fell to pieces in the hallway. And the casting lady came out and said, "Are you all right?" I said, "Yes. It's just that my own mother died recently." And she said, "Oh, I'm so sorry." So by the time I got home, my agent had gotten the call that I had gotten the part and she told me, and I said, "Oh." She said, "Well, you don't sound very happy." So then I told her what happened and she said, "Look. If this is going to be too rough on you, you don't have to do it." And I said, "No. Mother would have wanted me to." So I went ahead and did it. But I never could really play the part. I couldn't get out of Elinor's skin, and it was probably a mistake and I shouldn't have done it. It came out all right, but it wasn't great.

Tell me about your experience on *Ellen*.
I'm a very big fan of Ellen DeGeneres. She's a wonderful person and very funny. She's just as funny as she is on the Oscars and her own show. Her wit is very sharp. Never mean. Never mean-spirited. She's just funny. She knows what she wants. She knows what she wants to do. She was unhappy with some aspects of the script, but it had to do with toilet humor, and she doesn't like that kind of humor. They had to rewrite a good bit of it. She was very firm about how she felt about certain things. She's a wonderful woman. But a kind of funny thing happened. There are lots of people that didn't watch television when they grew up, and she was in that age range where I've found that people just didn't watch *Father Knows Best* and the kinds of shows that I was on. But when you do a show in front of an audience, the director or the warm-up person will introduce all the actors to the audience, and, of course, the star is introduced last. So they went around the table, and introduced the girls in the show, and they introduced the guy, and then they went around the table and they introduced me, and the audience just went *wild*. They went, "Oh, it's Elinor Donahue!" They were just screaming and yelling. And while all of that was dying down, she looked over at me and said, "Who *are* you?!" And one of the other girls said, "Oh, Ellen, for heaven's sake!" But she had honestly never seen me. I thought that was so funny. She was so cute.

One of your more recent roles was on *Dr. Quinn, Medicine Woman*.

Yes. I played Rebecca, Jane Seymour's older sister from Boston. I did one or two episodes a year during the last four years of the show. They were usually those two-hour episodes during sweeps week that dealt with a birth, or a death, or something of epic proportions.

Where was the series shot?

Usually at Paramount Ranch, but the last one I did was up in Canada. I didn't particularly enjoy the one in Canada because of the cold, but I really enjoyed doing the ones in California. Jane Seymour was wonderful. She's darling. And at that stage in time, we were not unlike sisters. We looked enough like sisters to actually be sisters.

How long would it take to shoot a *Dr. Quinn* episode?

Usually about ten days. The last one that we did in California was especially fun because we got to ride horseback. I hadn't ridden in quite a while, so I had to take lessons again with their wranglers, but we had so much fun that when we stopped shooting that day, we asked if we could take a couple of horses out, and the wrangler went with us and we rode all over the place just for fun. That was wonderful.

What have you been up to recently?

Last year, I did a *Cold Case* episode on CBS called "Colors." I enjoyed that. I was quite pleased with it, though they did age me quite a bit. I hope I don't look quite *that* old! (*Laughs.*) It had a baseball theme and they usually play it around the play-offs or the World Series. And in it, I played a very surprising role.

I'm going to look for that. Sounds interesting! So have you chosen to slow your acting career down?

I guess you could say I'm semi-retired. I really only do things if something comes up that I really want to do. I'm not averse to doing something, but I don't run up to town and seek it. If it works out within my schedule, then that's swell.

Still a "princess" in my book.

Well, for our sakes, let's hope something comes along you'd like to do again very soon.

Thank you!

[Elinor Donahue is semi-retired and lives with her husband Lew, in Palm Desert, California. She, Ken Beck and Jim Clark are co-authors of a wonderful memoir cookbook called *In the Kitchen with Elinor Donahue* [Cumberland House Publishing] that contains 250 photographs from her many years in the business and dozens of mouth-watering recipes from her own kitchen as well as from the co-stars of her many film and television appearances.]

Lynn Borden

Hazel: Barbara Baxter 1965-66

It was 1961 when television audiences first met the irrepressible Hazel Burke, the delightful domestic who could whip together a gourmet meal for unexpected guests in a moment's notice.

Always efficient, Hazel could keep the house as shiny and spotless as a newly-minted dime, bake cookies for the church social, and still find time to play touch football with the neighborhood kids. Although at times a busybody, viewers knew that Hazel's heart was *always* in the right place.

For five seasons, Oscar-winner Shirley Booth lovingly brought to life the *Saturday Evening Post* cartoon of the same name, created by Ted Key in 1943. [Booth would go on to win two Emmys for her work on the series.]

Through reruns and the release of the series on DVD, her endearing portrayal of America's favorite maid will continue to charm generations to come.

During the first four seasons on NBC, Hazel devotedly took care of George and Dorothy Baxter (Don DeFore and Whitney Blake) and their lovable young son Harold (Bobby Buntrock).

During the fifth and final season, the show changed premises and networks. *Hazel* moved to CBS, along with a brand-new family. Hazel became housemaid to George's younger brother Steve, his attractive wife Barbara (Ray Fulmer and Lynn Borden), daughter Susie (Julia Benjamin), and nephew Harold (Bobby Buntrock).

The change in premise was explained by sending George and Dorothy to the Middle East on an oil deal for one of George's clients. Hazel would move in with Mr. B's younger brother, manage their household, and bring along Harold so he wouldn't miss school.

Although best known from television for her role in *Hazel* and the 1972 shocker film *Frogs*, Borden has also appeared on many other small screen favorites such as *The Dick Van Dyke Show*, *Family Affair*, *Get Smart*, and *Starsky and Hutch*.

Recently, I spoke with Borden, who is as friendly and charming as the character she played on the series.

Lynn, how did you land the role of Barbara Baxter?
At the time, I was living in San Francisco, and was doing a play with Walter Pidgeon called *Take Her, She's Mine*. I got a call from my agent to come down and read for this series. Now mind you, we're in production with the play, so I would zip down in the morning, read, and then I came back up and had a performance at night. And I had to go back a couple of times because they were looking at everybody!

That's when I met Shirley. She came in on the casting toward the end. I think we were down to the last five groups of husbands and wives they were choosing from. We all chatted, and then they tested all of us again. Ray Fulmer and I originally read together, and I guess we looked good together or something, because they didn't change us around with different partners. They kept us together.

Then a little later, I got the call, and that was it! So I had to move from San Francisco to L.A. very quickly. In fact, my husband at the time sold his business and we relocated. I loved every minute of it!! I got up every single morning really, really early, went to work, and thought, "This has to be the most wonderful life in the entire world!!"

What was it like working with Shirley Booth?
I was so thrilled the whole time I did the show with her —we *all* were. She was fabulous! She was funny as a crutch, and so good, such a *professional* ... There wasn't a mean bone in this woman's body. She was very sincere, very down to earth, and generous. She was so good to me. She always gave me tips on things to do when we were acting. Then I'd run out and write them down in a little book that I still have. I just loved her!

Lynn Borden, Shirley Booth, and Ray Fulmer, 1965.

How was it working with the rest of the *Hazel* cast?

There was no one in our cast that wasn't great! We all got along so well, and I think it was because Shirley hand-picked her people. She owned the show and she picked who she wanted, and must have had an instinct because we all got along so well.

The little girl who played our daughter, Julia Benjamin, was a terrific little girl. She was brilliant. She and I did keep in touch, but I haven't seen her in a while.

What was a typical day like at the studio?
Well, on Monday, we would sit around a big table on the soundstage and read through our scripts that we got on Friday night, so we had the weekend to look at them. We would read through and make any corrections. But we really didn't do too much correcting, because the writers pretty much knew our characters.

There was only one writer, and I'll never forget his name, but I won't tell you . . . (*She laughs*) and every time we would do a read through, we'd go, "Oh, my God, this is so and so's script isn't it?!" I mean, we could tell!! Then we'd look and say, "Yep... that's who wrote it!" (*Laughs.*) Then we'd have to kind of improvise and change the way some of the words were written. He would write words that just didn't fit our characters. You could always tell. But everyone else was great. We had about three or four writers and the rest were great.

After the read through, I would meet with the costume designer. Barbara Baxter had some outfits that were made, some of them we would just get in wardrobe, and some we just went out and bought. Monday was the day we would do that. We usually went to Saks Fifth Avenue and got clothes. That way, I would know what I was wearing down to the shoes for the whole week. Some of them became my favorites, and I'd say, "Oh, I want to wear that again!"

Then we shot Tuesday through Friday. On those days, I'd get to the studio around seven, and go right into the make-up room and get make-up and hairdressing, because I had to be on the set by eight. Then they would be lighting when we got there, and I would go to my dressing room and change into my costume.

Then we'd block the set, how we were going to walk, and how we were going to do this and that. Then we'd have our stand-ins come in to make sure the lighting was right. We would begin shooting by nine o'clock, and we'd finish at seven.

So you worked a five-day week.
Yes, and we worked *hard*. By seven o'clock, all you'd want to do was go home and go to bed. Everybody thinks we worked nine to five, but it wasn't like that. It was a lot of hours and a lot of hard work.

Were there many retakes or did everyone pretty much know their lines?
We had that problem with one particular person who had trouble getting things out of their mouth. They could never quite get it. And I would become hysterical with laughter, and Shirley would take me aside, trying not to laugh with me, and say, "You can't do that! Stop it!" So she'd pull me into her dressing room and we would just die!

E. W. Swackhamer directed a lot of the episodes.
Yes. Swack! He was a fabulous director. Without a doubt, he was the *best*.

Why do you say that?
Because he *directed*! He knew what he wanted, he knew how he wanted it done, he knew the camera angles, and he knew the characters. He was just fantastic! Some of the other directors I didn't care for. They were older and had been doing it a while. I was new and I'd ask them what they wanted me to do, and they'd say, "Oh, just do what you're doing." Some of them would be more interested in just sitting back. I wanted them to tell me what they wanted.

Was the last season of *Hazel* still filmed on the Screen Gems lot?
Yes, it was always at Screen Gems. The only thing that changed was it went from NBC to CBS.

What other shows were being filmed there at the time?
Bewitched was there, because Elizabeth Montgomery and I would be sitting there together in make-up. In the morning, Sally Field would be in there too.

Was she nice?
Sally? Oh yes! She was always friendly. We would always chat when we were all sitting there getting made up. I think we all came from a really "glad we're working, happy people" backgrounds. We were all so glad to be there.

What was Elizabeth Montgomery like?
Oh, she was great!! We were very friendly. If we happened to see each other,

we would go have lunch or something like that. In fact, one day, I was at Paramount, and I pulled up in my car, which at the time had "Borden" plates on the back, and Elizabeth had "Lizzie" plates on the back of hers. And she happened to pull up later and saw my car and parked beside me on the left. She went in to do whatever she was doing there, and came out and was waiting on me, kind of giggling. Then I saw the "Lizzie Borden" plates right beside each other and just died laughing. And what is so funny, years later, she ended up doing the *Lizzie Borden* movie. [*The Legend of Lizzie Borden.*]

Do you have a favorite episode or can you really remember them?
Oh, I remember *all* of them ... There's one where Harold is getting into music ["My Son the Sheepdog"], but not the kind of music we want. So we decide to join in and make even *worse* music. We dressed up like beatniks and danced around. Shirley was dancing, and I never laughed so hard in all my life! We had this rock music on, and I had on tall boots and a short skirt and my hair pinned up above my head. Shirley had a scarf wrapped around her head. Oh my God, her outfit was unbelievable ... Then the kids come in, and, of course, our plan backfires because they loved what we were doing!! We had a lot of fun with that one. In fact, I used to take my camera with me, and I have pictures from that episode.

Do you keep in touch with your TV husband, Ray Fulmer?
Yes, I do. Every once in a while, we'll just go have lunch and touch base. But we do autograph shows, and he usually does them with me. I would love to find Julia to do some with us.

Does Ray still act, or is he retired?
I think he's wanting to work again. He was very big in theatre and has done some *great* theatre work. So he kind of got into theatre more. Once in a while I used to go see him in plays he was doing, and he was very, very good at that.

And sadly, Bobby Buntrock died in a car accident.
Yes. I was really sorry to hear he had been killed. I don't exactly remember *when* he was killed, of course, it was way after the show. I keep thinking it was on a

bridge or something. [According to the website *Former Child Star Central*, Buntrock, 21, was killed in an auto accident in April 1974 on a bridge in South Dakota. Ironically, it was the same bridge on which his mother was killed a year earlier.]

What was he like?
Oh, he was great!! He played ball. He was just a *regular* kid. He got along well with Ray and everybody. He was just so neat.

That's good to hear because sometimes you hear these horror stories about kids in the business, how they are horrors on the set ... How it affects them later ...
Yes, and I know a lot of kids that it *did* affect, but it didn't affect Bobby. I think because he had really good parents, and the kids were schooled on the set, and had a wholesome group around them. But his parents were great! I think we all came from good parents. I know I did. I couldn't have had a better childhood.

Speaking of parents, your father was a famous cartoonist.
Yes! [Bill Freyse.] He did *Our Boarding House with Major Hoople, Lone Ranger*, and *The Green Hornet*. And the man who created *Hazel* was a cartoonist named Ted Key. They were going to do a movie on Major Hoople, and W. C. Fields was going to be Hoople, and the person they got to do the script was Ted Key!

How's that for a coincidence?
Yes!! And I didn't know any of this at the time! So during my first episode, I see this man standing around in the shadows. So I finally went up and introduced myself, and he said, "Well, my name is Ted Key, and I'm the cartoonist that created *Hazel*, etc." And I said, "Oh, that's really great! My dad is a cartoonist. He did Major Hoople, etc." Then he just stopped and looked at me and said, "Oh my God! Bill Freyse is your dad?" And I said, "Yes!" At that time, he had no idea who I was, because I was going by my married name, Borden. So I got him and my father on the phone together, and it was really, really neat. I always kept in touch with him.

So Ted Key was there on the set when you began season five?
Yes. He lived back east, but he was there for the first episode with us as *new* people. I imagine he wanted to see how it was going to go, who these new people were and everything. He stayed the whole week and watched.

How did the premise change for season five come about?
They wanted a younger brother and sister-in-law, and a kind of a different business. So they wrote George and Dorothy out by sending them to the Saudi Arabia on an oil deal, and they would leave Harold with us so he could finish his school. Why they picked Saudi Arabia, I'll never know! It seemed so far-fetched to me. I thought," Nobody's gonna buy that!" But they did! Nobody even questioned it!

Why did the show come to a close at the end of season five?
Shirley called us all together one day and said, "I'm not going to be able to go on with the show. I was hoping it would go on forever, but I just can't do it anymore. I'm just going to have to close it down. It's not because of anybody, or anything. I just can't do it anymore. I'm too sick right now."

What was wrong with her?
I think it had something to do with her lungs. I'm not sure about that. I know she was getting some kind of shots. She got very sick all of a sudden. For a little while, we had to shoot around her. We had to shoot three episodes at one time and we didn't know which episode was which. Sometimes we'd be in the back lot and do one scene from one show, and then another scene from a different show. We had to make notes in our scripts about what we were wearing in each episode just to make sure we wore exactly the same thing.

You mentioned Shirley said she had hoped the series would go on forever. Do you think it would have been renewed?
Oh we *were* renewed. We knew we were, but then Shirley decided she couldn't do it.

7   CONTINUED: (2)   11
                                                                  7

HAZEL
(as someone answers)
Dolores? Hazel. I'm throwing a
party tonight. Can you come?...
Good. Call the rest of the girls
for me, will you...
(pauses briefly)
Who?...Everybody! The more the
merrier...

FADE OUT:

(COMMERCIAL)

FADE IN:

EXT. SPRINGER'S MUSIC STORE - DAY

8   MEDIUM SHOT BARBARA AND MONA   8
are chatting as they stroll into scene. Mona is concerned
although trying not to be -- and Barbara is attempting to
convince her that there is nothing to worry about.

BARBARA
He's bound to get the promotion,
so stop worrying!

MONA
I'm not worrying. I just can't
understand why we haven't heard
by now!

BARBARA
Who else are they going to give
it to? Steve says Fred is
absolutely tops in his field.
Steve says --

MONA
Steve isn't Fred's boss. Oh, I
know there's nothing to worry
about...

BARBARA
Then don't.
(stops)
Oh! Ukelele strings.

MONA
Ukelele strings!

Beige suit.
Bone 3/4 heel.
No slip
Beige Purse
Gloves.

One of Borden's script pages from *Hazel* ("285 Dollars by Saturday"). Notice the
attention to detail by the wardrobe items listed on the side in Borden's own
handwriting; Beige suit, Bone ¾ heels, No clip, Beige Purse, & gloves.

Still as pretty as a picture.

That had to be disappointing.

Oh, God, my world ended... When she told us, our faces dropped a mile. She was in tears, we were in tears. It had been so wonderful to get up in the morning and drive in and do the thing you wanted to do more on this earth than anything else, and be allowed to do it.

Did you keep in touch with her?

We wrote to each other when the show ended, and I would call her and talk to her. And she'd send me pictures of her new little poodle dog. She always wrote me back.

I hope you kept those letters!

Oh yes! I have them put up somewhere. I just need to remember where! (*Laughs.*)

Do you have any funny stories about Shirley?

I remember that Shirley would not go out to lunch with anybody. She was always in her trailer. So one day during lunch hour, I knocked on her trailer, and I *thought* she said, "Come in."... So I went in. So there she is lying on this built-in couch thing that was in all of our trailers, with her legs up in the air on a big pillow, and she was taking a nap. And I just died.... I was mortified!! I said," I'm so sorry!" And she said, "No, come in! Come in!"

Then she explained to me why she never went to lunch. She said she would take a nap during lunch hour for fifteen or twenty minutes, and by golly, she had the most energy of anyone by the end of the day. We worked twelve hours a day, and then she would still be full of energy when she left and went home, and by four o'clock the rest of us were just dragging! To this day, that's what I make sure I do -- take a little fifteen-minute nap, especially if I'm going out in the evening, or working. It's the most amazing thing. She taught me something that I have carried through my whole life!

[Lynn Borden lives in California and continues working in the field of entertainment. An active member of the Motion Picture Academy, she shares a seat on the Foreign Language Film Committee with another *Hazel* actress from the same season, Mala Powers [Mona Williams] [Powers recently died of complications from leukemia at age 76]. A talented French impressionist artist, Borden's works can be seen in galleries throughout the country.]

Ray Fulmer

Hazel: Steve Baxter 1965-66

Not long after I spoke with Lynn Borden about her days on *Hazel*, she called one afternoon and said, "Eddie, I have something funny to tell you! I had just come out of the Motion Picture Academy and was about to cross Wilshire Blvd. when I hear someone shout, 'Lynn Borden! Hello, Lynn Borden!' I look across the street and headed in my direction is Ray Fulmer! [Her TV husband from *Hazel*.] I ran out and met him in the middle, grabbed him, whirled him around, and pulled him back across the street to talk to him." He said pointing, "But I have an appointment over there"... "Well, you have to come this way for a minute and talk," she laughed.

"As I had mentioned to you, I hadn't seen him in quite a while, and I had *just* talked to you about the show. Then all of a sudden, I run into Ray. It's so weird. It's like *Hazel* is all around me again!"

Luckily for me, it was. Lynn told Ray about my interest in the show and he kindly agreed to take me along as he strolled down memory lane about his time on *Hazel*.

Still quite handsome, and looking much younger than his seventy-three years, Fulmer couldn't have been nicer and had some great stories to share.

Ray, what was your first impression of Shirley Booth?
Funny. (*Laughing.*) A little dumpy, which was cute. Very approachable, and so generous.

Lynn Borden used that same word to describe Shirley. Generous.

Oh, she was. She would even give you the benefit of the camera angles. When they would set up the camera and the lighting, they would always give her the benefit of the angle. She's the star. Why not? But she'd grab my arm and whisper, "I'm gonna move over about three inches, 'cause a shadow is falling on your nose. And your nose looks funny, Ray."

(*Laughing*) That certainly isn't the norm in the business, especially coming from the star.

That's how she was. Generous to a fault.

Tell me about the rest of the cast.

Bobby Buntrock was a good kid. He was a pro. I remember the kids got Christmas presents on the *Hazel* show, and I got Bobby a neat plastic helmet for his bicycle. And though I never got it in writing, I heard he was killed on his bicycle, and I was just sick about that. And Julia Benjamin, who played the new role of my daughter with Lynn, was a cute kid. Lynn Borden was great fun. And what was it? '65-'66? Lynn hates to be reminded of how long ago it was. She just quivers. (*Laughing.*)

Jim Fonda was the producer, and one day we were shooting a scene in the second or third episode, and Jim came up to me and said, "Hey, ever wonder why you got the part?" I looked at him and said, "Yeah, because I didn't trip over any cables and fall flat on my face." He said, "No, no, no. Shirley thought that you were funny. In fact, she said if she didn't watch her step, you were gonna cop a few scenes from under her."

What a compliment.

Those are flattering words coming from her. I thought, "Thank you. Thank you."

When I was growing up, I only knew her as Hazel.

It wasn't until many years later that I realized the talent she had when I saw some other things she had done, like *The Matchmaker* and *Come Back, Little Sheba*. I'd watch her and think, "My God, she's brilliant!" Any part she played

A *Hazel* Family Christmas. From L to R: Julia Benjamin, Lynn Borden, Shirley Booth, Ray Fulmer, and Bobby Buntrock.

was convincing. She was a natural. She just had it! She certainly did. Did you know that she starred in the *The Philadelphia Story* on Broadway?

No, I didn't.
She did the Ruth Hussey role. She had to be as funny as hell in that.

What were you doing when *Hazel* came along?
I had just finished playing the role of Patrick in *Auntie Mame* on Broadway.

Who was Auntie Mame when you were in the show?
Well Roz Russell originated the part, and I did work with her for a while, but then she had to come out west to do the movie [*Auntie Mame*]. Then Greer Garson replaced her. Greer was such a princess. She was wonderful! Terrific!

I've always heard nice things about Greer. On the other hand, I've also heard that Roz could be tough.
Tough lady. Tough lady. She was annoyed because she had to break in Patrick Dennis, which was my part, her nephew. Wisely, Greer Garson had it in her contract through the William Morris Agency that everybody had to be in the play at least two weeks before she came in, so they'd know what the hell they were doing. She was marvelous. I had such a crush on her! Oh my God, a gorgeous woman. [*He begins talking in a low sultry tone.*] And she had that *earthy* kind of voice... (*We laugh.*)

Did Roz make it tough on you?
No. She was very professional, but she was at the twilight of her career. Her big splash was about to be the movie version, and she didn't like having to break in a new featured player. Anyway, we did it with Roz, and then Greer, and then Bea Lillie. She was a gas! Funny gal. Very stylish. She would say lines in Act One that should have been done in Act Three.

(*Laughing.*) Really?
Yes. So if you weren't on your toes, you could make a reply that was totally incoherent. It pissed a lot of the actors off and they would blow it if they weren't

paying attention. So her run wasn't that splendorous. But I learned quickly, you listen for the lines, and you pay attention. By paying attention, you learn. That's how you find your niche as an actor... (*A pause.*) I forgot to mention the last person that I worked with in the role was Eve Arden.

Tell me about her.
She reminded me of a California Mame. Very home-grown and tall. She was like 5'10. She was great. Nice lady. Also very generous. It was a great thrill working with all four of these gals.

So *Auntie Mame* was a very rewarding part of your career.
Yes, very. (*A pause.*) Do you remember how they have a peek-a-boo spot on the curtain where you can look out and see who's in the audience?

Yes.
One night somebody said, "Hey, Bob Hope's in the audience." I'm thinking, "Damn! Bob Hope?!" So I look through the peephole and sure enough, there he was, bigger than shit. And I thought, "My God! Bob Hope's gonna see me perform!"

Did you keep anything from your *Hazel* days?
No, I didn't. Not a thing. Not even the rights. I sold my residuals back to Columbia Pictures for ten grand.

I didn't know you could do that.
Yes. They said, "If you don't sell them in a year and a half, you'll get fourteen grand including the residuals." But I thought for a couple-thousand dollars less, I'd just take the first deal, and it turned out to be a good move for me. I went to Italy and did a few things over there.

What other shows can you remember that were filming at Columbia when you were doing *Hazel*?
The Western *Rawhide* was there. The exteriors locations were being done out in the valley.

Is that the same place where the exteriors for the Baxter house and the neighborhood were shot?

That's right. I got to know Clint Eastwood fairly well. Nice fellow. In fact, the same time I was in Italy, he went to Rome and did those Spaghetti westerns and I ran into him out there. Getting back to your question, *Bewitched* with Elizabeth Montgomery was shooting there. (*He pauses a moment.*) You know, in New York a few years ago, I was picked by Walter Grauman, who's a director, to do a screen test for the television version of *Some Like It Hot*. I forget if it was the Tony Curtis role or the Jack Lemmon role, but half of the test was in drag.

(*Laughing.*) Yes, I was just picturing that.

I'm a pretty big guy. I'm six feet, and have a hairy chest, and I'm in this blond wig. But we finally did it, and the director yells, "Cut. Print." And I remember that the crew applauded, which was most flattering. Crews are *notorious* for not responding, so I was excited, and I'm heading back to the dressing room, and right behind me was Elizabeth Montgomery, who happened to have been on the set for some reason. And she's laughing and says, "Hi, Ray! Boy, that was a great test!"

And you're standing there in all this drag. (*Laughs.*)

Yes, and after all that, I didn't get the part. I came pretty close though, and I got a very flattering letter from Walter. I wish I had enough pull to get a copy of that test. That had to be hysterical. I'd love to see it.

Lynn told me you had a great Shirley Booth story that warrants attention.

Oh yes! As you know, The *Hazel* show was shot at the Columbia Picture Lot. So movies were being made there as well. So one day the cast was breaking for lunch, and I walk by Shirley's trailer, and she's putting on lipstick, and the hair and everything is hunky dory, so I said, "Shirley, it's lunch. What are you carrying on about?" And she said, "Cary Grant is on Stage 8 and he's shooting *Walk, Don't Run*! And I haven't seen him in fifteen years, so I'm gonna go see him." I said, "You're gonna go see Cary Grant?!" She said, "Yeah, he invited me over." So I said, "Oh! Oh! Can I go with you?!" And she was always so generous, she said, "Yeah, sure. Come on!"

"Steve Baxter" today.

So we're traipsing over to Stage 8 and I'm going, "Oh my God. I'm gonna meet Cary Grant!" And she's telling me, "The last time I saw him was in New York. We ran into each other in front of Tiffany's on the corner of Fifth Avenue. And Ray, we stood there for fifteen or twenty minutes swapping stories and *nobody* even approached him and asked him for his autograph."

That's hard to believe!

Yes. For fifteen or twenty minutes. Nobody! Then with a little chuckle, she added, "Coincidentally, nobody asked me either." We laughed and she said," Well, I was an entity. I was known in New York. And nobody ever approached us."

That *is* unbelievable.

I couldn't believe it either. So we get to Stage 8 and knock on his trailer door and his secretary answers and says, "Oh, Miss Booth. Do come in. Mr. Grant will be out in a minute." So she whispers to me, "Now watch how he pays attention. Watch how he listens." She was always giving acting lessons but in a nice way. All of a sudden, he bounds out, and says [*in an excellent Cary Grant impression*], "Shirley! Shirley! Good to see ya! My goodness, how many years has it been?" And sure enough, he turns to me and says, "Ray would you like a cup of tea?" I'm thinking, "Christ! My hero, Cary Grant, just offered me a cup of tea!" So the girl brings me out a cup and saucer, and I'm hoping there is adhesive on the bottom of the cup so I wouldn't rattle it! (*Laughs.*) But sure enough, Shirley was right. All of his attention was right at her, recounting old stories and friends and things. Like I mentioned earlier about listening, it pays off. So then we shook hands and he said, "Great to meet you, Ray!" You know, one of those kinds of things. I'm like, "Holy Christ! He made my day!"

That had to be the thrill of a lifetime.

That was definitely one of the highlights of working on the show for me. And it turned out to be his last picture.

Listening to these stories has been a highlight for me, and I very much appreciate it! Thank you, Ray.

You're welcome, my friend.

   [Ray Fulmer is semi-retired, and currently single. He lives in Beverly Hills, California.]

Keith Thibodeaux

I Love Lucy: Little Ricky 1956-60
The Andy Griffith Show: Johnny Paul Jason 1962-66

The name Keith Thibodeaux may not immediately ring a bell. If you're scratching your head, it's not your fault. Trivia buffs know that his real name was never used in the on-screen credits, and sporadically, the name Richard Keith was inserted in the closing credits. But it's highly improbable that (unless you've been living under a rock for the last half-century), you wouldn't recognize the name *Little Ricky*.

It was during the sixth season that this amazingly talented child prodigy joined the cast of the most popular sitcom in television history, *I Love Lucy*.

Unlike five-year-old Little Ricky, who began tapping out a cadenced pattern with his spoon on the side of an oatmeal bowl, Thibodeaux began his musical career at the remarkable age of two!

A year later, he was spotted in a talent contest by famous bandleader Horace Heidt, who hired him to join his Big Band Variety show. Thibodeaux and his father toured the nation in *The Horace Heidt Swift Premium Hour* for a year and a half before finally deciding to settle in California, which offered more opportunities in the field of entertainment.

Soon after, word reached Thibodeaux's father that a talent search was being conducted for a little boy to play the Ricardo's son on *I Love Lucy*, and, as they say, the rest is history.

Thibodeaux, born in Louisiana, and now living in Jackson, Mississippi, retains an accent that is a charming reminder of his southern roots.

Keith, what's the question you get asked the *most* about your time on *I Love Lucy*?
People always want to know, "What was Lucy like?"... Lucy wasn't like the Lucy you see on TV. She didn't think funny off camera. She was a great actress, but she definitely had her moments. She could be moody, and testy, and impatient with people. But I don't remember anytime she was really testy with me.

Is there anything you can particularly recall about your first days on the show?
When I first started on the show, I called Lucy "Miss Ball." And I remember her saying, "Don't call me Miss Ball. We're all on a first name basis here. Call me Lucy." So I did. I called all the cast by their first names: Vivian, Bill, Desi, and Lucy. That's what I did my whole life.

Tell me about Desi.
He was a very nice guy. Very warm. Very generous. He just had a problem with drinking, and because of that, he was kind of ostracized in a lot of ways in Hollywood because of it.

Did you stay in touch with him after the series?
Off and on. He sent me a graduation present when I graduated from high school, and I saw him at his son's wedding when Desi Jr. married Linda Purl.

What are your memories of Vivian Vance and William Frawley?
I thought they were perfect for their roles. They fit them to a tee. They were both nice to me, although Bill was a bit friendlier than Vivian. [According to reports, Vance used to retreat to her dressing room when she wasn't rehearsing and wasn't the warmest around children.] They were both consummate professionals who came to work and did their jobs.

During that period of time, were they as strict with the hours that child actors could work?
Yes. I think you could only work six hours a day back then. And you'd have to have three hours of school, so you'd have to sandwich in three hours of work inside that one day.

This cast needs no introduction.

Was it hard for you to memorize your lines?
Not really. My dad would help me. He would read the lines, and I'd speak the lines back.

I read where you used to go over to Lucy and Desi's house and play with Lucie and Desi Jr. Were they pretty easy to get along with?
Yeah. Pretty much. We were good childhood friends, and we spent a lot of time together.

What kind of things would you do when you'd visit?
We'd do everything kids like to do. We'd play, ride bikes, put on plays, have dances. We'd go to the movies, go to the beach, and sometimes we'd go to the racetrack with Desi. All kinds of things.

If the kids misbehaved when you were visiting, who would usually handle that?
It was usually their maid, Willie Mae. She had that part - the discipline. In fact, she took a switch to me and little Desi a couple of times. (Laughs.)

What did you do?
We jumped in the swimming pool when we weren't supposed to.

Did you keep anything from your days on *I Love Lucy*?
I have some scripts that someone gave me, but I don't think they're originals. I have a couple of Little Ricky dolls, and a 1956 set of Gretsch drums that Lucy gave me for my birthday which have been totally restored. That particular year made those drums a collector's item.

Not to mention the fact that Lucy gave them to you.
Yes. (*Laughs.*)

Is there anything in particular that you wish you *had* kept?
Oh, sure! I wish I had kept *everything*! (*Laughs.*)

Like the mini Conga drum?
Oh yeah. I wish I had kept that, my tuxedo... many, many things.

Is there anything that you *don't* get asked about your *Lucy* days that you wish people knew?
Probably the fact that I never got credit as *Little Ricky* on the show.

I wanted to ask you about that. I've always noticed that on the *Lucy-Desi Comedy Hour*, the credits always said, "Starring Lucille Ball, Desi Arnaz, Vivian

Vance, William Frawley, and "Little Ricky."

Yep, they wouldn't give my real name, so I really didn't get on-screen credit... which may be good or bad, depending on how you think about it. (*Laughs.*) But it was kind of an odd thing how they wanted people to think that Little Ricky was their real son.

When was the last time you spoke to Lucy?

The last time I saw Lucy was at Desi's funeral in Del Mar, at their beach house. The family had a get-together afterwards. When I got there, Lucy came over and hugged me for a real long time.

How was she holding up that day?

She was . . . well, you know . . . (*He pauses.*) It was a passing milestone in her life. But she got through it. She had a lot to do that day, a lot of people to meet, so I didn't get to talk to her that much. But she told me that she had seen me on *Good Morning, America* that morning talking about Desi, and that she was proud of me. That meant a lot coming from her.

How did you find out that Lucy had died?

A reporter from the Associated Press called and told me. It was quite a shock.

Yes, I think it was to everyone. We had all heard that she was in the hospital but the last reports said that she was doing much better, and everyone thought she was going to be fine.

Exactly. That was a sad day.

I remember. I was teaching school when we heard the news and everyone on our staff was so shocked and saddened. We all made black armbands and wore them that day. That's how much she meant to us who had grown up watching her. I'll never forget one of my colleagues calling her "our electronic baby sitter." The students asked why we were wearing the armbands, and we said, "Lucy died." And they knew who we were talking about. Even in elementary school, they knew who Lucy was.

It's amazing. She just had that kind of impact.

Let's talk about your time on *The Andy Griffith Show*. Did you have to audition for the role of Opie's best friend, Johnny Paul Jason?
Yes, I did. It wasn't much of an audition. It was just meeting the casting director and that was about it.

I'm sure he was familiar with your work on *Lucy*.
Right.

Was the *Andy Griffith Show* shot on the same lot as *I Love Lucy*?
Yes. It was actually shot at the Cahuenga Studios, which also filmed Dick Van Dyke, Danny Thomas, and a bunch of other shows.

Did you ever get to do any scenes on the old 40 acres back lot in Culver City where the exteriors of Mayberry were shot?
Yeah, I did. We did a lot out of scenes out there.

Keith today, still beatin' those drums.

I've read that it was an interesting lot to work on. The old *Gone with the Wind* house was out there, things like that. Were you able to look around much when you were there?
I didn't get to see a lot. You basically had to stay around where you were filming, within earshot of where they needed you. Although, on the RKO lot that Desi bought, I got to see the original King Kong they used in the movie.

Was it a miniature?
Actually, it was really huge. And I saw the airplanes and skyscrapers. They were all miniatures. That was neat! Now, if I could have obtained all *that* stuff from back then, that would be worth *A LOT* of money now!(*Laughs.*)

Tell me about Andy Griffith.
Andy was very much like his character. Very nice. Very down to earth. The whole show was like that.

Was it a lot different from the *Lucy* set?
Absolutely. It had a real *family* feel to it. Sometimes you'd see people sitting around playing checkers on the set between takes. Also, one of the biggest differences was that *Lucy* was filmed in front of a live audience, and *Andy* was not.

***Andy* was a one-camera show, I believe.**
Right.

Do you prefer one over the other?
Well, with one camera it's more laid back, and it gives you a little time to breathe. It wasn't as tense as it got on the *Lucy* set with a live audience. It depends what style you like. Working with three cameras is like shooting a play. Some people prefer the energy of a live audience.

When you were doing the *Andy's* at Desilu, did you ever run into Lucy on the lot?
No, because she wasn't on that particular lot anymore. By that time she had moved to the old RKO studios.

Did you keep any of the *Andy* scripts?
No, I don't think I did. You just never think about those kinds of things when you're doing it.

Do you have a favorite *Andy* episode that you were in?
Gosh... (*Thinking.*)

I was flicking channels the other night and caught you in "Opie and His Band of Merry Men" on TV Land. That episode had a lot of scenes around the lake that you see in the opening where Andy and Opie always went fishing.
Right. I believe that was filmed at a canyon out in L.A. somewhere.

The Miracle Salve episode ["A Deal is a Deal"] was funny. That's one of my favorites.
Yeah, that's a good one. Man, they were just *all* good. I just enjoyed being in every single one of 'em.

Do you have any of the *Andy's* you were in on DVD?
No, I don't. I've got the sixth season of *Lucy*. I did a voice-over on that one for the *Superman* episode.

I bought that set the other day. It was interesting listening to your comments about it.
That was one of my all-time favorite episodes. Meeting Superman was every kid's dream.

Have you ever run into Andy over the years?
No, I've actually not seen him since I've been on the show.

What about Ron Howard?
We were friends on the set, but I haven't run into him either since the show. But I did do a couple of things with Don Knotts.

What kinds of things?
Actually, I played back up for him when he was traveling in Alabama and North Carolina. He did a baseball routine, and I did a drum roll behind him, and some cymbal hits as part of it. That kind of stuff.

What was he like?
Very quiet, very soft-spoken, very unassuming. The characters he did were great. He was a funny guy, unlike Lucy, who off camera was not funny. She just wasn't a naturally funny person without the scripts.

And Don recently died.
Yes. I was surprised he lived as long as he did.

Why do you say that?
Because he was pretty sick when I last saw him, and that had to be seven or eight years ago.

Is there anything else you would like to be remembered for, other than being Little Ricky on I Love Lucy?
Well, the most important things in life to me are my faith in Jesus Christ, being a good husband to my wife Kathy, and to hopefully have been a good father to my daughter Tara.

Thank you, Keith. I appreciate you telling me about your days on two of the most famous sitcoms in television history.
You're welcome. Send me a signed copy when the book comes out!

You got it!
[Keith Thibodeaux lives in Jackson, Mississippi with his lovely wife Kathy. They are the founders and executive directors of *Ballet Magnificat*, a Christian Ballet Company. Keith's own book, *Life After Lucy*, is available at their website www.*Ballet Magnificat*.]

Marla Gibbs

The Jeffersons: Florence Johnston 1975-85
227: Mary Jenkins 1985-90

Marla Gibbs was a United Airlines worker and mother of three when she left Detroit and set out for the bright lights of Hollywood in 1969. Gibbs would strike sitcom gold when she landed the plum role of sassy, no-nonsense, domestic Florence Johnston on *The Jeffersons,* the highly successful and long-running Norman Lear comedy, in 1975.

The immense popularity of Gibbs' character was one of the reasons audiences kept tuning in week after week for ten years. After continuing in the role until cancellation of the series in the mid-eighties, Gibbs would again move right on up into another hit sitcom, this time as wife and mother Mary Jenkins on the 1985 NBC comedy *227.*

During the middle-eighties, NBC was the place to be on Saturday nights, as *227* immediately followed *The Golden Girls* for a hysterical hour of prime-time laughs.

When did your acting career begin, Marla?
My acting career really began when I moved from Detroit to Los Angeles in 1969. I had done one well-known TV show in Detroit called *Juvenile Court.* That came about when I ran into an ex-teacher in a grocery store, who belonged to the Screen Actors Guild, which I didn't know what that was, and he was doing this thing in the grocery store where you stop people and you let them try a product and you take what they say about it, and he liked what I did. He asked

me if I'd like to do this TV show, so he sent me the script, and I learned the *whole* script, not knowing that I wasn't supposed to memorize every word in it. But I did the part, and people liked what I did. My mother said, "Oh, that was good!" and that stayed in my mind. So I moved out to L.A. with my children in '69, and by '70 I was doing some work. I played extras and did a couple of bit parts. Like *Lady Sings the Blues* ...

You were in *Lady Sings the Blues*?
Yes.

Do you know I have never seen that movie? I hear it's a great movie, but I've never seen it.
(*In a snappy "Florence" retort*) Well, you won't see me either. It was that quick.

(*Laughing*) I won't?
No. And then I was in *Uptown Saturday Night,* and you won't see me in that either. (*Laughing*)You can barely see me as the camera panned. But I did a show called *Christmas Dream,* which turned out to be a reoccurring show every Christmas. It ran every Christmas for about four or five years.

Then I did a show called *Where Does It Hurt?,* which was the first TV show on breast mastectomy. I played a nurse with a couple of lines. Then I got involved with workshops and did some plays. Then I was in a playhouse called The Zodiac Theater, which I was excited to be in because it had won some critics awards here in L.A., and I was doing *The Gingerbread Lady* when the audition came up for *The Jeffersons.*

How long was it after the audition that you found out you had gotten the part?
It was all in the same day. I went in, and the part reminded me of my grandmother and my aunt, and that's how I delivered the lines. A couple of things that they used to say came to me, and I added that, and they liked it. So they took me over to the producers and I did it the same way I did it in the casting agent's office, and by the time I got home I had the part.

A pre-printed, autographed photo sent to fans who wrote the cast.

Is it true that you were working for an airline company at the time and kept that job for a while after you got the part on *The Jeffersons*?
Yes. I was working for United Airlines, and kept that job for two years.

Why?
(*Laughing.*) You know what they say. Two in the pan is worth twenty in the bush!

Your role on *The Jeffersons* was more semi-regular when the series first began.
Yes. I was only in seven or so episodes the first two years.

I was watching the first episode the other day and at the end of the show, Florence says...
(*Taking the cue.*) "How come we overcame and nobody told me?!"

Yes! (*Laughing.*) The audience exploded! That had to have been a signal to the producers that your character was going to be popular. I'm surprised that they didn't write you in more episodes.

Well, I think that in the beginning, my part was a lot like Mother Jefferson's [Zara Cully]. She was the antagonist for Louise and I was the antagonist for George.

I see. She passed away around the third season I believe.

Yes, I believe so.

Was that unexpected?

No. She had been ill for a while.

What were Sherman Hemsley and Isabel Sanford like to work with?

They were very loving people. But Sherman was extremely shy. I always said he was an extrovert on camera and an introvert off camera. He's gotten much better. Now I think he's balanced that out pretty well. He's been doing plays and shows and his manager became ill, and he has gotten more comfortable talking for himself. Isabel was a comedienne off stage. She actually was more like Florence.

Did you stay in touch after the show ended?

For the most part we did. Then she bought some other properties in other places, and generally your career goes where it goes, and your life goes where it goes. I stayed more in touch with Roxie [Roker].

Were you close?

Yes. Roxie was a very sophisticated, very fun, very loving person. We had a lot of fun together.

Mike Evans, who played Lionel, was replaced after the first season.

Yes. By Damon Evans.

Any relation?

No. Just a coincidence.

Why was that?

I'm not sure what the whole story was. I know there was some sort of disagreement, and he left and they hired Damon, who was really more of a Broadway actor and singer. I don't think he was as happy in the role toward the end. Mike eventually came back to the role. [Evans returned to the series in 1979 and played the role of Lionel until 1981. He passed away in 2006, just before this book went to press.]

How would you describe Florence?

Florence had common sense, which the majority of women have without benefit of formal education. She was down to earth. She didn't put on airs. She really loved the people she was with. She was happy they were affluent, but she couldn't see why they were putting on all these airs. She just told it like it was. Her take was, "Don't tell me to come out of the kitchen and open the door when you standing right next to it." That to her made sense.

Did the show have a heavy work schedule?

We worked five days a week, but the hours were light. We were pretty much up on what we did and were able to work it out pretty readily. It got to the point where Norman Lear wouldn't even come to our run-throughs. He'd say, "You guys have it together!" We were a very loving cast, like family. We came together to play, and out of that came a lot of lines and things that we wanted to do. Our production company was very open to that and allowed us to do a lot of things.

What are some of your favorite episodes?

(*Laughing*.) Oh, there were so many. There was the one with Gladys Knight, where we were in a salon with goop all over our faces and I didn't know she was a celebrity.

I just watched that episode last week. You got on the subject of singers and she asked you your favorite, and you said, "Diana Ross."
(*Laughing.*) Yes.

She sang a little for you, and you said, "Not bad, but I don't think you're ready for no church choir."
(*Laughing.*) Yes, yes. And there was the one with Billy Dee ["Me and Billy Dee"] and the one where I get fired, and I come back and put on the Aunt Jemima costume.

You in the Aunt Jemima costume was featured a lot in some clips of the opening credits. That was so funny.
And I liked the one where Ned Wertimer, Ralph the doorman, and I played the Willises. Mr. Jefferson has an interracial company rep come over that he wants to impress, and he's made the Willises mad, so he gets me and Ralph to play Helen and Tom Willis ["A Case of Black and White."]

Sounds funny. I've got to see that one.
Yes. That's a good one.

How did the spin-off *Checking In* come about?
A couple of the writers from the show wanted me to spin-off, but I didn't really want to do it. They were trying to talk me into it, so I made them agree to pay me for whatever I missed if it didn't work.

Why were only four episodes produced?
There was a writers strike, and they didn't have any more material. So I had it in my contract that I could go back to *The Jeffersons*.

That was a smart move on your part. Do you think the show would have gone on?
I don't know. I didn't have as much faith in that show simply because the premise was wrong. With Sherman and I, there was always the expectation that he might fire me, and how I would get out of it. He had some power over me. In *Checking In*, Larry Linville from M*A*S*H was playing the manager, but he

Florence and Weezy listen to a blustering George.

didn't have any real power. So he had to play frustrated, which he didn't like. It didn't work, because John Anderson was the owner of the hotel, and he was the one that hired me. So nobody could really fire me.

Liz Torres was also in the cast.
Yes. She was a doll. And Ruth Brown, the blues singer, was in it. She went on to Broadway and ended up winning the Tony. [Ruth Brown passed away at age 78 as this book was going to press.]

***The Jeffersons* ended in '85. Did you realize that the last show of that season would be the last one of the series?**
No. They canceled us. And it happened rather quickly.

Did you keep any of your scripts from the show?
I used to, but I sent most of them off to people who were doing auctions. But I have all the tapes that I'm now converting to DVD.

Did you go right from *The Jeffersons* into *227*?
Yes. Originally, though, we were going to hold *227* back for another year, because we didn't know *The Jeffersons* was going to be canceled. It happened so fast that they didn't tell any of us. So we were a little upset over that.

So there was no goodbye show or anything.
No.

How did you become involved with *227*?
It was originally a play, and my daughter [Christine Houston] was producing it. She cast me in it, and eventually talked me into getting the rights for the series.

Was the series different from the play?
Oh, we changed everything. The play was set in the fifties and had a lot of the problems of the fifties in it, which I didn't think made it viable for a television show. It would have been good for a movie of the week. When we shopped it around, Norman Lear saw it as a play, Brandon Tartikoff saw it as a TV show, and Universal saw it as a movie of the week. But by the time Norman came, he talked me into putting the play up again, so we did that. Once we put the play up, we found that NBC was the one that was still interested.

Did any of the cast members follow the play into the series?
Yes. Hal Williams was my husband in the play. I insisted in him being in the show because we had already worked out the chemistry between us. And Regina King was my daughter. Curtis Baldwin, who was originally on the production crew of the play, ended up playing Calvin [Dobbs]. Then everybody else that was in the play got a chance to come in as a guest.

Was Helen Martin's character [Pearl Shay] originally in the play?
No, she wasn't. But I wanted a senior citizen in it, so I suggested her.

She was wonderful in that part.
Yes, she really was.

That was you singing the theme song ["No Place Like Home"], wasn't it?
Yes. That's me singing.

Was that song written especially for the series?
Yes, it was.

It was a great cast.
Yes. I first met Alaina Reed when she auditioned for the show. And the same with Jackee'. I had never met her before the audition either.

Her character, Sandra, became very popular, much like your Florence on *The Jeffersons*.
Yes. She became the break-out character of the show. She was very funny.

I have read that, at times, she caused some rumblings on the set and could be a bit difficult.
That has been said, but Jackee's in a different place now. Sometimes when people come on a show and it's new, what they thought was going to be happening is a little different from what actually happens, and they don't adjust to that right away as well as they could, because they still have that other picture in their head. The fact that she was so good, and her people concurring that with her, made her move just a little too fast. I thought she had the ability to have a show, and be the star of it, but you can't go too fast, because you really have to learn about the business. Watching everything on *The Jeffersons* made it very easy for me to make the transition of having my own show, understanding what I needed to do, and how important it was that I recognized everybody on the show. But Jackee' has made a lot of changes and I think she really understands that now.

There was an episode in the first season of *227* where the residents are at a crime prevention meeting in the basement of the building, and while you're there, your apartment gets robbed.
Yes. They took all our stuff. (*Laughing.*)

And you ended up getting all new furniture. Did that just happen to be written in, or were you ready for a change of scenery?

We were all ready for some new furniture, so they came up with a way to get us some.

Describe Mary Jenkins.

Mary was a wife and a mother, unlike Florence, who never had a man. People used to ask me why they would never let me have a man on *The Jeffersons*. (*Laughing.*) So with Mary, I finally got one. Mary was very loving, and got into trouble all the time mostly thanks to Sandra. And on the show, we got to explore the things that go on between husbands and wives, and mothers and daughters. We were really trying to showcase what goes on in the world between *all* races. In fact, Hal Williams and I were in the airport in Vegas one time going to a convention where you sell your TV shows, and a Caucasian couple ran up to us and said, "You're doing us! You're doing us!" I just thought that was so profound.

Do you have a favorite between Florence and Mary?

I think I liked them both in their own ways because they were both so different.

Tell me about the jazz club you used to own.

I had it for about twenty years. We showcased some new talent, but generally it featured top-of-the-line jazz performers like Dizzy Gillespie, Kenny Burrell, and people like that.

What kind of things have you been doing recently?

I've been doing some television guest appearances. I recently did an *ER*, and an episode of *Cold Case*. I was on *Passions*, the soap opera, and I did the Neil Simon play, *Proposals,* which was just wonderful. And I've just finished my first Jazz CD called *It's Never Too Late*. I'm planning on perhaps touring and doing some major performances with that.

I love jazz! I'll have to look for that.

I'll just send you one.

Still crazy after all these years!

Wow! Great! And if Atlanta's on your touring itinerary, *please* let me know! (*Laughing.*) I certainly will. That's a promise!

[Marla Gibbs is an actor, singer, producer, and a great-grandmother of three. She lives in Inglewood, California. Gibbs was true to her word. Shortly after this interview, I received her Jazz CD *It's Never Too Late*. It was even better than I expected!]

Jon Provost

Lassie: Timmy Martin 1957-1964
The New Lassie: Steve McCullough 1989-1991

No Sunday night in our home would have ever been complete without watching a weekly episode of *Lassie*. Always in the top ten, it was a show that everyone watched where I grew up. You talked about Lassie's latest adventures at school the next day. You often wished you owned a dog that was so smart and so loving. To no one's surprise, Lassie and Timmy became a beloved part of our childhood.

Imagine the excitement that was created when it was announced that Lassie and company would be coming to film an episode at Alexander Springs, a beautifully wooded forest with a natural flowing spring, six miles from where I grew up in Central Florida.

Although Timmy and the Martins had recently sold the farm and moved to Australia, forest ranger Corey Stuart (Robert Bray) was now master and he and Lassie would actually be making a local appearance only a stone's throw from where I lived.

It seemed that it took forever, but *the* evening finally arrived. It was an unusual and exciting event for our tiny community, and I remember it as if it was yesterday. Almost everyone we knew was there. The crowd was thick and anxious. Excitement seemed to ripple through the air. Finally, Forest Ranger Corey (Robert Bray) appeared onstage but alone, and after moments of thunderous applause, quiet whisperings began churning throughout the crowd, "Where's Lassie? Where's Lassie?" We listened intently as he stepped up to the microphone to make an announcement. Unfortunately, it wasn't one we particularly wanted to hear.

Bray apologetically informed us that due to an exceptionally hard day of filming, Lassie was unable to appear that evening. A sea of moans and disappointed groans emanated from both children and parents alike. Soon after, our disappointments subsided and our enthusiasm began to resurface at the opportunity of shaking hands with Lassie's TV master.

As we waited in line, we were handed an autographed photo of everyone's favorite collie as a keepsake. Of course, Lassie's signature was a paw print stamped in ink, and I found it just recently as I was going through some boxes at my mother's as she was preparing to move.

We finally worked our way up to meet the familiar, smiling face that had appeared in our living room on a weekly basis. For posterity, my dad recorded the moment my sister and I made it to the front of the line with his Kodak super-eight movie camera. Later, I'll never forget watching the film on a brand-new movie screen that had recently replaced a wrinkled white sheet tacked to the living room wall. We watched as Lassie's master picked up my sister Mary Kay, and placed her on the bench right beside him. He was just leaning over to kiss her on the cheek, when, as luck would have it, the film ran out.

But for us, it was a thrilling and fascinating night, because not just anyone can boast that Lassie and company came to their hometown. It left us with one of those childhood memories that you hold so dear, the kind that can still make you smile years and years later.

Talking with Jon Provost for this book was an enjoyable addition to that Lassie adventure, a nostalgic trip down memory lane.

You began your career at a very young age.
Yes. The first thing I ever did was when I was barely three years old. Nobody in my family had ever been in the business. And how that came about was, my mother was from a small town in southern Texas, and her idol growing up was the actress Jane Wyman. She met my father in Los Angeles and they married there. Later, they were living in Pasadena at the time, and she read an article in Louella Parsons' newspaper column in the *L.A. Times* that said Warner Bros.

was looking for a two to three-year-old blond boy to be in this movie called *So Big* with Jane Wyman. Well, my mother literally thought that if she took me on this audition, she might meet Jane Wyman and get her autograph. She told my father, who thought she was crazy, but that didn't faze her a bit. So she took me to the audition and it was a real cattle call. There were over two-hundred little boys trying out, and I ended up getting the job. I have to say that I'm a real believer in being at the right place at the right time!

That is unbelievable.
She didn't know anything about the system or how it worked, or anything like that. So later in the day, this kind of heavy-set woman came over to her and said, "Excuse me, but I think your son is going to get this job. Can I ask who your agent is?" And this is how naive my mother was. She said, "Oh, thank you, but we just bought our house. We don't need an agent." The woman said, "No. You don't understand. I'm talking about a theatrical agent, because if your son gets this job, he needs an agent. I happen to be a very big child agent in Hollywood, so that's why I'm asking you." So Mom said, "Well, Lord no, we don't have an agent. But sure, if he gets the job, you can handle him." And it turned out that she really was a very big child agent. Her name was Lola Moore. She handled all of the early child stars through the years. She was my agent until '69, so she ended up having me the entire time. So that's how I got the first job.

So I assume your mother finally got to meet Jane Wyman.
(*Laughing.*) Oh yeah. She definitely got more than her autograph. My mom thought she was great. (*A pause.*) Remember how I said I believe in coincidences and being in the right place at the right time?

Yes.
Now, listen to this. In that first movie, *So Big*, I played the youngest of the character, and he grew up in the movie. The actor that played the character at an older age was Tommy Rettig, who I took over for in *Lassie*. Secondly, there was a dog in the movie and it was owned and trained by Rudd Weatherwax, who owned Lassie.

Amazing.

So here we are in '53, and then in '57 I get *Lassie*, and now I'm working with these same people again.

And how many times have we all seen Rudd Weatherwax's name on the *Lassie* credits?

Yes. He and his brother Jack were both big dog trainers and had Lassie, Old Yeller, Asta, all the famous dogs.

So that first movie led to others.

Yes. I did *The Country Girl* with Grace Kelly, *The Day They Gave Babies Away* [All Mine to Give] with Glynis Johns and Cameron Mitchell, *Back From Eternity* with Rod Steiger and Anita Ekberg, and then I did a movie for RKO called *Escapade in Japan*. This was in 1956, and I was six years old. We spent three and a half months filming in Japan. My mom stayed the whole time there with me. What a change and what a culture shock that was for a six-year-old! Great memories! I mention that because that was the movie that got me the part as Timmy on *Lassie*.

How did that come about?

The producers of the show wanted to replace Tommy Rettig, only because he was too old. He had outgrown the part. They wanted to get a new face in there. But they were having a hard time finding somebody that fit what they wanted. So they happened to see some of the outtakes of the movie that we were doing in Japan, and they said, "That's the kid! When he gets back, we want to meet him." So when I got back from Japan, I met with the writers and producers, and they said, "Yes. You're Timmy. We want you. But, how do you get along with big dogs?" They wanted to make sure that Lassie and I hit it off, because that was so important to the show, and something you couldn't fake. So I stayed with Rudd Weatherwax, on his sixty-acre ranch outside of Los Angeles, for about three or four days to see how Lassie and I got along. And, obviously, we got along well!

So there was no official audition.

No. They had a lot of other kids audition, but I didn't have to. They knew I could act, and I had the face that they wanted. So that's really how it came about.

How did they change the focus of the show from Jeff [Rettig] to you and the Martins?

I was written in as an orphan living with my grandparents, who had run away because I was a burden on them. They were old, and I felt guilty. So I ended up in the Martins' barn, and Lassie found me hiding in there. That's how they introduced me into the series. Then I worked with Tommy and Jan Clayton, and we did a transition period that lasted about a half season.

I don't remember ever seeing any of those very early episodes.

The early ones are really hard to find. Especially when Tommy finally left and his mom ended up selling the farm to the Martins -- who everybody remembers as being June Lockhart and Hugh Reilly, but my original parents were Cloris Leachman and Jon Sheppod. They played the same parts, Ruth and Paul Martin, but for less than a year. Cloris was not happy with the character and did not want to play it. So she got out of her contract, and, unfortunately, they didn't just let her go, they let Jon go also. Jon wanted to stay, but they decided to replace them both. Basically, Cloris said, "I'm not bakin' cookies for seven years."

(*Laughs*.) So then June and Hugh came in.

Yes. They came in and did the show for five years.

Where was the series filmed?

We filmed at Desilu studios, which used to be RKO, but now it's all Paramount. Paramount was right next door, and they bought it when Desilu sold out, and just knocked the walls down.

What other shows were filming there around the time you were doing *Lassie*?

We were on Stage 7, which was an end stage. Next to us was *Ben Casey* with

Vince Edwards, and on Stages 9 and 10 was *The Untouchables* with Robert Stack. That was very cool. We had a thing going between the two sets, that whenever they'd be doing a big gangster shoot-'em-up, they would come and get me and let me come and watch.

Really? How cool is that?!
Yes. It was very cool! I was a kid ten, eleven years old, and I wanted to see this stuff. It was also a way to let me have a little break. Maybe it was only once a week for ten minutes, but at least it was still something. Also, *My Three Sons* was filmed there, and, of course, *I Love Lucy*.

Did you ever meet Lucy or Desi?
You know, I never met either one of them. Never. I saw Lucy on the lot driving around in her golf cart quite a bit, but I never did meet her. But, again, we were so busy working.

Long hours?
We worked ten hours a day, five days a week, and nine months out of the year for seven years. I did over two-hundred fifty half-hour episodes. In those days, we did between thirty-seven and thirty-nine shows a year. And when I say ten hours a day, that was broken down into one hour for transportation, one hour for lunch, one hour of recreation, three hours of school, and four hours of work.

What kind of things did you get to do during recreation?
All recreation meant was, you weren't workin'. (*Laughs.*) I wasn't allowed to run around and get my clothes dirty and mess up my make-up. The only time that you were allowed to run around and do anything like that was at lunchtime. And at lunchtime, we ate! We didn't bring our lunch. We'd go out.

Did you eat at the commissary?
Desilu's commissary was really bad, so we didn't like to go there a lot. So a lot of times we would go next door to Paramount, and we'd eat in their commis-

sary, which was cool because you'd see different actors from different shows like *Bonanza*. And I'd see those guys like Dan Blocker and they'd say, "Hey, Jon! How you doin'?" It was cool. In fact, one time we were there and Bob Hope was filming a movie and he happened to be in the commissary. I was around eleven or twelve, and he called me over to his table and said, "Hey, kid, I like you on *Lassie*. That's a good show, but you know what? I want you to make me laugh. Show me what you got." Well, at the time, I was wearing false teeth. So what I did was, I pulled out my teeth in front of him and it cracked him up. In fact, I have this great picture hanging in my hallway signed by him of that moment. Somebody saw it as a photo op and took a picture. How the false teeth came about was, I had lost one of my front teeth, so the studio had dentists to make up false teeth to put in for continuity when we were shooting. A couple of times we would be filming a scene and thirty seconds into it somebody would yell, "Cut! Cut! He doesn't have his teeth in."

(*Laughs*.) You said you were allowed one hour for transportation. How did you get to work?
My mom usually drove me.

Was she usually on the set with you?
Yes, probably ninety percent of the time. And if she wasn't there, she had a woman that would be there to take care of me. But then they also had a social worker and a schoolteacher that was paid by the studio.

Did you go to school with any of the other kids on the lot, or were you tutored by yourself?
Most of the time my schooling was just me and my tutor when we were on the set. If some other kid would be working on an episode, then that would be different, but most of the time it was usually just me.

So you worked nine months of the year filming the show.
Yes, and for two of those three months that we weren't filming, Lassie and I would tour. We'd do the big parades, like Macy's Parade, the Rose Bowl Pa-

A boy and his dog.

rade. We would travel to major cities and do appearances. We'd go to rodeos and fairs, all those kinds of things.

Did you ever feel that you missed out on, quote, unquote, "a normal childhood?"

You know, I got to do stuff other kids didn't get to do, and they got to do stuff I didn't get to do. But it's hard to say. I didn't get to play soccer, or be a Cub Scout or Boy Scout. I was working. That's the way it was. It's just what you did.

So do you consider it as balancing out? A sort of trade off?

Exactly!

Was *Lassie* a one-camera show?

Yes. We only did one show with multiple cameras, and that was at the very end. It was a five-parter, shown on five consecutive Sundays, and it was filmed in color. It was the only one we ever filmed in color, and the reason is because it was released as a movie called *Lassie's Great Adventure*. It was in black and white on TV, but as a movie, it was released in color. That was the only thing we used multiple cameras on.

How many different Lassies did you work with?

In the seven years that I did the show, I worked with three different dogs. The first was the son of the original Lassie, and that was the dog that Tommy Rettig worked with. Tommy worked with him for three years, and I worked with him for a year and a half. Then his son took over, but I only worked with him for one year. Then the grandson took over and I worked with him for another five. His nickname was Baby, and he and I really bonded and grew up together. He and I could be anywhere, at the ranch, or wherever, and I could tell him, "Hey, Baby, lay down. Shake hands. Do whatever." And he would look at me like, "You're not my trainer."

Really? (*Laughing.*)

Oh yeah. He wouldn't do a thing. Wouldn't shake hands, wouldn't speak, but that's the way it had to be, because the dog couldn't be distracted by other people saying things. It all had to be the trainer or his assistants. For instance, if we were doing a scene, I might say to Lassie, "Lassie, I'm hurt. Run. Go get help." Right after I would say that, the trainer would say, "Lassie, run," or whatever. Then they would cut his voice out. So, as actors, if it was a scene with June and Hugh and Lassie and me, we would have to space our dialogue so the trainer could do his commands, and there would be room so they could cut his voice out.

I see. I always wondered if the trainer was beside the camera using hand signals or exactly how that was done.
Some of his commands were just visual, hand signals. And some were voice. It was probably fifty-fifty.

How did they get Lassie to look so vicious when there was a fight scene?
If there was a scene where Lassie was fighting a wolf or another dog and they had to make him look mean, they would take a rubber band and put it on his upper lip and then put it around the back of his ears, so it would lift up that lip so all of those teeth are exposed.

Really?!
It looks like they're growling, but they're not. If you ever watch a fight scene, look at their tails. They're wagging!

(*Laughing.*) The magic of television. Tell me about Hugh Reilly.
Hugh was great. He was really mellow. He was a very calm and easy-going guy.

Sounds like he was a bit like his character.
Yes. Very much so. Unfortunately, he passed away about eight years ago.

Did you keep in touch with him?
I did, but I didn't as much as June Lockhart. Hugh and I kind of lost contact. But I'm very happy to say that in the last three or four years of his life, we did reestablish that contact. He was a really great guy. Unfortunately, he smoked too much and that's what killed him.

Is June Lockhart anything like the character of Ruth Martin?
June is a *bit* more flamboyant than her character. June and I have stayed in touch forever. What's funny is, there have been times when my birthday came and my mom would forget, and she'd call a couple of days later and say, "Oh my God, I love you! I'm sorry your card is late!" But June never forgot a birthday, never forgot a Christmas card. That's how it's been the whole time.

She had parents who were actors and grew up in the business.
Yes. Both parents were very famous actors [Gene and Kathleen Lockhart].

Speaking of Christmas, I especially remember all three of them in *A Christmas Carol* [MGM, 1938]. Her mother and father played the parts of her parents in the movie.
Right. That was actually her film debut. She was twelve years old at the time. Her daughter, Anne Lockhart, is an actor and they have done things together as well. [Another daughter, Lizabeth Lockhart, was also briefly an actress.]

So she continues the tradition of keeping it in the family.
Yes.

You also worked with Andy Clyde on the series. [Andy was a former Keystone Kop and great character actor often recognized for his role as George MacMichael on *The Real McCoys*.]
Yes. He was a kick! He was just a little wiry guy, and couldn't have weighed more than ninety-five pounds. I knew a little about him because I had seen The Keystone Kops and stuff as a kid. So I did know who he was. He was so funny. Andy was great!

Did you ever get hurt doing the show?
Yes. I almost drowned. That was in the five-parter, *Lassie's Great Adventure*. We were doing a multiple-camera shot that we couldn't rehearse. It was a one shot deal. We were in the Sierra's on the Senora River and it was wintertime. And Lassie and I were on a raft and we were going down this whitewater and the raft

was supposed to break up, and Lassie and I would be thrown into the rapids and get separated. That was supposed to be the shot. They had a safety rope tied across the river past the cameras that I was supposed to grab and hang onto as I went by. They had two men in wet suits that would jump in and pull Lassie out. The water was freezing, so under my clothing I was wearing a wet suit, which luckily gave me some buoyancy. Well, we're thrown into the rapids, and I'm immediately thrown into a sinkhole. I hit my chest on a rock under the water, and it knocks all the air out of me and I come popping back up to the surface, and I'm screaming and yelling and hollering, but that's exactly what I'm supposed to be doing.

So they have no idea you've been hurt.
Oh no. They had no idea. So the scene goes on. The guys jump in, they pull Lassie out, and Timmy goes by. There was a stunt double there and he recognized something was wrong. He said, "He's in trouble," and he jumps into the water with all of his clothes on, grabs me, and then we both got sucked under one of these sinkholes. He told me later that he was literally standing on the bottom of the river and was pushing me up so I could get air. Somehow he managed to get us loose and we were pulled out and saved. Later, he told me that some locals in the area had come up and asked what we were doing, and he told them. And they told him to be careful; that it was very dangerous there and not as calm as it looked.

Luckily for you he was paying close attention. Was he your stunt double?
He had been my stunt double and he was going to be my stunt double for this show, but they couldn't use him because it was a one shot deal.

Was that your only close call?
No. Strangely enough, there was another show where we had this chimpanzee and he was old. And when chimps get old, they get angry and mean. It took us three and a half days to do one half-hour show, and this was the second day, so we were through filming for the day, and I was going home. And the chimp was sitting on a stool and his handler was next to him. Picture this. His handler

looked just like he was out of Barnum & Bailey Circus. He had the English pith helmet on, the riding boots, and he had a gun strapped to his side, which only had blanks. But he's there, so as I'm getting ready to leave, I'm walking by and I go up to the chimp and take my hand and rub it on his head and say, "I'll see ya tomorrow, Buddy." Well, as soon as I said that, he grabs my hand, puts my thumb into his mouth, and proceeds to chew it off!

Good Lord!
I'm screaming, blood is flowing, and the chimp jumps off the stool and starts running. So he's running and I'm running with him because I have to, and his trainer is running after him, and finally he pulls out his gun and shoots it in the air three times. Luckily, that startled the chimp and he let go of me. So they immediately rushed me to the studio infirmary and sewed me up.

Unbelievable.
But true. And I still have the scars on my thumb.

Amazing. Did Lassie ever use a stunt double?
Actually, yes. A lot of people think that we had like five Lassies to do the show, but that's not the way it was. We had the real Lassie, a stand in, which you never saw, and a double that would do fighting, swimming, running across the fields, or whatever.

Was Lassie ever hurt doing the show?
We did have one incident. I mentioned the three dogs I worked with. The reason that I only worked with the second dog for a year was, we had a scene with June, Lassie, and me, and it was set up where the camera was on this big dolly, and it was to come straight toward us. There were three men and a camera on the dolly, the camera operator, the assistant, and the guy that controls the machine. Well, this thing probably weighs two-thousand pounds, and the controller of the dolly was coming toward us when he tripped. He let go of the dolly and the whole thing kept coming, and it hit a couple of big lights and fell over. Nobody got hurt or hit, but it spooked the dog, so whenever we had a scene

that was similar and set up like that, he would get very nervous. They couldn't cure that, so then Rudd had to quickly replace him with his son, Baby, the one that I worked with for five years.

Was Baby his real name?
They all went by Lassie, but they all had their nicknames. When you called them Lassie, they knew that was their name.

What other kinds of animals did you work with on the show?
We worked with alligators, ostriches, elephants, lions, tigers, cougars, mountain lions, snakes, eagles, bears, everything. Every type of animal you could imagine.

Did you have pets when you were growing up?
Oh yeah. Always. Now everybody asks me, "What kind of dog do you have now?" and I tell them that I now have a beagle.

Do you have brothers and sisters?
Yes. I was the youngest of three. My brother is six years older, and my sister is four years older.

You mentioned that you were the only one in the business. How did they adjust to having a famous sibling?
Well, it had its ups and downs. In fact, my wife Laurie and I are actually writing my autobiography right now about that. It's called *Timmy's in the Well*.

(*Laughs*.) Perfect title!
It's the whole history before, during, and after *Lassie*. But the main thrust of the book is the effect that it had on a family of five living with this very public figure.

Did you all watch the show when it was originally on Sunday nights?
Oh yeah. I didn't watch a lot of television as a kid, but I watched *Lassie*, for sure.

Definitely not Lassie's signature.

What are some of your favorite episodes?

You know, we did so many, but we did one that was a three-parter called "The Odyssey." I think it was done around '62. It was about Lassie getting separated from the family, and by episode three, we never thought we'd ever see Lassie again. So at the very end of that third episode, I'm burying all of Lassie's toys up on the hillside, and then in the background you hear this bark, bark, and Lassie comes running up over the hill. It's great.

God, that had to be a tear-jerker.

Oh, listen, I still cry when I see it today.

Some of my favorites were the Christmas episodes. In one particular episode, the big field where you and Lassie always ran around went from summer to winter right before your eyes on camera, and was all covered in snow. How was that done?

Back then, they used soap suds. (*Laughing.*) They would have something like a fire truck and it would squirt out all these soap suds.

Where were most of the outside scenes shot?

Most everything was shot in the San Fernando Valley. We never traveled out of L.A. much. But we did go to the Grand Canyon, and also filmed in Lake Tahoe and Lake Arrowhead. But most of it was within an hour of L.A.

Did Desilu have a back lot?

No. Not on the one we were on. There were a couple of Desilu lots, but we were on the one on Melrose and Gower, and we had no back lot. Their other studio was in Culver City, but we never went there. We always went out on location. One place I'm sure you might have heard about is Vasquez Rocks. It was named after a Mexican bandit whose last name was Vasquez. Supposedly, there's millions and millions of dollars worth of his booty still buried there. It's like *Pirates of the Caribbean*! When we would go out there and be doing a show, at lunchtime I'd be crawling in all the rocks digging up stuff thinking, "Oh God! Maybe I'm gonna find some gold!"

(*Laughing.*) Is it still there?

Oh yeah. They still use it a lot, and, unlike most of California, it hasn't been developed.

Did you save anything from the show?

No. But, luckily, my mom saved a lot of stuff.

Do you have any red-checkered shirts? (*Laughs.*)

As a matter of fact, yes. In fact, about twelve years ago, I got a letter from the Smithsonian, and they were opening this exhibit in the American History Museum called *The History of Television in the United States*, and they wanted to know if I had anything I could donate. So I immediately called my mom, and said, "Mom, this is incredible. Do we have anything?" And then there's this pause and she says, "I never told you, but I have your whole outfit."

Wow! And she never told you?!

No, never told me! She said, "I have your shirt, I have your tennis shoes, and I have your jeans." And I couldn't believe it. I said, "Oh my God. Please send them to me." So she sent them up to me. Well, Eddie, when I opened that box, the smell and the deja vu and all of that was overwhelming. My son Ryan was standing there and said, "Daddy, I want those tennis shoes!" They were the high top Keds, but the studio had to rip off the round Ked label.

We all did that anyway!

(*Laughing.*) Oh yeah! And I said, "Ryan, I'm donating all of this to the most incredible museum in the United States, but I promise that tomorrow we'll go to the mall and we'll buy you some high tops." So my outfit from the show is now in the Smithsonian.

Man! What luck your mom saved it. And now it will be preserved as a part of history!

Yes. I know, I know! And, luckily, she saved a couple of other shirts, and so I do have those. And I have almost every script.

Now, that's unusual. You'd be surprised at the number of people I talk with who don't have *anything*. They always say they didn't have the foresight to think of that, and, of course, who would?

Right, and it's in your face everyday. You just don't think about it. That's why I couldn't believe my mom saved this stuff. I never had a lot of stuff. In fact, I buy stuff off of eBay all the time. The other day, somebody had my original contract. My original, thirteen-page contract! I couldn't believe it.

Were you able to get it?
Unfortunately, no.

You did a couple of episodes of *Mr. Ed*.
Yes. They were fun.

So can you tell me how they got Ed to talk?
Okay, I'll tell you the secret. (*Laughs.*) They had fishing line tied around and under his lip, and the trainer would be behind him, and when he would tug on the line, it would irritate his lip a little and he would raise his lip and look like he was talking.

So that's how they did it!
Yes.

Was the ASPCA on the set back then like they are today?
Oh yeah. They were always around. (*He pauses.*) In fact, sometimes I think they were more concerned about the health and well being of the animals than they were about the kids.

You're not the first person I've heard say that... How old were you when you began the role of Timmy?
Seven, and I was on for seven years.

How did you memorize your lines at seven?
When I was really young and I really couldn't read, my mother would read me

the lines the night before, and I would memorize them. Then, the next day, we'd go to shoot and we'd have the rehearsal and that was it. They said that I had a photographic memory. If I was told something, then I remembered it.

That had to come in handy!
Oh yeah!

So you were fourteen when you left the show.
Yes. And they wanted me to go for three more years, because our show had always been in the top ten. I had done my seven years and when they were up, they asked if I wanted to go for three more. So my parents came to me and told me about the offer, but they said that it was my decision and that I had the option of saying yes or no. Well, I was fourteen, I was going through puberty, I was looking at girls, and I'm playin' Timmy and sayin', "This don't sound right." So I told my parents that I didn't want to do Timmy anymore, and they said that was fine. So that's what ended the Martin family.

How were they written out of the show?
They shipped us off to Australia. Paul was a farmer, so he got this great deal where you get a thousand acres if you come over to start a farm, or something like that.

Did you ever regret not continuing with the show?
No. You have to make decisions in life, and it was the right thing to do at the time.

You played Steve McCullough on *The New Lassie* in the late eighties and early nineties. What was that experience like compared to your time on the original *Lassie*? Was there a big difference in the technology?
Well, the cameras were smaller and quieter, and the lights were smaller, but everything else was the same. It still took three and a half days to do a half-hour show. A little bit of the new technology blew me away, but everything else was the same. The last thing I had done was *The Computer Wore Tennis Shoes* with Kurt Russell for Disney in '70. So then it's '89, and the first day on the set when

I went into costume and makeup, I thought, "Man, this is like going home to your old bedroom." It was incredible.

Are there any plans to release the different seasons of *Lassie* on DVD?
I don't know. I think if they're smart, what they should do is release a season at a time. That's what so many people are doing, and that's what people want. And they probably will do that, but right now, I don't know if that's in the works.

Do you have many of the episodes?
Oh yeah, but only from taping them off of TV. So I can't wait for them to come out on DVD.

The quality of DVD is amazing, and nothing will be cut out of the original program so they can stick in more commercials.
Right. What they should do is show them as they were shown originally with the original commercials. That would be so much fun.

A lot of series back then did commercials for their sponsors. Did you do commercials?
Yes. Campbell's Soup was our only sponsor for the entire seven years, so we always did Campbell's Soup commercials. I would love to see some of those.

What do people usually say when they meet you?
A lot of people usually have one special episode that really touched them, and they talk about that. And as I said earlier, we did over two-hundred-fifty episodes, and on any given day, we could be filming from three different scripts. So I would not know what they're talking about when they mention this one special episode. For me, they all kind of blend together, and that's kind of tough. But the number one thing people say is, "I always cried. Lassie always made me cry." And I say, "Yes, but it was a good cry, wasn't it? Everything always turned out okay. Everything got rectified and turned out all right, and you learned something from it."

Jon with Barney the Beagle.

Good point.
And if you think about it, we were also pioneers in that we touched on a lot of different issues that a lot of people had not talked about before, such as the environment, animal rights. Things like that.

What kind of things are you doing now?
I've been involved with an organization for about twenty years now called Canine Companions for Independence. It's kind of like guide dogs for the blind. We supply service dogs to people that have other disabilities. Most of the people are quadriplegics or wheelchair-bound. It's a nationwide organization. I'm on the Board of Directors here in California. We cover about six different states. It's a volunteer thing I like to do. I'm also still doing a little bit of acting here and there, and as I said, we're writing a book.

Timmy's in the Well. (*Laughs.*)
Yes.

Well, I have one last question for you.
Okay.

Was there ever an episode when Timmy really was down a well?
(*Laughs.*) It's so funny. I don't know how this Timmy and the well thing got started. It's become this myth, this kind of urban legend. You know, I'm not really sure, but if not, it was close. There were mine shafts and culverts, and storm drains, all those kinds of things! Unfortunately, I'm not ready to sit down and watch all two-hundred and fifty episodes to find out. (*Laughs.*)

So until you do, the legend will continue . . .
Yes! (*Laughing.*)
    [Jon Provost and wife Laurie Jacobsen live in California. Provost continues to act and make appearances around the country, in addition to his work with Canine Companions for Independence. Jon and Laurie own a beagle named Barney.]

Barbara Billingsley

Leave It to Beaver: June Cleaver 1957-1963
Still the Beaver 1984-85
The New Leave It to Beaver 1985-89

Barbara Billingsley's loving portrayal of June Cleaver in the classic 1950s situation comedy *Leave It to Beaver*, has become as much a part of our American culture as apple pie.

It was 1957 when the mother of *all* TV moms began the role in which she will forever be remembered. Almost thirty years later, she would resume the beloved character in the 1983 reunion movie *Still the Beaver*. High ratings would propel the cast into updated versions of the original series, *Still the Beaver* and *The New Leave It to Beaver*.

The love affair still continues as new generations tune into the Cleavers and their friends, and find them as endearing as their parents and grandparents did.

Not only have Ward, June, Wally, the Beav, and Eddie Haskell become pop-culture icons, more importantly, they are charming reminders of childhood -- a simpler, sweeter period of time.

Barbara, how did you get started in the business?
I had always been in shows in school but the first thing I really got that's worth mentioning was a contract at MGM.

When were you at MGM?
Oh, good grief. (*Laughing.*) Too far back!!

So you began in movies, but found that your niche was in television.

Yes, I was in some movies, but my goodness, they were small parts. Then I did *a lot* of television. Television was very good to me. You know, there were so many anthology series then, like *Schlitz Playhouse of Stars* and *Four Star Playhouse*, all of those, and they changed the cast each week, not like series today. Now, most of them use the same people. It was a lot different then. Of course, you didn't make as much money then either.

What do you think of the salaries of TV stars today?

I think they're pricing themselves right out of the market. They have to put so many commercials in to pay for the actors now! It's ridiculous!

Do you watch much television now?

I don't watch much, but I do look at *Jeopardy*. I don't look at too many series though.

How did the role of June Cleaver come about?

How I got *Beaver* was a fluke! My agent called and sent me to see Joe Connelly and Bob Mosher, who were the creators and producers of *Beaver*, and they wanted me to come down and improvise a part with Buddy Ebsen. They were going to be doing a show with Buddy, and they wanted me to audition for the part of his wife. Well, we had a fine time. We were acting up a storm. I was running down the stairs and embracing him and greeting him, and running up the stairs and all this stuff. But when I left, I thought, "That was pretty dumb! I doubt this goes anywhere." And it didn't. The series was never made. Well, that was on Thursday, and I was on my way to Spain with my husband to make a picture. He was a director. So on Saturday, would you believe, my husband had a heart attack and was gone?

Oh my.

So about six months later, Joe Connelly and Bob Mosher got in touch with me again and they wanted to see how I looked for a part they had me in mind for. So I went over, and they gave me a script and said they were going to make a

Christmas with the Cleavers. Eagle-eyed fans will recognize this shot as pure publicity as there were no Christmas episodes ever produced during the original series.

pilot, and it was *Beaver*! And that's how difficult it was! (*Laughing*.) Isn't that remarkable? I had been very unhappy at the time, but that cheered me up after a bit, and that's how I started.

What was your schedule like?
Hugh [Beaumont] and I had long hours because the kids couldn't work too many hours. They were very strict in those days. They came in at nine o'clock and left at five o'clock. They had to get school in there as well, so they would save all of our close-ups until after the kids went home.

It would take a week to do one show. We got a script on Friday night and read it, then went into the studio Monday morning and read it for the creators sitting around the table. They'd hear us read it and then they'd change some things. And then we'd get clothes fitted, then we'd go home and get a new script that night with rewrites. Then we'd go in Tuesday and rehearse, and then we shot Wednesday, Thursday, and Friday.

Did you ever suggest any storylines or ideas?
No. I didn't want to and I didn't try. Everybody else did, particularly Ward [Hugh Beaumont]. There were people that would question things, but Joe Connelly and Bob Mosher always had a good answer because the shows were all based on fact. Joe had six kids, so he had plenty of opportunities to pick up things for the show.

That's why it rang so true.
Oh yes. I think it rang true not only because of good writing, but, as I said, they based it on *fact*.

What were Jerry and Tony like as kids?
They were pretty much the same as their characters. Tony was always a nice kid but he could sometimes get himself in some trouble with his parents.

It's remarkable. Both the boys came from completely different kinds of families. There were two completely different sets of parents for these kids. When Tony was much younger, when we started the show, his parents used to

The Cleavers leaf through a family album in this rarely seen publicity still.

go to a lot of nightclubs and they'd just as soon bring the orchestra home with them!

Jerry's family was the total opposite. Jerry's father was a principal of a high school, so their home atmospheres were quite different. But it didn't seem to hurt either one, though. They both turned out great!

In real life, you're the mother of two sons as well.
Yes. Just like Wally and the Beav. Same ages.

There's no doubt that people must have constantly kidded you through the years about June doing housework in her pearls and high heels.
Oh God in heaven!! (*Laughing.*)

How did that come about?
Well, when I was photographed, I actually had a hollow in my neck, and that made a shadow. That's why I wore them. At the beginning, it used to be a necklace of some kind. Then it evolved into pearls. I happen to be a pearl woman so it ended up being pearls.

June always looked immaculate, even when she was doing housework.
Believe it or not, they weren't always expensive clothes. The trick is to fit them! And as for the heels, for pity's sake! (*Laughing.*) The kids grew, so I *had* to be taller!

Did they buy your clothes or make them?
They bought them from every kind of store, from wholesale, to a place like Penney's. From good clothes to very inexpensive. Then they would fit them. Now if men only knew that about their suits! How much better something looks if it fits!

(*Laughing.*) What do you remember about Ken Osmond [Eddie Haskell]?
He was over here two days ago! He was fine. He wasn't anything at all like Eddie. The interesting part about it is, he has two of the best kids in the world. One of his sons, Christian, is a veterinary surgeon, and the other, Eric, is a film editor.

Wally and June, in her ever-present pearls.

Eric also played Eddie's son in the new series during the eighties.
Yes, indeed. That was Eric.

Tell me about Hugh Beaumont.
We got along fine, but it took us a little while at first. He would call me "Pol-lyanna" and he didn't mean it in the nicest way. (*Laughing.*)

Why do you think he called you that?
I'm not quite sure, but I think it was because just before we did the show, I had lost my husband and I was trying to keep up a brave front and a good spirit. But then we got to where we really liked each other, and we worked well together, because we did like each other.

There was great chemistry between the two of you.
Well, he was a very nice man. I don't know if you knew that he was also a Methodist lay minister. I enjoyed him very much and I think he was the *best* father on television.

Tony told me that after a couple of seasons, Hugh wanted to get out of his contract because he was a bit unhappy in the role.
Yes. He wanted to get on with this show so he could get on to something else. I don't think he had any idea of what a good show he was making at the time, but I think he realized it after he made so many of them, and realized what a good show it was. He had done a lot of things prior. He had played a well-known running part as a detective [Michael Shayne], and he had been in a lot of movies. He wanted to get on to something else, but he was so much better off where he was. I thought he was just the best!

Did you keep in touch with each over the years?
Yes, we did. In fact, he and Drew, one of my sons, became good friends. My sons both have restaurants, and he used to go over to Drew's restaurant in the Valley. You know he had a stroke, so he didn't walk too well, and he'd have one drink too many, so Drew would have to take him home. They became fast

friends, and then Hugh and I became even better friends. He was divorced then, and I had lost my other husband I had married. [*A pause.*] I don't know... I'm bad on men, aren't I?!

(*Laughing.*) Did you ever watch the reruns when they were on?
I watched the show when it was *originally* on. Then as far as reruns, I have a number of them that my son brought me on DVD, so I can look at those, but if I really want to have the whole set for posterity, I'll have to buy them as they come out.

What goes through your mind when you see yourself?
To tell you the truth, I haven't looked at it in a long time, but the first time I'm very critical. But after that, I can sit and enjoy it and stop picking myself to pieces.

Are you anything like June Cleaver?
I think through the years, we kind of got mixed up. What I mean by that is, I think that some of my personality was in there as well as the June Cleaver they wrote. My sons seem to think that I *am* June Cleaver, the June Cleaver from back in the olden days.

Tony Dow said the same thing. I asked him what you were like, and he said, "She's June Cleaver."
Well, that's what my sons say.

What kind of things do people say to you when they meet you?
It's funny. Most are very nice. But there's a few that will say, "I don't like you. I have to bring my children up and it's too hard trying to keep up with you! I can't keep a clean house like you did." Things like that. But those are very few.

What did you think of how the character of June was written for the updated series?
She was the same thing, only older. She was just a grandmother instead of a mother.

(*Laughs.*) Yes, but she was doing things that the June of the fifties never did, like running for city council and things like that.

Who's to say she couldn't have when she was younger?! (*Chuckles.*) But, yes, she did run for city council and tried to beat that Eddie Haskell!

(*Laughs.*) What did you think of the new series?

I don't think it was as good a show. I love Brian Levant [executive producer of the new series], and he loved the show so much that he wanted to do an update. And we did it, and I was very grateful and always happy doing it, but I don't think it was as good a show.

Even so, it has never been rerun.

Right. I've never heard of it being rerun, I've never seen it. Maybe they're going to bring it out and surprise everybody one day, I don't know. They'd have to pay us residuals on that one, though. On the first *Beaver*, they paid us for six runs, and that was one year. It's on every day, so they've been running it free forever. They can't do that with the second one. Maybe that's why they don't show it. But you'd think they'd slip it in someplace.

Do you have any favorite episodes?

I just like so many of them, that I don't really have a favorite, but I can tell you the people's favorite. They like the one where Beaver fell in the cup and they had to call the fire department.

So you really don't have a favorite?

Well, now that you ask, what comes to mind is the one where it was my birthday ["June's Birthday"], and Beaver bought me a horrible silk blouse that had the Eiffel Tower on it or something, and all these sayings written all over it.

I remember one in particular…"Ooh La La!"

Yes! And he wanted me to wear it to a PTA meeting or something at school, and I was too embarrassed to wear it and it really hurt his feelings.

I remember because that is one of my all-time favorites. That was such a good episode.

Yes. I liked that one.

Tell me about Miss Landers [Sue Randall].

Everybody loved her. And she died very young. I don't think I ever knew why she died, but she did die young. [Randall died of lung cancer at the age of 49 in 1984.] So often people would ask me about Miss Landers. She was a pretty thing and everyone seemed to like her. And certainly Beaver did!

Did you keep any scripts or mementos from the show?

I have a few scripts, but not many. I do have something that I'm very proud of though . . . My grandson works for NASA, and he got the astronauts to take a *Beaver* book up in space, and they gave me a letter the crew signed, and there's a picture of them in the spacecraft holding up the *Beaver* book. Then my son and his wife had it put in a shadow box for me. That's kind of neat, that it went up in space! (*Laughing*.)

That is something to be proud of! It's not everyone who can say that they have something that was on a spacecraft in outer space!

(*Laughing*.) Yes.

You were on a 1995 episode of *Roseanne* ["All About Rosey"] with some other TV moms [June Lockhart, Alley Mills, Isabel Sanford, Pat Crowley]. What was that experience like?

You know, I was with Joan Rivers on the *Tonight Show* or somewhere, and I don't remember who else was on it now, but everybody said, "She's [Roseanne] gonna eat you alive!" And do you know, she couldn't have been nicer?! She was the nicest person!

It was funny. She was pregnant at the time, and she wanted a chocolate cake that she had gotten before from some bakery. So they sent out for it, and they finally got there with it, and they cut it and gave her a big slice and she said,

"Well, don't just stand there. Give the mothers a piece!" (*Laughs.*)

The only thing she said that we kind of expected from Roseanne was, she didn't make an entrance on cue and they stopped the camera and asked where she was, and she called out, "For Christ Sakes! Give me a little time!" (*Laughs.*)

You surprised everyone as the Jive-talking lady in the movie *Airplane!* Was it hard to learn to talk jive?
No, believe it or not. The only thing is, they changed it at the last minute! But strangely enough, it wasn't hard. I must have a little of that dark blood in me! It came so easy! (*Laughs.*) What's funny is, I was married to an honest to goodness Englishman, and I still can't do an English accent!

That scene was great. I have no idea what you said, but it was funny.
Well, that's why they changed it. They didn't want anyone to really understand it.

You played Aunt Martha in the 1997 movie, *Leave It to Beaver*. What was that experience like?
It was awful. That was a terrible movie. Brian Levant was supposed to do it, but he opted to leave to do a Schwarzenegger movie and we were left with this director from Canada who'd never even seen the show! He would cut stuff out and say, "Oh, we don't need that." It was just a fiasco! But I thought the one person that was good in it was the girl who played me. She was wonderful. The father, who played Hugh's part, was terrible. He would whistle between his fingers when he was calling the Beaver. Can you imagine Ward doing that?!

Not in a million years. I understand that it was also set in the nineties and not in the fifties. Do you think that was a mistake?
I think the *whole thing* was a mistake! It wasn't good.

Were you the only cast member in it?
No. Ken Osmond was in it. He played the same old character [Eddie Haskell], but, my God, he was funny. He was really good. Tony and Jerry wouldn't be in it. They wanted more money than they would pay them, so they wouldn't do it. They wanted

them to play firemen. It would have been a funny bit, but I saw their point of view.

I know you keep in touch with Tony, but do you see Jerry very often?
I don't get to see Jerry that much. I've heard wonderful things about him. I hear he's gotten thin, and has a wonderful girlfriend. When they have us do anything together, and I don't know if we're ever gonna do anything together again, but that's when I see him. Jerry's great and I always love seeing him.

What do you think is the reason people love *Leave It to Beaver* so much? What has made it endure all these years?
I think people just related to it. An awful lot of people wish they had a family like that.

Do you ever get tired of talking about June Cleaver, or the show?
No. But I don't talk about it as much as I used to because it's getting to be a long ways off now, and I don't look quite as good as I used to. (*Laughs.*)

I saw you on the TV Land awards, and I thought you looked great.
Well, I've had a couple of physical problems in the last year, but it's all right. Listen, I've had a good run. I'm happy!

You said you thought that Hugh Beaumont was the best dad on TV, but I think it's no secret that *you* are considered *the* definitive TV Mom of all time. Everyone knows who June Cleaver is and what a wonderful mother she was. How does it make you feel to know that you're going to be remembered as that character for posterity?
Oh, I think it's wonderful! I wished for something like this. We have to decide what we want to do with our lives and if you really have faith and believe, it usually happens. I used to be in bed at night and I'd think, "Now, what would I like to do?" And in answering that, I used to describe the *Beaver* show, in that it was something my children could look at and they would like, and something that I would be proud of, and it was a family situation. I had it pretty well described. And one day, a few months after we started doing the show, I thought, "My

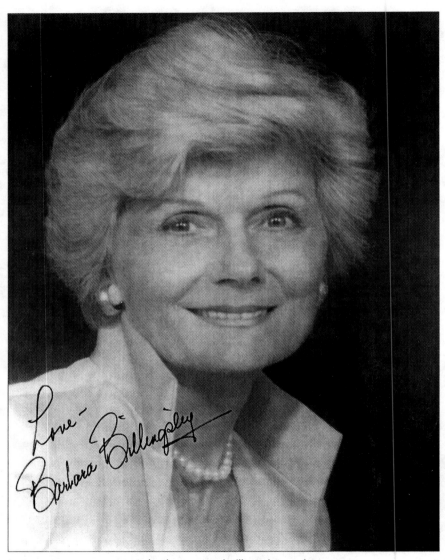

As lovely as ever and still wearing pearls.

goodness! I'm doing the show I always dreamed about!"

That is amazing!
And it's true. It's absolutely true. We have to work toward things. We have to believe, and decide what it is we want to do, and it can happen.

I don't think any mother in the world could ever top that kind of advice!
Thank you, Barbara.
It was my pleasure, dear.

[Barbara Billingsley is a mother, grandmother, and great-grandmother. A resident of Santa Monica, California, Billingsley divides her time working with the Foot-lighters and other charitable organizations for children.]

Tony Dow

Leave It to Beaver: Wally Cleaver: 1957-1963
Still the Beaver 1984-85
The New Leave It to Beaver 1985-89

I was born in 1957, the year that *Leave It to Beaver* made its television premiere. Growing up without brothers or close-by pals, Wally and the Beaver became my after-school friends, along with Lumpy Rutherford, Larry Mondello, and even Eddie Haskell.

Ward and June Cleaver, my favorite TV parents, left a lasting impression of wisdom and guidance, and emanated a calming influence during my adolescence, the era somewhere between the Cuban Missile Crisis and the Vietnam War.

Many years later as a college student majoring in broadcasting journalism, correspondence for a term paper eventually opened a door into a very familiar world, 211 Pine Street, the home of the Cleavers.

Tony Dow (Wally Cleaver), with the help of his lovely wife Lauren, assisted me in answering questions for a college research paper about what it was like to have literally grown up in living rooms across America.

After a few years of letters, Christmas cards, and phone calls, I visited Dow and his wife at their beautiful home in California during the summer of 1986.

What followed became what any true *Beaver* fan would call the opportunity of a lifetime. *The New Leave It to Beaver* series was currently in production at Universal Studios, the original home of the Cleavers. I was invited to visit the studio the next day and watch Beaver, June, Wally, and the rest of the gang tape an episode.

Tony and I on the way to the studio, July 1986.

Walking into the Cleaver living room was almost a surreal experience. Decorating the staircase wall were pictures of Ward, June, the boys, and now, the Cleaver grandchildren. Looking up the staircase that Wally and the Beav had run up and down so many times before, I couldn't help but picture June standing at the bottom in her high heels and pearls, handing the boys their lunches as they made a mad dash out the front door to school.

To my left was the Cleaver den where Beaver had once taken Ward's prized autographed baseball off of a shelf and after ruining it, replaced it with a not-so-convincing signature of "Baby" Ruth.

Behind the cameras, it was fascinating to watch a quiet but friendly Ken Osmond transform himself into the loud and obnoxious Eddie Haskell the minute he walked on camera.

During a break in shooting, Barbara Billingsley graciously invited me into

The Cleaver living room; immaculate as ever. (June always did keep a clean house.)

her trailer for a chat. I took pictures and she signed a photo that I had brought along of her as June Cleaver standing in the kitchen holding a tray of freshly baked chocolate chip cookies.

Jerry Mathers, the Beaver himself, amiably chatted with me as we sat in directors chairs while waiting for the crew to set up lights for the next scene. After lunch in the commissary, and a ride around the Universal back lot, I was given a Beaver script of the episode they were shooting that day, signed by the entire cast.

My only regret is that Hugh Beaumont (Ward) was not there. He had passed away four years earlier, and his presence was sorely missed. I would have given anything to have walked into that den to hear him bestow the fatherly wisdom and understanding for which he was so admired and respected.

My visit was an astonishing glimpse into a world few have seldom seen and one that I'll always remember. For any true *Beaver* fan, it doesn't get any better than this.

Barbara Billingsley and I on the back lot at Universal.

Twenty years later, in the summer of 2006, I interviewed Dow for this book.

Tony, you started out in the business accidentally, didn't you?
Yes. I went with a friend to an audition for a pilot for a television series called *Johnny Wildlife* and I ended up getting the part, but the pilot didn't sell. So, a little while after that, the guy who was the executive producer on that show got assigned to *Leave It to Beaver* and when they needed to replace the older brother, he remembered having worked with me, so he suggested me.

Did you have to audition for the role?
I'm sure I had to go in and meet the producers, but there was no test or anything like that. They were really in a bind because they needed to get started in production, and they needed to find somebody.

What was your working schedule like back then?
It was an eight-hour day with a one-hour lunch. Basically, you'd go in at eight and you'd be through at five if you took an hour lunch. If you went in at nine, you'd be through by six.

How many hours a day were you required to go to school?
Three hours a day. Theoretically, there was three hours of school a day, one hour of recreation, and four hours of work. But it isn't like we went to school for three hours, then went out in the yard and played for an hour, then worked four hours. It was all mixed together.

Did you usually complete an episode a week?
Yes. We did one a week in most cases.

Most people are familiar with the three- or four-camera technique used for taping in front of a live audience. But can you describe, for people that don't know, how a scene would be filmed when you're working with one camera and no audience?
The traditional way, and the way we usually did it on *Leave It to Beaver,* was you'd shoot what's called a master. That's sort of a wide shot that includes everybody in

the scene. Sometimes the camera moves, and sometimes it doesn't. Once you've completed that, then you go into coverage, depending on who's in the scene. Let's say if it was a dining room scene, you would have a close up for each person, and in many cases there'd be a two shot with Beaver and Ward, or something. We did a lot of two shots on *Beaver*. So we'd start out with a master, then we'd do a two shot, then we'd keep moving closer and closer until you have a close up on everybody.

Let's say you were by yourself in a scene but you were supposed to be talking to Ward. How would that work?
He would deliver his lines off camera and whosoever close up it is would deliver theirs. That's one of the gripes when you're an adult and you're working with kids. What ends up happening is the kids can only work so many hours, so usually the adults' coverage or close ups are saved until later in the day. Then the kids go home and the adults have to stay and do all their coverage for the scenes. Then you'd have a script supervisor reading the kids lines back to you, which makes it more difficult to do if you're not with the actual person.

Was it like that for you when you became the adult on *The New Leave It to Beaver*?
Yes. Sometimes.

Was there a classroom on the lot?
There was a classroom at Universal so, if we weren't shooting, we'd go to school in that classroom. There were other kids there, but the other kids had their own teachers, so it was kind of a weird situation. For the first year or so, Jerry and I had the same teacher and then because there was such a disparity between our ages and the subject matter, we ended up with two different teachers. So in the beginning, there was one area set aside for the schoolroom, and any kids that were on our show would all go to school with us in the same room. But, again, it got a little disruptive, so we later ended up with two classrooms.

Did you have different teachers throughout the run of the show?
Usually we did. Theoretically, you'd want to have a different teacher every year.

There's only a select group of teachers that are qualified to teach all the different subjects, especially when you're in high school. You have to be able to teach Art, Algebra, English Lit., and all these other things. There aren't that many teachers that are qualified to do all that, so some of them would have shortcomings in one area. But I had one teacher for two years because she happened to be particularly interesting and knew her subjects well.

What were some of your favorite subjects?
(*A pause, then he laughs.*)

(*Laughing.*) **Or did you have any?**
(*Chuckling.*) I don't remember having favorite subjects.

Were there any areas in school that you did particularly well in?
I did real well in school, but again, it was a one-on-one situation, so basically you could make of it what you wanted. You'd go at your own pace. But I was always good in Math, and Algebra, and Geometry. I wasn't as good in Trigonometry or Calculus, math of that level. I don't read real well, so anything that required a lot of reading I wasn't particularly fond of, but I liked Art. I did a lot of projects that I enjoyed, and I liked History depending on what era it was. I really like the Civil War era.

Did you get progress reports or report cards like students in public school?
Yes. If I remember correctly, we got a quarterly report and one report card for each semester.

When people meet you, what do they usually say or want to know?
They usually say, "Where's Beaver?" or "Where's Eddie Haskell?" It's interesting. People in general are usually taken by surprise when they see you; so many times they end up saying stupid things.

Do they call you Wally?
Yes. Not so much anymore, but when I was younger.

211 Pine Street, Mayfield; the second and most recognizable home of the Cleavers.

The first house the Cleavers lived in was the two-story house with the fence in the yard, and then they moved into the last house which most people more closely identify with the show. Why did the Cleavers move?
That first house was at a completely different studio. We started out shooting at Republic Studios, and Revue, which was the overall production company, just rented space there. Then a couple of years or so into the show, Revue got so big that they ended up buying space at Universal Studios, so we moved there. That's why they changed houses.

I remember when you were showing me around the Universal lot, you mentioned that the Cleaver house was not on the same street as it was when you were making the old series. Why was it moved?
Colonial Street, which had traditionally looked a particular way, had the *Munster's* house, all the stuff that we used on the new show, and it had the *Beaver* house. It originally started out being used as Ronald Reagan's house in *Bedtime for Bonzo*. Then it was the *Beaver* house.

Wasn't it also used for Marcus Welby's house?

Yes, it was, and now it's used on *Desperate Housewives*. But to answer your question, a few years ago, when Ronny Howard was doing a movie called *The 'burbs* [1989], he evidentially blew up a house. So they took our house and moved it somewhere else and they built a house to be blown up on that location. And when the movie was popular, people would remember that part of the movie, so Universal left that house there a while for their tour. I don't think they ever moved our house back. I think they just built a new one that looked the same.

What are your memories of Hugh Beaumont? What was he like when he wasn't playing Ward?

He was kind of a serious guy. He had written some books and he was a Methodist Minister. He was really a nice guy. I got to know him later in life. We became really good friends, but when he was working, he wasn't real happy doing the show.

How come?

He had been a lead on some other series, he was in a ton of things, so basically getting tied down to just being a father in a series that is basically about a couple of boys, and having to play second fiddle to Jerry and I, he wasn't real happy.

After the first or second year he tried to get out of his contract, and they wouldn't let him. He was kind of a guy's guy. He played a lot of golf with the boys at the country club, and he had an island up in Minnesota that he bought and grew Christmas trees. So every year during our off time, which I believe was two weeks, he'd go up there and tend the Christmas tree farm and during the holidays he'd go up and cut the trees down and bring them back down here to sell.

Later on in his life he had a stroke. That was a very frustrating thing for him because it affected one side of his body, so he had trouble writing and walking. He walked with a cane, and he had trouble with speech. The mind worked as fast as ever, but the mouth didn't, so he was always a little frustrated about that. But one time after he had had the stroke, he was directing a play at a theater in the community he lived in, and he called me because the kid that was gonna play one of the roles turned out to be a real flake or something. So he asked me to take over, and I did. That was a fun experience.

For people that only know Barbara Billingsley as June Cleaver, how would you describe her?
She's like June Cleaver. (*Laughs.*) She's really beautiful, and very proper; although she can surprise you sometimes with her sense of humor. She's very funny, and fun-loving. She has an amazing positive attitude. For example, I've seen her when she had some personal things to have to deal with, and she keeps it positive. I'll sometimes see her start thinking about something that she may start feeling a little melancholy over and she'll purposely make herself smile. Her whole demeanor is always one of pleasantness.

How is she doing?
She had a little bit of illness, and had a hip replacement, but she's doing much better now.

Did you ever catch the show in reruns when you were flipping channels?
Not very often. Once in a while.

I've talked with people who are critical when watching themselves. Are you critical when you watch yourself, or is it more like old memories?
It's more like old memories. If I criticized myself, then I've have to kill myself, because I was so bad in the beginning.

You really think so?
Yeah. I mean, there are a lot of things I liked. But the style of acting back in that time was usually pretty broad. I came along about the time Brando and James Dean were making their movies, so I was always fascinated by how *real* they looked. So that was one of the things I was doing; trying to make everything look real, and basically I underplayed things instead of overplaying them.

It didn't seem that way to me. I think it came across as real. I actually felt like I was looking in on this family and these two brothers and their friends. It never seemed like you all were "acting."
Well, a lot of people have said that's one of the things that made the show so

endearing; that it seemed so real. But for me, at the beginning, I was just sort of trying to survive, and I felt I was bad.

Did you and your family watch the show when it was originally on in prime-time?
No. The producers didn't want us to watch it. They thought that if we watched it, we might start thinking we were funny, and they were afraid we would start thinking in terms of being a celebrity, and one of the things they wanted were the kids next door. They didn't want "Hollywood celebrities." So I never watched the show. That's why when people sometimes ask me about an episode, I've never seen it. I vaguely remember doing it, but I never watched them until I'd occasionally be flipping through and catch one. The oddest thing that happened was many times I'd be in Japan or Mexico just on a vacation where there were no phones, no electricity for like two weeks, then we'd come out and be ready to go home and we'd be staying at a regular hotel the night before we'd be flying to come home, and we'd turn on the TV and the first thing that came up on television would be June Cleaver's voice. So there would be kind of weird things like that that would sometimes happen.

I bet it was weird to see yourself speaking Japanese.
Yeah. It was. And what was weirder was they used little girls' voices for Jerry and me. (*Laughs.*)

Of the episodes you *do* remember [*we laugh*] do you have a favorite?
I think it was the episode where Ward wanted to take the kids up to a cabin with a lake ["Happy Weekend"], and get everybody away from spending Saturdays inside a movie theater or reading comic books in their room. He has to talk everybody into going, because the boys wanted to go see a movie, and June doesn't have any clothes to go camping. So we go, and the cabin is all messy and dusty, and we go fishing and catch a bunch of fish, but then we find out the pond has been stocked. (*Laughs.*) That disappoints Ward. It's a show that had a theme that I thought was really interesting, and it was done in an interesting way. That's probably my favorite that I remember.

Everybody's favorite older brother.

That's also the one where you and Beaver were laying on the ground looking through binoculars and Ward comes up behind you, and he thinks you're nature watching or something. He's proudly thinking, "Great! I've finally gotten through to them."
Yeah, and come to find out we're looking at a drive-in movie. (*Laughing.*)

Do people mention any episodes in particular when they're talking to you?
Yes. They mention the tea cup episode. Or was it a coffee cup?

It was a giant bowl of soup. ["In the Soup."]
(*Laughs.*) That's right. That's the one that people seem to remember the most. That was also the one that we spent the most amount of money on. When we did our show, we basically spent the same budget on each show. When we'd go outside, or do different things, that was a luxury.

There was an episode where Wally gets a job as a lifeguard at Friends Lake ["Wally the Lifeguard"], but finds out too late that he isn't old enough, so he ends up selling hot dogs or ice cream or something. Was that lake on the Universal lot?
Yes. We had a lake on the lot. In fact, there was a couple.

Norman Tokar directed a lot of episodes on the show. What was he like to work with?
Norm directed most of the first hundred shows we did. Then he went on to work at Disney, and he became Disney's second highest box office director. He was a very good director and really good with kids because he had been a child actor. The only problem was that he was intimidating because he directed kids by showing them how to read the lines. In today's world, you don't want to show people how to do it. You let them find it for themselves. Actors find it demeaning if they get line readings from people. But for me it was great because I was just starting out. Had he given me an intellectual direction, I wouldn't have known what the hell he was talking about. So he would show us, and he was so darn funny that it was impossible for us to be as funny as he was. In fact, I have

a picture in my hallway here, that has him sitting on a couch by a girl, and he's got a chocolate chip cookie in his hand, and he's showing me how to look intimidated by this girl. He was really good. He was also a lifelong friend. In fact, I have his first hundred or so *Leave It to Beaver* scripts.

I remember seeing those. They were the ones that were leather bound.
Yes, and they have his notes, but he didn't make many. If you look at the scripts I've directed, there's scribbling everywhere. But I think it was easier then. You didn't have to do as much because you'd just go in, rehearse the scene, and once the scene is rehearsed, there was usually only one place to put the camera that fit everybody in, and then it was just the matter of getting the close ups. It was the kind of show where you didn't need to get too technically involved. All you really had to do was make sure that the writing was funny, and people delivered the lines in a funny way.

Was there much time spent on rewrites?
Sometimes. What happened was usually on a Monday we'd read the script at a table. That was usually a half day. We'd go to school for three hours, then read, or vice-versa, and then we were pretty much done unless we had to go shopping for wardrobe, but that was the day to take care of all that.

Then, Tuesday, we rehearsed, so they'd listen to the show at the table reading and then rewrite something if it didn't work. Tuesdays were their regular writing days because these guys were the executive producers, Joe Connelly and Bob Mosher. They did most of the writing on the show, especially the first few seasons. They would generally write an episode in a day. I don't know how they did it. So Monday was the day they would do rewrites on the show, based on the reading. Tuesday, when we were rehearsing that show, they would write the next week's show. Then we'd rehearse all day, and at the end of the day, they'd come down on the set and watch all the scenes. Then they would rewrite Tuesday night what they thought worked or what didn't. So our biggest rewrites came on Tuesday nights. We'd usually get them after dinner on Tuesdays. It was very organized. Since then, I've directed shows that aren't nearly as organized. I directed *Star Trek: Deep Space Nine* and I remember getting rewrites every day.

On a couple of occasions I remember being handed a rewrite, and I said, "Well, that's okay, but we already shot it." (*Laughs.*)

I did *Babylon 5*, and it was really well organized. Joe Straczynski wrote all of them, and I'd get a script like a month in advance when I was directing it, and it would never change until we had a production meeting, and then if something needed to change, there might be some rewrites but they were practically line for line. I've done other shows where I haven't gotten the third act until the second day in.

You directed some episodes of *Coach*. What was that set like?
We'd get rewrites late, but a lot of that had to do with the performers. Craig [T. Nelson] was difficult because he was looking to improve things. He's a really talented guy and he came from doing movies and working with very competent people. Television is not the same business. It's a completely different procedure because of the lack of time and the lack of money. So because he wanted things to be better, he was difficult to work with. But from a director's point of view, I'd rather have somebody who is a bit difficult because they want to make it better, rather than someone who just walks through it and doesn't give a crap. There are a lot of those kinds of people around. So you put up with the temperament to get somebody good to work with, so I always thought that was a good trade off.

I did one *Coach* which probably turned out to be one of the best I ever did. The script got thrown out on Tuesday night, and on Wednesday we got a little bit of a first act, and we didn't get the rest until Thursday, when we were shooting it on Friday.

When you were doing *Beaver*, how did you memorize your lines? What works for you?
What works now is different than what used to. I'm not sure anything works now. (*Laughs.*) It's a practiced skill like everything else. When you're doing it every week, it's a lot easier to keep doing. When I was doing *Beaver*, we'd get our shooting schedule so I would always go over my scenes the night before. In the beginning, my mom would run lines with me for probably the first season. Then after that, I would cover my line, then read the line before it. Then I would check

to make sure it was right. Then I'd go to the next one. Generally speaking, I've have it down pretty well by the time we'd shoot. There were times when I didn't always have time to do it like that. I might have homework or be signing photographs, and sometimes I just didn't get to it. But if not, you'd always have time on the set while they were setting up. And after rehearsing it a couple of times, then you'd know it by the time they were ready to shoot it. It's not as if the lines were one-page monologues. They were kind of short utterances in most cases.

I read somewhere that at one time during the show, you were getting close to two-thousand letters a week.
Yes.

How did you handle all that mail?
My mom handled it all. She read every one and responded, and then if they wanted a photograph, I'd sign it to the person.

Did you ever suggest any storylines or ideas for the show?
Not really. A lot of times we'd change the language. If something was not cool to say, or hard to say and didn't seem natural, we'd make suggestions about that. But the guys who wrote it had like nine kids between them, so consequently, they didn't have any trouble coming up with ideas and writing dialogue. All the shows were usually based on something one of their kids did, or one of their kids' friends did. Especially the first couple of seasons, it was pretty much based on real life. So we didn't have a lot of input from that respect, but we had a lot of how things were said, and making the dialogue seem natural.

So you didn't necessarily have to follow the script verbatim. If you came up with a better way to say something, you were allowed to do that.
Yes, and sometimes not. If it had to do with a rhythm of a joke, you couldn't change it. But I added a lot of "wells" and "you knows," those kinds of things.

And "gee's."
Yeah. (*Laughs.*)

What was it like growing up on the Universal lot?
It was great. We basically had the run of the whole lot. What was interesting was when we came back to do the new show, it was also at Universal, and we ended up having the run of the lot then again. I remember doing a play at the time, and I needed some things, so I got 'em from the prop department. It was sort of like a big resource for me.

I know that you have scripts from the show. Do you have anything else from
Leave It to Beaver?
I have a basketball trophy with "Wally Cleaver" engraved on it. I think I got that when we did the new show.

I remember seeing that when I was at your house.
Yeah. They went back in the prop room and dug everything out that had to do with the old show. I also have one of the shirts that Wally wore.

Did they buy those clothes or make them?
They bought 'em. We'd go shopping maybe once a month. They wanted us to wear clothes that we were comfortable with, sort of everyday clothes. I always hated wearing new clothes. First, they're uncomfortable, and second, it just didn't seem natural. I kept lobbying for a rack of clothes like somebody would have in their closet that we could pull from all the time, and finally that started to happen toward the middle to the end of the show. Then we didn't have to go shopping as much and the clothes were more comfortable.

Where did they go shopping?
We had an account at Desmond's, which was a sort of department store that was popular back then.

You and Dobie Gillis kind of wore the same kinds of clothes, checked shirts and khaki pants. But I rarely saw Wally wearing jeans.
No. Wally never did wear jeans. I might have worn them a couple of times like on that camping show we were talking about.

The bullfrog episode. Look closely. Is our Wally wearing jeans?!

Right. And in the one where you're in the pond catching bullfrogs.
Right. For some reason, jeans were sort of identified with hoodlums. (*Laughs.*)
And they also didn't want to do anything that was too stylish, because they
didn't want to intentionally date the show. It's dated obviously from the time
period, but they didn't want it to become fashion-dated.

Did they save outtakes back then?
No. That kind of thing was considered unprofessional. We didn't do any of that.
They're fun to watch, but what ends up happening, depending on who it is, a
lot of times people are conscience that they're doing things for the gag reel.

What are some of your favorite memories from your time on the show?
The thing I remember most was we'd play football or baseball between the

soundstages, especially when all the guys were there. I remember Steve Mc-Queen had a racing jaguar and he parked it by his soundstage where he was working, and I think we broke his windshield at one point in time.

And you'd be throwing the ball around and at lunchtime, maybe Robert Mitchum or Rock Hudson would wander by and you'd throw the ball to 'em and they'd throw it back. It was like a big family there.

What other shows were being filmed on the lot?
Wagon Train, Tales of Wells Fargo with Dale Robertson, *Riverboat* with Darren Mc-Gavin and Burt Reynolds, and a show called *Checkmate.* Generally speaking, Universal would have around eight shows a season. The only show I remember being there forever was *Wagon Train* because they were on the same years that *Beaver* was.

Do you ever get tired of talking about Wally or the show?
There was a period in my life when I did. Now I have more of an appreciation for the show; its longevity and quality. And I'm actually grateful that I was a part of it. I've always been grateful that I was on it, but, at some point, you get to where you want to be recognized for all the other things you've done. There was a large period of time between the end of the first *Beaver* and the new show, and if you just count episodes, I've done more episodes of other things than the 234 episodes of *Leave It to Beaver.* I was on a soap opera called *Never Too Young* and I've done way more episodes just of that.

Do you have any of the DVD releases of *Beaver*?
(*Chuckles.*) They never sent us any, so then my wife Lauren called them and said, "What's the deal?" Then they sent us some.

Do you know why there were no extras on the DVDs? I was really hoping there would be.
Yeah. I went to Universal maybe a total of four times, and made that suggestion. It was always met with disinterest. The last time I went, I had a whole package to present. I got a little more sophisticated in my pitching techniques. (*Laughs.*)

There were about six additional features they could've added, like Jerry and I walking through the back lot at Universal and talking about where we filmed episodes and how the studio had changed. Then I had commentary on specific shows and interviews with each of the people who were in the shows. I thought it would have been a much better package with all the added bonus features. That's what makes DVDs really shine.

Those are the kinds of things fans of the show want to see. It would have made the releases so much better!
I thought so. So I made that proposal, and they made it clear that they weren't interested. I even suggested possibly colorizing a couple of episodes, only because nowadays, kids have trouble watching black and white.

And the technology for that is getting much better than it used to be.
The studio's response was that they didn't think anyone would be interested in that. My response was, "Well, it's only one of a few shows from the fifties that's actually still broadcast on television," along with *I Love Lucy* and *The Honeymooners*. So what happened was, they said nobody cared, and I figured that was that. So about six months later, I got a call from someone at the studio who said they wanted me to come down to the Ambassador Hotel and spend a couple of days and talk about the show. That's typical of a big studio. It's so big that no one knows who's talked to who. I asked what kind of compensation there would be for us, and they said, "Oh, we don't pay for that." So I thought, I'm not gonna go spend two days of my life so you guys can make a hell of a lot more money for something that I've been trying to keep alive for all these years anyway. So none of the cast ended up doing it. They expected us to show up and get nothing. The studios always think it's in the actor's best interest to do these things, but expects us to do it for free. The studios have never really been fair about things like that, so what happens is, the longer you're in the business, the less prone you are to want to do things they ask. They don't seem to realize it doesn't help you get anything in terms of work. And we would have all gladly done it. Jerry really keeps the character alive. That's what he does. He travels around and makes appearances, and I've done a few things like that. Barbara

loves the character and is more than happy to talk about it. It's been a huge part of her career, and her life. I'm always amazed that so many people asked when it was coming out on video or DVD, because they wanted to have the episodes because it was really a big part of their childhood, and wanted their kids to see them.

But don't you get paid something from the sale of the DVDs?
Nothing. That's a real bone of contention for me. I believe the studios pay for DVDs based on some kind of formula, and it didn't really kick in until 1960 or so. The *Beaver* shows that are released right now are from '57-'58, so we haven't gotten anything.

At least fans who read this will know that you wanted to do some extras, and that you all love the characters and would have been more than willing. It's not as if you all said, "We don't want to do it. We don't want to be associated with the show."
Right.

I assumed that a show as popular as *Beaver* would have some extras on it, and I was disappointed to find out that there weren't any. That's the kind of things fans look forward to. We like to see and hear things that happened behind the scenes and commentaries from the actors. The studios don't have a clue about what the fans really want. When are they going to realize that, in the end, they're just hurting themselves?
Exactly. It was the same way with the *Leave It to Beaver* movie. Brian Levant, who did the new show, wrote the film. He was supposed to direct it, but he got an offer to do a Schwarzenegger movie, *Jingle All The Way*, so he couldn't turn that down. But technically he was still a producer, so he wanted me to direct it, because I'd been directing, and I knew more about the show than anybody else. So I went in and met with them, and, of course, they weren't interested. So I figured well, that's okay. It's a big project. They probably want a big film director, so I understand that. Then I find out they get this TV director who'd never worked with kids. It didn't piss me off because I know the business, but what

did piss me off was (*chuckling*) I got a call one day from Universal saying, "Your call time is Sept. 23, and we'll want to do wardrobe on the 20th", etc. etc." For a long time, my manager had been trying to negotiate something about being in the movie. They wanted everybody from the show to be in it. Well, they would never negotiate, and they wait until the last minute when they're under pressure, so they had never talked to me about it. So I said, "I don't know anything about this. I'm going to have to call my manager." So I did, and they offered some ridiculous sum like $1200 to work on the movie. So Barbara, Frank, and Ken are in it, but Jerry and I aren't. I just felt that from the beginning that it wasn't going to be any good. It basically wasn't going to be *Leave it to Beaver*. I thought it would depreciate the value of the show, so I didn't want to be part of it.

Did you watch it?

I heard it was horrible, and I'd catch it on cable occasionally, but I never watched the whole thing from beginning to end. In the first place, if I had done it, I would have done it as a nostalgic piece. They did it as late nineties with guys in baggy pants and all that. It just doesn't translate. There's no value to *Leave It to Beaver* if you're going to do that kind of movie. The only value at all is the recollection of the sweetness and a sensibility of the show. All they see is a franchise, thinking that the value is just in the name.

Earlier, you mentioned that you had thought about colorizing a few episodes if they had used your package ideas for the DVD release. Speaking as a fan, I would have liked to have seen what the Cleavers' world looked like in color.

Generally, I'm against it, but with our show, the only reason we weren't in color was that color wasn't around. Television shows weren't done in color then. *Wagon Train* was one of the first shows that went to color, and that was probably '58 or '59. It also required a ton of extra lighting because the film stock they used then wasn't as sophisticated as today. It required an awful lot of light, maybe twice as much as black and white, so it would have taken longer to set up, and it would have made our schedule really difficult to complete in three days. Not to mention the fact that it's very uncomfortable on the set because it's so hot. As we were finishing up the last season, the network wanted us to go to color and to expand to an hour, and those are two of the main reasons it went off the air.

An hour?
Yes. I don't know what the hell they were thinking. The producers wouldn't do it. They decided to let it go. Jerry and I were getting up in age where it was getting difficult to do as well.

So you were ready for it to end.
Yes. I was ready.

Did you enjoy doing the reunion movie and the new series?
Yes, I did.

Did you have input into that show?
No, I didn't. Brian Levant, who was an executive on *Happy Days*, and his partner, came to Jerry and me and said they wanted to do a remake of the show. Jerry and I had already approached Universal about that and they weren't interested. So, basically, our attitude was, "Hey, knock yourself out! But you're not gonna get anywhere." (*Laughs.*) So when they actually got somewhere, it was really a surprise. I thought the movie script [*Still the Beaver*] was pretty good. I'm not so sure about Wally and the impotence part, but in any case, I thought it was well written. But then they hired a guy to direct it who had never seen the show, and that was a bone of contention for a while. Brian wanted to direct it, but the studio wouldn't let him. It was interesting the way this new guy approached it. He didn't approach it from a comedy point of view. He approached it from a film point of view, and it was much more honest than it would have been otherwise. I thought the reunion movie wasn't bad. Then Brian produced the series and started directing some of those.

Did you like the way Wally and Beaver turned out as adults?
The only thing I think I would have done differently is I would have much rather had seen Wally end up being a coach instead of an attorney. Or if he was going to be an attorney, I'd rather have him work in one of those places where he did

pro bono work. He came home in three-piece suits and did all that attorney kind of stuff, and attorneys are my least favorite kind of people. I would have rather been *anything* but an attorney. (*Laughs.*) But I can understand Wally becoming one. He always came out on top and was level headed and successful.

The show got a bad rap for not being like the old series. What was your take on that?
I think, the fact is, you can't go back. It's impossible to recreate something from a different time period. The writing was so good on *Leave it to Beaver*; you're probably not going to ever get that kind of writing. That was Joe and Bob's style. Whoever's doing the new show has their style, and things they're comfortable with. But the thing that I did think was interesting about the show was how many different types of episodes we tried to create. We did a musical episode with Brian Wilson. We did flashback episodes. We did some very huge things production wise. The show got knocked for not having the sweetness or the relevance of the original *Leave it to Beaver* and that's probably true, but, on the other hand, I think it brought a lot of other things to the table.

It first premiered on the Disney Channel, correct?
Yes. It was *Still the Beaver* when it was on Disney, and then when it went to TBS, it became *The New Leave It to Beaver*.

I'm always surprised that it's never been rerun. I mean, there are so many different outlets now.

Exactly. You'd think that by now it would have found its niche somewhere.
I know fans from the eighties would like to see it again. Disney has its own channel, so I don't know why they haven't rerun it.
Yes, and we took the Disney Channel from being a channel with one a half million subscribers to one with five million because of the popularity of the show.

Why did the show leave Disney and move to TBS?
Negotiations between Universal and Disney are usually a pain at best. They couldn't come to an agreement.

How did you get into directing?
When I was approached to do *The New Leave It to Beaver*, I was actually supposed to have done another show. It was called *High School U.S.A.* and they had big hopes of making it a series.

I played the principal of the school.

I remember. That was the TV movie with Michael J. Fox and a lot of earlier sitcom stars. [Angela Cartwright, Elinor Donahue, Dawn Wells, Dwayne Hickman, David Nelson, Ken Osmond].
Right. So because of that, I was sort of in an okay position to ask for things, so one of the things I wanted to do was direct. So that was in the original contract. So I wrote a show and they allowed me to direct it. Then I wrote two more shows and then gave them a story for a third, and then I directed seven or eight of them.

What other shows have you directed?
I did a half-hour Universal show called *Swamp Thing*, *Harry and the Hendersons*, *The New Lassie*. I also did a show with Chris Elliot called *Get a Life*. Then, eventually, I got into more of the episodic hour shows because those are more like shooting a film. I tried to go in that direction. Then I did a lot of the *Babylon Fives*, which I thought was a really good show, then the subsequent spin-off which was called *Crusade*. Then I did a show called *Cover Me* that was about an FBI family and it was based on a true story. That was a good show.

What is your directing style? Is there any Norman Tokar in you?
Well, I've given line readings for kids if the kids are real inexperienced, but I try to stay away from that and only use it as a last resort.

The first thing you have to know about directing is whenever you say something, it's going to concern the actors. They immediately think, "Oh, I'm doing it wrong" or "What the hell is he talking about?" So you want to steer people in an abstract way. For example, a lot of directors will block scenes. They'll tell a person to start at a particular place, and on a particular line to cross over there, and do this on this line, and so-and-so. What I try to do is set up the sets and sort of guide them into doing something. For example, if a person has to have a certain prop in their hand and I want them to start at the window, rather then telling them to start at the window, I'll put the prop over at the window. Then they'll go over to the window and pick up the prop and think this will be the place to start. So you do things like that, as opposed to telling people what to do because if you tell somebody what to do, first they have to assimilate why and how come, and then they have to incorporate that into the performance and think about their lines, while thinking, "Where was I supposed to move? What was I supposed to do?" So if they do it themselves, that's already taken care of. They've solved that problem. They don't have to think about it anymore.

Usually I have everything blocked out in my head and down on paper to a certain extent, of where I want people to be. If there's a specific place and time that I want them to be at a specific location doing a specific thing, I can sometimes say, "I had this idea. What if you took these papers and did this?"

Oh, more like a suggestion.
Exactly. Sometimes they'll take right to it and other times they won't. But I'm more than happy to look at it another way. There are so many resources on a set, and I want to use every resource there is. So that means allowing the actor to do their job and many times what they're going to do are things that I never thought of, or things that are better for their character. Because in most cases, they know the character better than I do, especially on episodic shows because they've been doing it. The same with the cameraman. I know what I want it to look like, but if he comes up with a better idea, I'm happy to take credit for that. (*Laughs.*) It's that kind of a balancing act between everyone.

I mentioned that I had done *Babylon Five*. That was a great show to direct. On *Babylon Five*, all the actors were committed and very professional. They knew their lines. They knew their characters extremely well and so if I set up a shot, for example, and I wanted it to be a "walk and talk," because the sets on that show were so long, they went with it. They'd figure it out and stop when it felt right to stop, and if they don't, I can help him with that.

Another show I did after that [which I was asked not to identify] was an interesting example, after working on *Babylon Five*. It was the end of the season. Nobody wanted to be there. Half of the people hadn't even read the script before they came in to shoot it. I remember one scene which was ridiculous. It was a joke on that show. They wouldn't come out of their dressing rooms until everybody was absolutely ready, and if they came out and somebody was setting a light or something, they'd go back into their dressing rooms. It would take ten minutes from the time that you were ready to get them on the set. We got ready to do the scene and one of the guys literally hadn't read it. So he's got the script in his hand and he's kind of reading it. In that kind of circumstance, the actor is not a resource at all. They're actually just a pain in the ass. So, he's aimlessly not knowing where to go or what to do. So in this case, I gave him some directions, and then the scene would start to take place. He'd start in his chair, and then I'd say, "Now, why don't you move over to the window and if you're comfortable, direct some of the lines out of the window? That might be interesting." So that's the kind of dialogue that I would have with someone that wouldn't be ready. So we get finished blocking the scene and it seemed fine to me. So we shoot the master, and we shoot the coverage of everybody except this one guy, and now we're ready to shoot his coverage, and we start shooting his close-up when he's sitting down and he gets up and walks to the window, and the camera is pulling back and following him to the window and we're starting to shoot it and he says, "I don't think I get up here." I said, "Well, we shot the master and you did it then." And he says, "Well, this isn't comfortable. I wouldn't do it like that." And we got into this big discussion like, well, we've got to do it that way or otherwise, we'll have to go back and shoot the whole scene if you're going to do it differently. So my attitude was if you'd read the script and come in with something prepared, then maybe you wouldn't have gotten up at that ridiculous point, but you did, so we need to go ahead with it.

Did he do it?

Yeah. He had to. There are all different levels of commitment from actors. Some actors like to be directed with where to move, what to do with props. Some actors don't like to work with props. Some do. And some, as soon as you tell them to do something, immediately go into fear, because they think what they're doing is wrong. So you almost have to preface everything by "That was great. I think it was terrific. Your attitude here is wonderful, but I have an idea. Why don't you try it with more anger?" That would be a direction that I would use. Or if that doesn't work, you can do little technical things. I could say, "Pick up your cues quicker and louder. That would give the appearance of being angry."

Well, that was my next question. What if someone is just absolutely reading it wrong, and you know it's not gonna work. What do you do then?
There are times when I give line readings where they might have put the emphasis on one word and it should be on another.

Sometimes, I've had actors that just couldn't make the change from the emphasis from one word to another, and because of expediency, you just have to shoot it, and hope that you can fix it in post-production. You can create the emphasis by changing the volume or sometimes you can use the actual reading from the master, things like that.

So would you describe yourself as a more laid-back type of director?
Kind of. There's no yelling and screaming, things like that. I've worked with directors who like to work in chaos, and thrive under pressure. I find that most actors don't respond to that. I like it to be a much more intellectual and analytical process. I don't even say, "Action," anymore. I use the Clint Eastwood approach. I'll say, "All right, everybody ready? Okay, let's take it nice and slow, ready and action."

Did you work with directors who yelled and screamed on *Leave It to Beaver*?
Not for the most part.

So it sounds like you've always responded better to directors who were more analytical than emotional.
Yes, and that's what I try to be. But I'd probably be a lot more successful if I was more demanding. I sometimes let things slip that I shouldn't. (*Laughs.*)

What are you most proud of about *Leave It to Beaver*?
That it has endured for so long, and will continue to do so.

Tony today.

So you don't mind that you will most likely forever be remembered as Wally Cleaver?

Nope. Not a bit.

[Tony Dow and wife Lauren live in Topanga, California. They co-produced a documentary for the A&E network called *Child Stars: Their Story,* which examined the lives of former child TV and film stars and their experiences in show business. Still frequently shown, it has become the channel's highest-rated documentary in the history of the A&E network.]

Dwayne Hickman

The Many Loves of Dobie Gillis: Dobie Gillis 1959-1963

Dwayne Hickman is most notably remembered as TV's perpetual teenager; first as nephew Chuck MacDonald in the 1955-59 sitcom *The Bob Cummings Show* (also known as *Love That Bob*), then as the title character in the CBS comedy series *The Many Loves of Dobie Gillis*.

Dobie Gillis was an average, American teenager whose life revolved around cars, money, and most importantly, girls. His sidekick and good buddy was a bongo-beating beatnik named Maynard G. Krebs (the G. stands for "Walter"), brilliantly played by Bob "Gilligan" Denver.

Dobie lived with parents Herbert T. and Winnifred (Frank Faylen and Florida Friebus) over the family grocery store, and was incessantly infatuated by Thalia Menniger (Tuesday Weld), an unattainable and self-absorbed beauty, who caused unceasing heartaches for the daydreaming Dobie.

Getting the girls was much easier for his rich and spoiled nemeses, Milton Armitage (Warren Beatty) and Chatsworth Osborne, Jr. (Steve Franken) and being constantly pursued by the unattractive but zealous Zelda Gilroy only added to Dobie's daily dilemma's.

After successfully portraying teenagers for a ten-year stint on the small screen and then graduating to co-star in films such as the Academy Award winning *Cat Ballou*, Hickman eventually ended up on the other side of the camera as a television director and a CBS executive.

Still exuding an easy-going nature and boyishly youthful appearance, Hickman talked with me about his days on *Dobie*.

Dwayne, who were your heroes growing up?

Jack Benny. I loved radio when I was a little kid. *The Jack Benny Program* on radio was my favorite. To me, he was so much fun; he and Rochester, Dennis Day, Phil Harris, and all those people that nobody seems to know about today. He made a big impression on me.

I've always felt that radio was the ultimate entertainment because with radio you had to use your imagination. I thought that was really kind of special. As it turned out, I didn't realize back then that Benny was such a big star. I was just a little kid. Then later, I got to know him a little bit. He was a lovely man.

How did you meet him?

George Burns was one of the owners of *The Bob Cummings Show*, and kind of a producer of the show. He and Paul Henning, who did *The Beverly Hillbillies* and *Petticoat Junction*, wrote it. So George was always around. He'd look at our run-throughs, and give us notes. Burns was a great man to look at your run-through and look at your scripts and give you help. He was terrific. So every once in a while Benny would show up. They had been friends over the years, from vaudeville to radio to TV. They were very close, so I got to meet Jack, and George I also got to know pretty well. I had no idea when I was little that I would someday meet Jack Benny and George Burns, and get their input into what comedy was and what it ought to be.

Before *Dobie* came along, you did *The Bob Cummings Show*. How did you get that role?

I had been an actor as a child. I had done movies at MGM, *The Boy with Green Hair*, *The Sun Comes Up* with Jeanette McDonald, and *The Secret Heart* with Claudette Colbert. I had worked around, and I had an agent. Then when I went to high school, I kind of let acting go and didn't do any work and concentrated on school. Then when I got out of high school, I went to college at Loyola University. An agent that I had many years before called me one day and said, "Do you want to go on an audition for *The Bob Cummings Show* pilot?" I said, "Well, you know I haven't been acting, and it's summer vacation." And I didn't tell him, but I had just taken a civil service exam for the Department of Water and Power here in Los Angeles. I was gonna go to work for the city for a couple of months in the summer, and would go back to school in the fall. So he said, "Well, just go see him." So I went on the audition and they kind of liked me. Then they called me back, and I read with Bob and Rosemary DeCamp, and then they offered me the part. In the meantime, I'd taken the job with the Department of Water and Power, so I called the guy downtown and said, "I'm so sorry. I can't take the job. I'm gonna do a TV pilot with Bob Cummings." And he was kind of put out. It was a question of whether I should work the whole summer and make four or five-hundred dollars, or work two days and make two-hundred. My father said, "Always take the most money for the least amount of work," so that's how I got *The Bob Cummings Show.*

What are your memories of Bob? What was he like?
Well, Bob was a perfectionist. He was like a mentor and a parent. He was a teacher. I was pretty green in terms of comedy, and he really helped me a great deal and taught me so much. But he was very demanding. He was a real perfectionist. He believed in a lot of rehearsal, and you showed up, and you knew your lines, you knew what you were supposed to do, and if you didn't, he'd let you know! So he was very parental. But I liked Bob. I got along with him very well. He really knew comedy. He knew from the stage, to theater, to radio, to television. And he'd been a movie star. So he knew what he was doing. He was a very bright guy. They said that I later kind of acted like him, which I suppose I did. Cause he'd say, "No. Do it like this. Do it like that." I, for years, was doing it like he did it, so it became sort of a thing that seemed like I was imitating him.

Was that a one-camera show?
The Bob Cummings Show was two cameras, as *Dobie* was a two-camera show.

I've never heard of that.
Yes. Two cameras were kind of the interim of one and four, like Desi Arnaz invented the four-camera system, and with an audience. We had no audience on *Cummings* and no audience on *Dobie.* We just had the two cameras; a flat shot and a closer-angled shot.

So they would be filming at the same time.
Yes. And then if they had to, they would do pick-ups or go in for close-ups later. It was basically the transition from one to four cameras. It worked pretty well.

We did the *Cummings* show in one day. One *endless* day. We were there until midnight sometimes. It was a hard, hard job.

How much rehearsal time did you get?
We got a lot of rehearsal on Monday. We started on Monday, and worked very hard. And, of course, everyone knew their lines because of Bob. He expected it and demanded it. We would rehearse all day long, and then George Burns would come and look at a run-through, and then we'd come the next day and film. But it was worth it because it was a really good show.

Tell me about Rosemary DeCamp.
Rosemary was a very nice lady. She was a very good actress. She was a radio actress as well. She was on the show *Dr. Christian*. That show I never much listened to, but she was on it for years. She had played everybody's mother. She played James Cagney's mother, Ronald Reagan's mother, Sabu's mother from *Jungle Book*, my mother. She was a lovely person. Very nice. I got very close to her. We were good friends and she was very nice to work with. She was a dear.

I remember her as Marlo Thomas' mother on *That Girl*.
Yes. She was very maternal. And Bob was paternal, and Ann Davis was kind of like a buddy. Ann was good. I saw her a couple of years ago. I was in San Antonio doing an art show and she lives down there, so she came to it. She looked good, and it was good to see her. So we've been friends forever.

Did you and Rosemary stay in touch?
Yes, we did. Her husband was a judge, a man named John Schnieder, and a very nice man. They were good people. They lived down in one of the beach cities here. We stayed in touch, as I did with Ann B. Davis and Cummings.

What did you like most about the character of Chuck MacDonald?
What I liked most was that Chuck wasn't a silly kid. A lot of times when writers write a teenager, they write him as voice-cracking and kind of odd. Very silly. Do you remember Dick Crenna? He played in *Our Miss Brooks*.

The Bob Cummings Show cast: From L to R: Ann B. Davis (Schultzy),
Bob Cummings (Bob Collins/Grandpa), Dwayne Hickman (Chuck MacDonald),
and Rosemary DeCamp (Margaret McDonald.)

Of course.

He played that kind of a silly teenager. Dick, who I love, had to play one of those silly characters. But Chuck was just kind of a regular kid. He wasn't silly and all. He was just a good kid who wanted to be like his Uncle Bob. I liked the honesty of the character.

Dobie Gillis was a little more of an exaggerated character. Not quite as real, but still, the thing I liked about Chuck was he was kind of straight. Kind of real. And with Dobie, he may not have been as real, but he was very sincere and honest. There was a lot of honesty in Dobie Gillis. He was very likeable, and used to tell it like it was. He told it to the audience at the Thinker Statue.

When the *Cummings* show ended, did you go right into *Dobie*?
The *Dobie Gillis* property had been floating around and was owned by Max Shulman, who created it. George Burns had an option on it and I think that's how Max knew about me. He had seen me and thought I was kind of right for the part. I think George wanted his son Ronnie Burns to play the role, but I don't know what happened to that. Anyway, *Dobie Gillis*, the property, left Burns and went to Fox and my agent got a call and said they wanted to see me about it. Really, I think that my part in the *Cummings* show was an audition for it. Everybody had seen me playing a similar kind of role. So I went out to see Max, and Rod Amateur, who I'd known for years. He was the producer-director, but he had also produced and directed *The Bob Cummings Show*. He even worked for Burns. He directed *Burns & Allen*. So I knew Rod, and he was now gonna do *Dobie Gillis*. So I read for them, got called back, and read again. Then they offered me the part, and I was thrilled, because it was a big, plum role. Everybody wanted it. It was a much coveted role for a young person back then. In fact, Michael Landon was heartbroken, I'm told. He wanted it very badly.

I can't even begin to picture *that*; Little Joe and Maynard!
(*Laughing.*) I think he was better off waiting and doing what he did.

Why did they make you change your hair color when the show began?
You know, when a thing doesn't work very well, it's hard to find the people that thought of it. As the old saying goes, "Success has many fathers, failures, and orphans." I think that Max and Fox, or the network, or someone, decided that I should look different than I looked on the *Cummings* show. That was their reasoning. So they bleached it. I had dark brown hair. So they took the color out and then put something on to make it look blond. And I'd have to have it done every week because I had a crew cut, and then, of course, the roots came back in look-

Dobie (with blond hair and a sore scalp) ponders life in front of the Thinker statue.

ing very black. It was a pain, and it didn't look that great, I don't think. It looked strange. So at the end of the first year I said, "I've got to quit doing this because my hair is falling out! My scalp's all raw, and scabbed over. It's ruining my head." And they said, "You have to do it." So I said, "Well, you'll have to get somebody else then." So they said they would work out something for me, and they did. They let me go back to kind of a medium brown, which lasted a few months, and then it was back to my normal hair color. And nobody said a word. Nobody said anything about it at all. It was just an idea that didn't work. The public didn't seem to mind. I guess they figured I was a victim of executives.

Speaking of executives, did the network execs come in and watch run-throughs back then?
Not to the extent that they did later. Occasionally, somebody would show up from the network, but they weren't as involved and hands-on as they later became, as I was when I went to work for CBS in '77.

What were some of the shows you worked with?
I supervised *Maude, Good Times, All in the Family, M*A*S*H, WKRP in Cincinnati, The Incredible Hulk, The Dukes of Hazzard,* all kinds of shows like that. I was at the readings, I was at the run-throughs, and I was at the tapings. I was very active and very involved. That's the way they wanted it, but I think so much of that has hurt things a bit. I think you have to hire good people and then leave 'em alone.

Television was really great in those days, compared to what it is today. I think it's because each show had its own look, and its own producers and writers, and they were left alone to make it or not.

And each show didn't have fifteen writers!
No! Max Shulman had three or four people that he would farm script ideas out to. And they'd write a script and then he'd do a little polish on it and then it was ready. We went to the table, and read it, and shot it. Now you go, and there's ten or fifteen people that write it. You go to the table on a Monday and you're gonna shoot it on Friday, and it's no good. Each day you have a new script. I've directed these shows. I directed *Designing Women* a few times. It's very difficult. You keep changing your scenes and your blocking. The show changes. They can't seem to get it how they want it. And sometimes by the end of the week, it's worse! Now it takes them a week to do a show that we did in two days.

Paul Henning sat and wrote *The Bob Cummings Show* and then he brought the script down to the set and we took it home and learned it and shot it. And it was terrific! Both of the shows I did had excellent writers and I was very fortunate. It's all in the writing. Now, they get all these people involved, and, frankly, I think it's hurt television.

So you didn't have to go through a lot of rewrites.
No. No. Thank God. (*Laughs.*)

You mentioned that you worked on *Designing Women*. Was all that turmoil going on with the show when you were there?
Yes, it was. But, you know, for some reason when you're at the network, they keep it from you. They don't want the network involved. So I never really got the straight of anything. When I was directing, I got a little more, but not a lot. They keep it to themselves. I know they wanted Delta to lose some weight. And Gerald McRaney didn't think she should have to do anything that they said. It was all kind of stuff like that. I kind of stayed out of it. Most series have a lot of behind-the-scenes stuff going on like that. Except maybe the ones I did. I don't remember a lot of that going on. Today, it seems everybody hates everybody and they fight and feud. And I don't remember that when I was doing it.

Do you remember if it was the producers or the network that wanted to let Delta go?
I don't remember them ever saying they wanted her to leave. I think it was a mistake to get rid of her, because she was terrific on the show. I don't know. I really don't. And I'd tell you, because it's after the fact now. I was with the network and then I left to direct and kind of lost touch with what they wanted.

Tell me about Bob Denver.
Bob was a good friend. Kind of shy. I loved Bob. We got along very well but we were kind of different. We were different like Dobie and Maynard were different. He was kind of like a hippie. We were the Odd Couple, but we got along beautifully. We really liked each other and I don't think we ever had a cross word. I stayed close to him until he passed away. I think Bob was very talented.

He used to entertain me. I used to laugh at what he'd say, and how he'd say it and do it. I loved him. He was a good guy.

What were Frank Faylen and Florida Friebus like?
Very nice. Very good. Hard working. Frank was kind of a curmudgeon. He was a lot like he was on the screen, but he was a good guy and I always got along very well with him. And Florida was a very nice person. They were both very good. They were perfect for their roles. They did their roles well.

I remember the episode with Francis X. Bushman, the famous silent screen star. That was a very big deal, wasn't it?
Yes, he was a *very* big star. He was in the original *Ben-Hur*. "The Flying Millicans" was the name of the episode he did. Yvonne Craig [Batgirl] played the daughter. They were gymnasts or circus people. They were gonna try to toughen me up, and work me out, and do the circus tricks, the high-wire acrobat stuff. That was a good show.

Do you keep in touch with Sheila James?
Sheila and I have also stayed good friends. I love Sheila. I just got an e-mail from her a couple of days ago. She was telling me that a columnist in the *L.A. Times* wrote that when he went to buy clothes, he always bought clothes like *Dobie Gillis*, Khaki pants and checked shirts. I e-mailed the guy and said not to worry; that I was still wearing the same thing too. I talk to her all the time. She's a state senator, and one of the brightest people I know. I'm crazy about Sheila.

I read that you got a bit upset with Tuesday Weld when she was on the show, because she was somewhat unprofessional.
Well, Tuesday was only fifteen. She was a baby, and I was kind of impatient with her. We didn't get along all that great, but, in all fairness to her, she was very young, and she was so pretty, and so good. She was terrific in the show. She brought a lot to the show. I thought she was very good. Again, I was under a lot of pressure trying to make the show as good as I could. And she seemed kind of like a kid, which she was, and not too serious about the whole thing.

And you were brought up under Bob Cummings where that kind of business just didn't fly.
Right. I was brought up under Bob. You rehearsed and rehearsed. Tuesday wasn't much into all that work. But, again, she was so cute and very good. She's probably the best person we ever had on that show, she and Sheila.

Warren Beatty was on a few episodes as well.
Yes. He was on four or five shows. He played Milton Armitage, the rich boy. Warren was pretty much like he is now. He was very good in the show and brought a lot to it. But he had the ambition to be a movie actor, and he left us and did *Splendor in the Grass*. And you can't blame him for that! He hasn't talked about it a great deal. Maybe he didn't want to be identified with television. That was true for a lot of people back then. Some thought that you couldn't have a film career and be in television. But I don't think that's true. There are people like Jim Garner, Roger Moore, and Steve McQueen, who was on the next street beside me at Fox Western shooting *Wanted: Dead or Alive*. He went on to become a very big film star.

Now, it's the complete opposite. Most stars would love to have their own TV show.
Yes. It's gone back. It's different now.

You mentioned that *Wanted: Dead or Alive* was being shot on the next street. What other shows were being done on the lot at the time?
Let's see... *Perry Mason* with Raymond Burr, and there was one with Cynthia Pepper. I think it was called *Margie*. It only ran one season. Shows came and went all the time.

Do you have any favorite episodes of *Dobie*?
Yes. One of my favorites is a thing called "The Chicken from Outer Space." That was a show where Maynard and I were supposed to do a lab experiment for school. We had a chicken, and we were supposed to give it one CC of hormone a day to see how it grew. So we had this chicken in the basement of the store, and at the end of the show, it turns out that Denver had given the chicken one

cup of hormone a day, thinking a CC is a cup. So the chicken comes up out of the basement and it's like ten feet tall.

How did they do that?
It was rear process, rear screen projection.

Oh, I see.
And Frank ends up shooting it with a shotgun. (*Laughing.*) It was so funny. I *loved* that show. There were a lot of really good ones. We did a thing called "The Best Dressed Man," where Warren Beatty and I compete for Thalia's affections, Tuesday Weld, by dressing up in more faddish clothes each day. I took a job at a clothing store so I could wear their clothes. Remember?

Yes.
Finally, he says, "I'm quitting this," because it was getting so ridiculous. The one you mentioned, "The Flying Millicans," with Francis X. Bushman, that was a favorite. There were a lot of clever shows.

You had a lot of people on the show who were just starting out.
Yes, like Marlo Thomas, who was very good, Michelle Lee, Ryan O'Neal, Bill Bixby. They were all terrific, by the way. They were all on the show because it was a great place that hired a lot of young actors.

Were you ready for the show to end when it did?
I felt it was time. I'd worked very hard. In those days, you did thirty-nine shows a season, so it was a hard go when you have that much of a part like I did. I was just as happy to see it end. Of course you're out of work, and then you wish you could come back. (*Laughs.*)

Did you enjoy making the reunion movies?
Yeah, I did. Actually, the first one was a half-hour pilot ["Whatever Happened to Dobie Gillis?"] but I didn't think it was very good. Lorenzo Lamas was in it, and he was good. The acting was okay, but it just didn't work.

What was it about?

It was about whatever happened to me, and it told where I was, and that I was married to Zelda. It was kind of odd. The script was not very good. Do you remember Jimmy Komack?

Yes. He was on *The Courtship of Eddie's Father*, and did *Welcome Back, Kotter*.

Yes. Well, Max Shulman wrote the script and Komack didn't like it, so, again, writers came in and began working on it and they ruined it. It's all in the writing. It really is. It was like saying Max Shulman didn't know how to write the script, and he created the character and the whole premise!

Was Bob Denver in that one?

Yes. Bob was in that one.

So you liked the second one better? ["Bring Me the Head of Dobie Gillis," 1988]

Well, yes, but I didn't like it that much either, cause I didn't like that script. I didn't like that premise, and I felt bad that we couldn't get Tuesday Weld. She couldn't do it for whatever reason. I was just kind of disappointed in that show too. It did very well, but it had a darkness to it. It wasn't the fun that the series had been. It just didn't work for me.

Were you given the opportunity to add your input?

Well, I did. I had input, but it's very hard to make a change. In other words, you've got dates that you have to begin production, you have a script maybe that isn't right, and you're working on it, and you've got people helping because you can't do everything yourself. It kind of gets away from you, you know? It's kind of hard to make it work out. You have to have a lot of help, and you have to have good people working with you. If you don't, then you're in trouble.

I ask everyone this, because I'm always curious. Did you keep any of your *Bob Cummings* or *Dobie* scripts?

I wish to God I had. I had this kind of spring-loaded binder that I would keep them in, and by the time I finished shooting, I'd already have the next script, and

I'd go home, open it up, dump the old one in the trash, and then stick the new one in. Isn't that awful?

Oh, no.
You don't realize that someday you'd love to own those.

You don't have *any*?
Not a one. Not a one. I have some of the movies I did. I have my *Cat Ballou* one downstairs, but no *Dobie's*. Now I think it was the dumbest thing I ever did. And I know of people that save everything, and I always thought it was kind of silly, but it's not silly. It's smart.

What kind of things did you do after *Dobie*?
I did a bunch of things. I did movies in the late sixties. Like *Cat Ballou*.

That was a great movie! Your first scene on the train where you pretend to be the drunken minister was *funny*. You looked like you were having a great time.
Thank you! That was a big-deal movie. Lee Marvin won an Academy Award. It made a lot of money, and it's still popular. It was fun to make because it was comedy. I had been doing *Dobie Gillis* and it gave me a chance to do a Western with guns, and horses, and all that. We went to Colorado on location. Lee Marvin was a lot of fun. A crazy guy. It was kind of different for me, and I really enjoyed it.

I got to the point where I was working all the time and got kind of tired of it, and wanted to get away from things, so I moved to Las Vegas for a couple of years and worked for Howard Hughes. I booked entertainment for the Landmark Hotel, which has been since been torn down, or imploded, or whatever they do to make things disappear. I did that from '70 to '72.

Did you ever meet Howard Hughes?
Nope, never. I never saw him.

As reclusive as he was, I didn't think you would have, but I had to ask.
In fact, the guy who was the head of the whole operation in Nevada, never met him either. Hughes just shut himself away. Isn't that strange?

Very.
So after I did that, I went back to acting for a while, and then I thought, "Well, maybe I need to learn more about production," so I went to work for CBS as a programming director. I liked that. It was a good change. I had been acting since I was a kid, and I was on TV for like ten years every week. So it was a good change. However, when I left CBS in '87, I wanted to do the *Bring Me the Head* movie, and I wanted to direct, which I did. I directed a bunch of other shows, *Head of the Class, Designing Women*. Then I started my painting career in the late eighties and I've been painting for about twenty years now.

How did you get into painting? Did you always have a talent for that?
Well, I never knew I did. I always liked doing it. How it all started was, as a child, like all kids do, I liked to draw and I played around with it all through my growing-up years in school. But I never really did anything with it. I got into high school and then when I was a freshman at Loyola University, here in Los Angeles, I really got diverted into show business doing the *Cummings* show. So any art ideas went down the drain. I didn't pursue them at all.

So years later, after I left CBS as an executive, and did *Bring Me the Head of Dobie Gillis*, all of a sudden, I was no longer in a regular job. So I decided to do a little acting and directing on the side, and pursue my art; something that I'd put off my whole life. So I went to an art school over in Brentwood, California called The Brentwood Art Center, and I started taking classes in pencil drawing and so forth, and it just kind of developed. I enjoyed it. I went a day or two a week and it was like a hobby. I started painting the next year or so, because they won't let you start right in with the oil paintings, because you need a background in drawing and perspective and all those different things. So I started painting about 1988-89, and then I had all these paintings that were hanging in the house, so I decided to rent a place, and then I had all these paintings, and people would say, "Gee. Those are kind of nice.

Dwayne in his art studio.

Dwayne today. (Dobie must have stumbled upon the Fountain of Youth!)

I'd like to have one. Will you sell it?" And finally, after doing that on a very small scale for several years, I did my first art show in La Jolla, California about 1999-2000, and I sold everything in the show!

Wow!
All of a sudden, it was like, I was a professional! And it's been going on ever since.

What kind of things do you paint?
Landscapes and things. Punch up my website. It tells you about all that.

How often do you paint?
I'm painting most every day when I'm not traveling doing art shows. I've maybe painted fifty, sixty, seventy pictures.

What do you enjoy about it?
I don't know. (*Laughs.*) It's an expression of ideas in my head of art. People say, "It must be very relaxing." But it can be very tedious and hard. Whenever you do anything all the time and you have to do it, some days it goes easy, and other times it's harder. I'm sure writing for you is the same way. You're searching for the right words and the right way to say something. It's the same way with art.

So, what do I get out of it? Satisfaction. It's something I've always wanted to do. I enjoy it when it's finished and it's there forever.

Are you still acting?
Yes and no. A couple of years ago I did *Surviving Gilligan's Island* with Bob Denver. I played the head of the network. That's the last thing I did. I enjoyed it, and I'm available. If someone calls up and has something good, I'll be glad to do it. But in the meantime, it's good that I have my art. I don't want to be retired! (*Laughs.*)

[Dwayne Hickman lives in Encino, California with wife, Joan Roberts, and fourteen-year-old son, Oliver. His artwork is available in fine galleries throughout the United States and can also be found on his website at www.dwayne hickman.com.]

Peter Lupus

Mission: Impossible: Willy Armitage 1966-1973

If you take tall, dark, handsome, then add muscular, you pretty much have just described actor Peter Lupus. Lupus played character strongman Willy Armitage on the popular CBS Action/Adventure series *Mission: Impossible*.

The series followed the adventures of the IMF (Impossible Mission Force); an elite group of secret government agents, spies, and specialists who were given a nearly "impossible" mission to complete every week.

Along with Lupus, other cast members included team leader Stephen Hill as Dan Briggs [season one] and Peter Graves, who subsequently replaced Hill as team boss Jim Phelps for the remainder of the series. Martin Landau (Master of Disguise Rollin Hand), femme-fatale Barbara Bain (fashion model Cinnamon Carter), and Greg Morris (electronics expert Barney Collier) rounded out the cast.

Lupus and Morris were the only two original characters to stay with the series from its premiere in 1966 until the series ended its seven-year run in 1973.

The series was immensely popular during its initial prime-time run and can still be seen in as many as 35 countries around the world.

Peter, how did you get into acting?
I started out to be a teacher in college at Butler University in Indianapolis. I wanted to teach Phys. Ed. I was playing football, and basketball, and running track, so I thought that would be a good extension because I wanted to be a coach. About halfway through the first semester, they were casting for a play called *Antigone* and they needed someone to play the part of King Creon. They

were just establishing a big drama department and the dean wanted to get more athletes into it so people wouldn't see it as a sissy thing, so they came to me and asked me if I'd read for the part of King Creon. So I read, and they asked me to do it. So I agreed. It's a Greek tragedy, and there was a scene in the battlefield where my son got killed and I had to go out on the battlefield and retrieve his body. So they always used a dummy. I asked how much the guy was gonna weigh that I was supposed to retrieve, and they said around 165 pounds, so I said, "Well, why don't I just pick him up instead of replacing him with a dummy?" And they said, "Could you do that?" And I told them I could. So the first show that we did was on a Saturday afternoon and it was mostly all women. So during this scene, I went out there and I bent over and got kind of emotional and picked him up and carried him off. And because it was a theater in the round, you walked right by people. And these ladies were kind of sniffling, and there were little tears here and there, and it just moved me. I thought, "Wow. It's fantastic to be able to move people and do something like this." So I got very interested, so I switched my major over to radio and television and drama.

When did you get into bodybuilding?
I started working out when I was fourteen because I was getting ready to start high school and I wanted to play athletics. I had never been able to participate, so I wanted to get stronger, and bigger, and more coordinated.

Were you the skinny kid who got sand kicked on him by the muscle guys?
Actually, I was kind of heavy up until twelve, and then between twelve and fourteen, I grew about four inches and then I got very lean. In fact, I was growing so fast that my joints hurt. So I started working out with weights to put on some strength. This was about 1951 and back then the coaches didn't want you to work out with weights. They thought it would slow you down and make you too cumbersome. They were all dead against it. No sports used weights to train back then. So I thought to myself, "Well, it must be working, because I'm getting stronger, and faster, and more coordinated, so I'm gonna do it and just not tell them about it." I used to go work out at the gym about ten o'clock at night when

nobody was there. And I just kept doing what I was doing, and it just turned out to be the way to go. At the same time, I got very involved in taking supplements, vitamins, minerals, proteins, herbs. And back then, there were two schools of thought. You worked out and you didn't worry about nutrition, or you worried about nutrition and you didn't worry about exercise. They both thought they had the perfect answer. So I started taking vitamins, and minerals, along with working out and that worked for me. I was kind of a pioneer in doing that. And now, that's what doctors recommend. Now it's working around the world.

What did you do after college?

I was bodybuilding and I had won some contests like Mr. Indianapolis, Mr. Indiana, and Mr. Hercules. One day I happened to run into some people from California, and they told me that I should go out to Hollywood because there weren't that many people in my physical category. So I went out there, and I remember the first job I went on. I was sitting at the famous Schwab's Drug Store where Lana Turner was discovered, and this guy came up to me and said, "Where have you been?" I said, "What do you mean?" He said, "We've been looking for somebody like you." I told him that I had just gotten there from Indiana three weeks ago. He asked me if I had an agent and I told him no. So he asked if he could be my agent if he got me this job he was talking about. So I said, "Sure." So he took me over to Desilu, and they were casting for a part in a sitcom called *I'm Dickens, He's Fenster,* with Marty Ingals, John Astin, and Emmaline Henry [best known as Mrs. Bellows in *I Dream of Jeannie*]. The scene with Emmaline Henry was walking up a ladder and she gets startled when this guy comes in and says something, and she falls, and he catches her. So they had already hired an actor, but Emmaline was kind of tall and this guy crumbled when she fell. He fell down. He couldn't hold her. So they got very worried and were going to cut the whole scene out. But then I walked in with this guy and they saw me and immediately called for Emmaline to come down on the set. Then they asked me if I would catch her if she fell off the ladder. So I said, "Sure. Go ahead. Walk up the ladder." So she did and I caught her. She only weighed like 135 pounds, which was like a feather to me, so I got the job right there. That was my very first job I can remember getting.

**When we were setting up this interview, you mentioned that you had done a
Dobie Gillis episode. Tell me about that.**
I met this fellow one day at the Beverly Hills Health Club for Men, and we just
started talking. I'd go in there four or five days a week, and he was in there two
or three days, and I started helping him with some exercises. A very nice guy.
So about three months after I had met him, someone called and asked me if I'd
come in and read for this part. So I go in and this guy tells me that it's a roman-
tic milkman part and he told me to just read a few lines. So I did, and he said
that was fine and that he wanted to introduce me to the producer. So I walk in
and the producer is Rod Amateau, the guy I had been helping at the gym! He
was the producer and writer of *Dobie Gillis*. Now that's a small world.

It sure is. You did some movies before *Mission: Impossible* came along.
I did a thing called *Muscle Beach Party* with Frankie Avalon, and Annette Funicello. My agent at the time was Jack Gilardi and he came on the set to see me,
and he met Annette Funicello, and they ended up getting married.

Buddy Hackett was also in it, and he and I got along famously. I just loved
him. It broke my heart when he passed away. And Don Rickles was in it also. That
was [one of] Don's first movie[s], and I remember we used to run to this circle in
the morning on the beach where you'd sit down to start the morning out. So I'd
get my place in the circle, and everyone would try to get there before Don Rickles
sat down. So he'd come sit down, and he'd start one at a time, just beating up on
everybody with those comments of his, and he got to me and he said, "You big
dummy. What am I supposed to say to you?" He used to use that "big dummy" a
lot and years later he told me that I was the first one he used that on.

After *Muscle Beach Party*, American International signed me to a five-year
contract, so I was over in Rome doing a film and I was at the American Embassy
on a Saturday or Sunday morning and there was almost nobody on the street,
so I'm walking to my car when I see this couple on the sidewalk and this guy has
a movie camera and he's filming. And he's got it in front of his face and he keeps
walking right toward me. So I kind of stepped to the right a little bit and he
walks right over to me and sticks this camera in my face. I was about to strangle
the guy, when he put down the camera and it was Don Rickles.

How funny.

I said, "What are you doing here?" And he said, "Meet my wife. We just got married." And they really had just gotten married. Can you believe it? I'm walking down the street in Rome and I run into Don Rickles. (*Laughing.*)

Tell me how *Mission: Impossible* came about.

I had just finished filming in Rome and we were going to Northern Italy to film this pirate picture. About a week before we left Rome, my agent called and told me that I needed to come back to California so they could talk to me about a possible series at Desilu. I said, "Jack, are you crazy? I have three years left on my contract. Why would I want to come back there and do a series that may not go anywhere?" He said, "Well, look at it as a free trip back." So I agreed. I had some time before the next film started, so I went back. I went into Desilu and Lucille Ball was there, and Bruce Geller, who created the show, and four or five other people. So I walked in there in a sport coat and a skin tight shirt and took my coat off and said hello to everybody, and they were all looking at each other. And I'm thinking, "They must like me. Oh my God. They're gonna offer me the part and I can't take it." So after that meeting, Bruce ended up following me out and he told me that he really wanted me to do this part. So to be polite, I told him to talk with my agent and work it all out. But I called my agent and told him that I was not going to leave my contract to try a series that may not go. And he said, "Well, take my word for it. This could be a blockbuster. I've read a lot of scripts and this really reads right." So I said, "Okay, but ask for more money than they want to pay." So he did, and they agreed. Lucille Ball ended up okaying the deal. So I went back to Rome and Jack worked it out where I would finish the film and then I could get out of the agreement. So I came back, and in November of '65, we filmed the pilot. In fact, at the time they filmed it, it was the most expensive pilot they ever filmed in Hollywood. It went three or four days over the budget. But we finished it, and it went on the air in September of '66. The ratings were okay at first, not fantastic, and people didn't quite understand it. People thought they were dumb, but it was all written that way. It was written so you were left at a suspenseful time right before the commercials. So the sponsors loved it because nobody left. They watched the commercials so they wouldn't miss one frame of it. It was all timed that way. A lot of people don't know this, but at the end of the first year, we were actually not penciled in for the next season. By chance, at the end of a board meeting, Mr. Paley, who ran CBS, said, "I just want to thank you fellows for coming up with my wife's and my all-time favorite show, *Mission: Impossible*." So guess what? We were inked in for the next year, and we ended up getting nominated for fourteen Emmys, and the rest is history. We ended up being in 108 countries at one time. We're still in 30 or 35 countries today around the world.

What was your impression of Lucille Ball?

She was a fantastic lady and a lot of people don't know what a business woman she was. You know, when she did *Mission*, they wanted her to renew her contract for three more years on *The Lucy Show*. They had already worked out the money, but she wanted a bonus. So she basically said, "Here's the deal. I'll renew, but I want you to finance three pilots. You pay for them, and you get first choice. If you want 'em, you get 'em, but if you don't want 'em, I can take 'em anywhere I want and I own them." So CBS agreed, and do you know what the three series were?

No. Tell me.

Mission: Impossible, Star Trek, and *Mannix.*

Three very successful shows!

How's that for a blockbuster! Those are the three she picked.

Did Lucy have much interaction with the show when it was being produced?

No, not really. Bruce Geller kind of held the reins the first three years, and he was a real stickler about getting everything right. He wanted to make sure that everything on the show was possible to do; that everything on there could be done. For instance, in the pilot we had to smuggle somebody into a vault in the Caribbean that contained these atomic bomb heads that were hidden in there, and our mission was to try to get them out. It was impossible to break into the safe, but we found out you could break out if you got locked in. So I had these two big cases of jewelry, and we asked the hotel if we could leave them in the safe overnight. So we got a safecracking expert, played by Wally Cox, who could break out of there if we could get him in. So we put him in one of the cases to smuggle him in. Those cases weighed like sixty pounds empty, so they wouldn't fall apart. And on camera, he had to be able to break out from the inside. So he was in one of the cases, and I tried to pick him up, and it was like I was lop-sided. He was about 125 or 130 pounds. So I was carrying 200 pounds in one case and sixty in the other. It's not possible. So I told them to put some lead weights in the other one so they would balance out. So Bruce came down to the set and said, "Peter, the shot is you have to carry both of these suitcases into the vault without breaking away, so we can see what happens with him getting out." So I said that I'd try it and I did. I was able to carry the two-hundred pounds, but I had to make it look like it wasn't that hard.

So Wally Cox really was in one of the cases you were carrying on camera?
He absolutely was. They didn't want to do a cutaway. In fact, it took two days to shoot it and the first day we shot it, when they called lunch, I set the cases down, and everybody started running for lunch, and I hear this tapping, and I said, "Oh my God, Wally's still in there." So I had to go back and let him out. (*Laughing.*)

How would you describe the character of Willy?
Willy was a secret agent, but what they needed from him were certain feats of strength that you couldn't get from anyone else. It took strength to do certain things, and it helped make the mission successful. The character turned out to be very popular with people, and I didn't know this at the time, but Willy was only originally written in the first episode to make it work. But when they tested it, he was so popular, and got such a positive reaction, they decided to write him in as a regular character.

You must have gotten a lot of fan mail.
Yes.

Did you have time to read any of it?
Oh yeah. I tried to read everything; I just couldn't answer it all. A lot of people

PETER LUPUS as *Willy Armitage*
MISSION IMPOSSIBLE

were always asking me about vitamins, and nutrition and exercise. In fact, one letter I got, and I wish I could remember the name of this fellow, but it's so hard to save all those letters. But at the time he was a freshman in high school, and he wanted to get bigger because he wanted to play high school football. So I wrote him back and put him on a muscle mass increasing workout with the diet and the supplements. Anyway, about nine or ten years later, I get a letter, and it said, "You may not remember me, but I wrote to you years ago," and he sent me a copy of the letter with the program that I had written out for him when he was in high school. And he said, "I would like for you to be my guest in two weeks when we play the Los Angeles Rams. I'm the second string linebacker for the Dallas Cowboys."

Unbelievable!
Can you imagine? He wanted to send me a ticket, but, unfortunately, I was going out of town and couldn't go. But I really felt good to think of this little kid trying to get big enough to play high school football, and ends up playing professional.

What a great story!
It was kind of a thrill to read that.

Peter Graves was not in the first season of *Mission*.
Right. He replaced Stephen Hill. Do you remember Stephen Hill from *Law & Order*?

Sure. That's one of my favorite shows. Why was he replaced?
Well, what happened was, Stephen had become an Orthodox Jew, and he had to leave at four o'clock to be home before sundown, and he didn't do anything at all until sundown the next day. So here's what happened. It was about the third or fourth show, and we've got over 200 people on the set for this scene, and at four o'clock on the dot, his agent walked in front of the camera and said, "Mr. Hill has to leave now." And they left in the middle of the scene and walked off the set.

I'm sure that didn't go over well.
Here's the thing though, Eddie. It was in his contract that he had to leave at four o'clock and everybody knew it. It just so happened that day it was in the middle of a shot, and it was just chaos. So they kept trying to shoot around him to honor his contract, but they finally decided that they just couldn't live with it. On Fridays, we used to shoot until twelve or one o'clock in the morning and catch up for the week and he couldn't be there. So by the end of the first year, he kind of wanted to leave, and they kind of wanted him to leave, so they let him out of his contract, so he was happy. He was a wonderful actor. I enjoyed working with him and I learned a lot from him. He was from the Actor's Studio. He was from the time of Marlon Brando, James Dean, George C. Scott, Paul Newman, Joanne Woodward, Martin Landau. You name 'em. They were all in that era. He loved his craft, and he was wonderful at it. He's a good man. Very solid in his convictions.

So that's how Peter Graves ended up coming on the show.
Yes. Peter came in the second year and stayed till the seventh. Greg Morris and I were the only two cast members that did the whole seven years. Marty and Barbara left at the end of the third year.

Why did they leave?
It was money. They had promised Marty more money and they had a change of who was running the television department at Paramount, and they had a new regime that came in and they said, "We can't afford to give you that kind of money, and we're not going to." And it became sort of a moral thing with Marty. He said, "You know, you made a promise, and that's it." And they did the same thing with Barbara. It wasn't Marty and Barbara's fault. They weren't given what they were supposed to get, so they both left.

Well, you can't blame them for that.
No, not at all. Marty had a very original deal that I've never heard of before or since in television. He signed a year-to-year contract because he didn't know if he wanted to keep doing the show.

That's unheard of.

Yes. He could leave. Barbara got out of hers because she just didn't come to work. She said, "Hey, you promised me this. You're not going to do this. From now on, count me out." And I want to tell you, when they left, it really hurt the show. It came back, but it took a while. They were very important to the show. Marty and I became very close. Marty comes to our house every year for Thanksgiving and Christmas, and I see Barbara at the Actor's Studio on Fridays when I go over there. And Greg passed away about a few years ago [Morris succumbed to brain and lung cancer in 1996].

What were your hours like?

Normally, you'd go in about seven o'clock for wardrobe and make up to be on the set by eight or eight-thirty ready to film. If you were going out on location, you usually had to be at the studio by four or five a.m. Speaking of being on location, here's a funny story. One day I was shooting up in Hollywood Hills about four blocks from my house, and because of the restrictions of insurance and the unions, I had to go clear back to Paramount to get into a limo so they could bring me back home and I was only four blocks from my house.

That's kind of crazy.

It was a union thing. You had to be driven from the studio by a union member. But when you were on location, you wouldn't get back to the studio until probably seven or eight o'clock at night. Sometimes later. Our normal day was from seven in the morning until seven or eight o'clock at night. It was a tough show to shoot. We always went over budget. You put a lot of hours in there whether you're actually filming or not. You have to be there.

How many days did it take to complete an episode?

Seven working days.

Some people I've spoken with said that their shows had a lot of rewrites and some didn't have any at all. What about *Mission*?

We had rewrites up until the time you got in front of the camera. They never really finished writing a scene until you were actually ready to shoot it. One time Bruce was watching a scene, and we had been to make up, wardrobe, and rehearsed, and he changed it. He didn't do that a lot, but I'm telling you, he was a stickler. It had to be right. That's one reason why it was such a success. To tell you how popular it was, I went over to Japan in '74 for the Department of Defense to see the service men that were coming back from the front. The first day I was there, I asked the driver to take me to a department store, and I got out at one to look at something in the window, and three or four people started gathering around me looking up at me, and pretty soon the sidewalk was full, then the whole street came to a stop, and finally the police arrived. When they saw who it was, they asked me not to go out during the day anymore because it caused riots. (*Laughs.*)

They just loved Willy. They had a press conference and as a surprise they brought in the guy who dubbed my voice on the show in Japanese. What a great voice. He was about five-foot-eight and really husky. He told the interpreter to tell me that he appreciated my supporting his family for the last seven years.

Are there any episodes of the show that really stick out in your mind?
A lot of them I don't remember, but there was one where I had to rescue Lee Meriwether. There was a scene where I had to slip into this place and get her out through this big chimney. I was on some kind of rope platform thing that had an automatic button where I could go up and down. She had to go up it, and then I had to go up it so we could climb out of the chimney and escape. So I worked this thing to take us clear up to the top. So they had tested it up to 2500 pounds to make sure it was safe. Well, we did one rehearsal, came down, and then got ready to shoot. The camera was at the bottom shooting up at an angle. And it was about thirty feet up to the top. So we start shooting, and about halfway up, I felt this plastic cable stretch, and I thought, "Crap. What's going on?" And just then I fell and barely missed the camera. Then Lee fell on top of me. I thought I had broken my neck, and she thought she had broken her back. And you talk about 9-11? They sealed this set and wouldn't let anyone on or off. Then they brought in the medics and took us to the hospital. Within an hour, I felt fine, but the doctor told me that if I hadn't been working out, she

would have absolutely broken my neck. I wouldn't be here. And if she hadn't fallen on me, she absolutely would have broken her back.

Was she okay?
Yes. I never went totally unconscious, but she was out. I went back to work that day, because I had to go back and do some other shots but, of course, she didn't. So they had to rebuild the whole thing on another set, but this time they only built it up about a third of the way. But she had to come back because we had to film the scene again. So just approaching it, she got tears in her eyes, she was so afraid. It was just a horrible experience. We got through it, though.

Those are the kinds of things that happen and nobody ever knows about. That's part of why I wanted to do this book. These kinds of things are interesting to fans.
Right, because we only show what really works. There was this one time when I was driving a motorcycle up in the hills doing a getaway shot, and all I had to do was go past the camera. I didn't want to wear a helmet because it was just a run-by shot, but I'll never forget Wes Eckerd. He was our wardrobe guy, and he came over in front of the motorcycle and said, "Peter, I've been in this business for thirty years and so I've seen a lot of accidents. We're up here in the hills, and anything could happen. So put this helmet on, or you're gonna have to run over me." So I balked a little, but I put it on, got on the motorcycle, drove past the camera, and, wouldn't you know, I lost control of the thing! I went over a cliff and down a sixty-foot embankment and ended up hitting my head on a rock that caved in the helmet. I'm rolling down, and I got my foot caught in a bush. Then the motorcycle came down and landed about a foot away from me, went over the top of me, and then burst into flames when it hit the bottom.

Talk about a close call.
You're not kiddin'. There was also another time when we were filming out in the ocean at San Pedro. We went pretty far out, and in the scene, I had to dive off the boat and into the ocean to get away because a couple of guys were trying to kill me on the boat. It was absolutely freezing and the water was like ice, and

A photo collage of Peter Lupus.

I didn't really realize that. The stunt men, who were going to do the far away shots, where you couldn't see their faces on camera, were dumping cold water on themselves to get used to the water. I had been below deck because I had gotten seasick and wasn't feeling good. It was on one of those great big PT boats, the one like John Wayne turned into his yacht. I had gotten so sick that I just wanted to get the shot done. I didn't want anyone dumping cold water on me, I just wanted to jump in and get it over with. So I dove in, and went too deep and it immediately felt like somebody had a chain around my chest and was pulling it tight. So when I finally came up, I couldn't even breathe. And then I hear this bing, bing, bing. And they had this sharpshooter on top of the boat, and he was trying to kill a shark that was about fifty yards away and was coming right after me. My stunt double had his wetsuit on, and he sensed that something was wrong, so he dove in and swam to me. I rested my arms on his shoulders, and I started getting my breath back again. So he and I both got back to the boat all right, and, believe it or not, they did get the scene.

Did you do a lot of your own stunts or were there restrictions against that?
There were, but I would try, and if I could do them, I did them. But after about the first year, I started getting to know the stunt men and I realized that I was taking jobs away from them. So I said, "You guys do 'em, and I'll do the close ups."

Tell me about Barbara Bain.
She's a dream. There's so many things about her. She was such a great mom. She called her kids every hour of the day to make sure they were okay, and they had two maids, one for each of the kids. And she had to talk to each of them each day. She was another one that was very professional. They would bring the girls in an hour earlier to do the hair and all, and if she had a six o'clock call, she'd get there at five to make sure she'd be on the set by seven. Nobody ever waited for her. She was always prepared, and a lot of people don't remember, but for the three years she was on the show, she won the Best Actress Emmy every year. Three years in a row! If she'd been on five years, she might have won five! She was just a doll to be with. As a matter of fact, she and I did an autograph show at the Hilton last year, and she and I got to sit by each other, and we had a ball.

What was Peter Graves like to work with?
He's a terrific guy. He was always on time, always knew his lines, and easy to be around. I remember the most angry I saw him in six years was this time when we were brought in at five o'clock in the morning to go on location, and at seven o'clock that night, they had still not used him in a scene. So he finally went up to the second assistant director and said, "Look. I haven't done one scene all day. I would appreciate it very much if you guys would get your schedule a little more organized." And that was about as mad as he got! (*Laughs.*)

You and Greg Morris had a lot of scenes together.
Yes. We were super buddies. Once we were on *The Mike Douglas Show*, and we were talking about all the tight spots we'd been in together like holes and tunnels and the backs of trucks. And I said, "Well, Mike, it looks like if Morris and I are in one more tight spot together, we're going to have to get engaged." We both started laughing and the audience was just laughing and laughing. We were always so serious on the show that they had never really seen us out of character and they were enjoying finally seeing us smiling.

For the first couple of seasons, Bruce Geller asked us not to do any talk shows. He said that he wanted people to believe that these characters were real. So I didn't do any shows for the first couple of years.

Did you save anything from the show?
Unfortunately, no. I wish I had. I don't even have a script. I remember one time when we were shooting down in Hollywood and they had our portable trailers out there, and I went out to do a shot and when I came back, my script was gone. So about two hours later, some lady comes up and says, "Peter, will you sign this for me?" And she handed me my script! She snuck it out of the dog-gone trailer and she got so excited she wanted me to sign it!

Did you sign it?
Yes. I said, "Okay, sure." (*Laughs.*) I had a lot of missing things, missing ties, missing everything. Everything was a memento to someone, so I didn't save a lot. (*Laughing.*)

What did you think about the *Mission: Impossible* movies?
The entire original cast was supposed to be in the first one, and what was supposed to happen was, they get a hold of Peter Graves, and they want him to get the group together for this special mission. So he's got to round up the group. He finds Barbara owning a modeling agency, and he finds Marty Landau doing some kind of a mind reading act in the circus or someplace, and Greg owned an electronics store, and I owned a chain of Golden Arch Health Clubs. So it worked in all of our backgrounds. So we're in the apartment with Peter Graves, and he says, "By the way, I'm bringing in one more guest expert." And, of course, that's Tom Cruise.

What a storyline!
Yes! So we go out on the mission and get in trouble and get caught. I remember telling the writers to make sure that I didn't get killed because I want to do the sequel. (*Laughs.*) So Cruise has to bring in some of his other people to rescue us and make the mission work. I thought it was fabulous, but what it turned into was a sort of James Bond, one man Mission Impossible. I heard that Barbara was taller than Cruise in heels, so he nixed that, and I'm 6'4, and Peter's 6'3, and Greg's 6'3, so he probably would have gotten lost in the middle of us. They were going to give us all two-hundred fifty-thousand dollars for four weeks' work. We were all to get the same thing. It was a favored Nations contract. But it didn't work out and that's the way it went.

That would have made such a great movie, seeing the old gang together again, working on a mission.
Yes. Everybody was very upset about the original cast members not being in it.

Did you end up seeing it?
Yes. *TV Guide* asked me to review it for them, so I went to the screening and I saw it. And I said that I thought it was going to be a hit.

People loved that show. It was one of the all time hit shows in the world of television. In fact, in Japan, in the past forty years, it was shown three different times in prime time as a *new* show. By the way, this is our fortieth anniversary of when we started the show in '66. It's amazing.

What kinds of things did you do after *Mission*?

For ten years or so I did plays all around the country. And I intentionally chose plays that were different from Willy, my character on *Mission*. I did kind of light stuff, plays like *Same Time Next Year,* and *Boeing, Boeing.* Then I got into the health food and exercise industry. Then my son and I decided to start our own company in Arizona, and that's what we're doing now. In fact, we're building houses two blocks from each other. Arizona is wonderful!

[Besides being right up there as one of the nicest people I interviewed for this book, Lupus maintains a much respected name in the health food and exercise industry. He divides his time between California and Arizona and continues to travel the country promoting health, energy, and exercise through his company Peter Lupus Enterprises.]

Kaye Ballard

The Mothers-In-Law: Kaye Buell 1967-69

Actress, singer, and comedienne Kaye Ballard has done it all from Burlesque to Broadway. Her first break came in the 1940s when she was hired as a singer by popular bandleader Spike Jones. Her thunderous singing voice and comedic talents eventually led to nightclub acts and roles on Broadway in such winners as *Touch and Go*, *Three to Get Ready*, and *The Golden Apple*.

Ballard's movie credits include *A House is Not a Home* with Shelley Winters, *The Girl Most Likely* with Jane Powell, and *Which Way to the Front?* with Jerry Lewis. But it was *television* that made her a household name when she landed the role of Kaye Buell in the Desi Arnaz comedy, *The Mothers-In-Law*.

Created by the talented writers of *I Love Lucy* (Bob Carroll Jr. and Madelyn Pugh Davis), *The Mothers-In-Law* premiered on September 10, 1967 and, according to Ballard, was never out of the top-fifteen Nielsens during its two-year run on NBC.

The premise followed the hilarious escapades of the Hubbards and the Buells, two bickering next door neighbors who become in-laws when their children decide to get married.

Herb Hubbard (Herbert Rudley), a well-to-do attorney, and wife Eve (Eve Arden), a sophisticated housewife who studied interior design, were a respectable suburban couple with a lovely daughter named Suzie (Deborah Walley).

Roger Buell (Roger C. Carmel), a palpably cheap television writer, and wife Kaye (Ballard), a loud-mouthed, Italian housewife, were their pushy, exasperating neighbors. When son Jerry marries next door neighbor Suzie and move into the Hubbards' garage apartment, the laughs begin as the meddling mother-in-laws get into one side-splitting situation after the other. [Carmel would later be replaced by *Dick Van Dyke Show* alumnus Richard Deacon over a salary dispute at the end of season one.]

Ballard, who is as friendly and down-to-earth as you'd hope she'd be, talked proudly about her days on *The Mothers-In-Law*.

Tell me how you landed the role of Kaye Buell.
I was doing a nightclub act at the Blue Angel in New York, and Lucille Ball came in with Gary Morton one night. As a matter of fact, I think it was their first date! I was a nervous wreck because they were sitting right in front of me. So after the show, I went over to their table to tell Lucy how much I loved her, and she said in that tough way she had, "You know something? You're funny."

What a compliment coming from her!
Right! And when Desi Arnaz was casting *The Mothers-In-Law*, she remembered me and told Desi about me. So Desi sent Bob Carroll and Madelyn [Davis], to see me in Detroit and that's how I got the part.

It had to be a bit intimidating having Lucille Ball sitting right in front of you while you were performing. Don't take this the wrong way, but did you notice if she ever laughed?
(*Laughs.*) I know what you mean. Once in a while. You know, she had this *poker face*, then all of a sudden she'd go "HA!!" (*Laughs.*)

So the writers saw you perform, and that was it. No audition.
Right. I didn't have to.

I read that in the beginning Ann Sothern was being considered for the role. Is that true?
That's right, but they decided that Ann Sothern was too much like Eve Arden. They needed the exact opposite to play against Eve, which I was. I was ethnic and she was very American.

THE MOTHERS-IN-LAW   produced by DESI ARNAZ PRODUCTIONS, INC.   a UNITED ARTISTS presentation

Kaye and Eve in *Mothers-in-Law*.

What was your schedule like during the week?
It was absolutely fabulous! When people complain about series, I'd like to slap them silly! Because it's a wonderful way to live! I mean compared to the show business I've known, where you have to travel and work at all hours of the night. No, No, No! It was a great, great life!

You'd go in on a Monday, they'd hand you the script, and you'd do a read through. Then in the afternoon Desi would stage the first act, and the next day he'd stage the second act. The third day we'd do run-throughs, and Thursday was the camera rehearsal. On Friday we'd tape it once in the afternoon as a dress rehearsal, and then again that evening.

Did they use the best of both shows?
Yes.

Was Desi Arnaz a "hands-on" director?
Yes, he was, and, I'll tell you, Desi was the most *tasteful* man in the world. He didn't like anything *forced*. He was a wonderful, wonderful editor, and a brilliant man. Brilliant!

And only recently is he finally getting the credit he deserves.
That's right, but he got the money and that's always good! (*We laugh.*)

I read where he used to let you use his home in the desert.
Yes. It was so funny. The first year on the show, he gave everyone presents for Christmas but me, and he said to me, "You get no present." And I said, "That's okay." "But," he said, "you can use my house in Palm Springs." So the first time I went there to use it, I opened the door, and there was a money tree sitting on the table, a Styrofoam Santa Claus floating in the pool out back, and in the refrigerator was champagne and caviar, with a little note that said, "Have a good time. Desi."

That was a present worth waiting for!
Yes! Oh, he was a classy man. I know why Lucy was in love with him. I don't think she ever got over her love for him either.

I understand that you eventually ended up buying that house.
Yes. I bought his little house in the desert. It's an itty-bitty house with big houses all around. And this little one stands alone, but I love it.

Did you have any input on any of the storylines on the show?
Oh, yes. I gave them three storylines, and I never got any credit, and I never got paid for them either! (*Laughs.*) At the time I didn't think about getting paid for something! One of my idea's was "Who's Afraid of Elizabeth Taylor?" "The Wig Story" was my idea, and also the grandmother coming to visit ["Here Comes the Bride Again"] was my idea.

The laughter on that episode where Jeanette Nolan played Nana Balotta was
unbelievable... **The audience was in hysterics!**
Oh, Jeanette Nolan was an absolute *genius* actress.

One of the all-time great character actresses! And she returned to play the nanny in another episode after Suzie had the babies. ["Nanny Go Home."]
Yes! She was brilliant!

The writers put you and Eve into some hilarious situations! The chemistry between the two of you was superb. Perfect comic foils.
Oh, thank you. I'm glad you care about things like that. So many of the young people don't care about what *was...* That show was a *funny* show. Today when they say, "Oh, *Everybody Loves Raymond...* greatness, greatness . . ." No. You just can't beat *I Love Lucy* and *The Mothers-In-Law*, because they were written by the same writers. And do you know "Nick at Nite" turned it down because they said it was too dated? I mean is *Gilligan's Island* dated?! (*She pauses.*) But you know what I'm proudest of about our little show? The laughs you hear on *The Mothers-In-Law* were *legitimate.* That's one thing Desi hated. Sweetening the laughs. Desi never used canned laughter. There was no sweetening on *The Mothers-In-Law*. And we didn't keep taping till three in the morning, like some of these new shows, redoing takes. With Desi, there was no redoing. That was it!

I think that has to ruin it for the audience when you hear something a million times. By then, the jokes have grown stale and it's not funny anymore.
That's right. How in the world do they expect them to keep laughing? It's just crazy today.

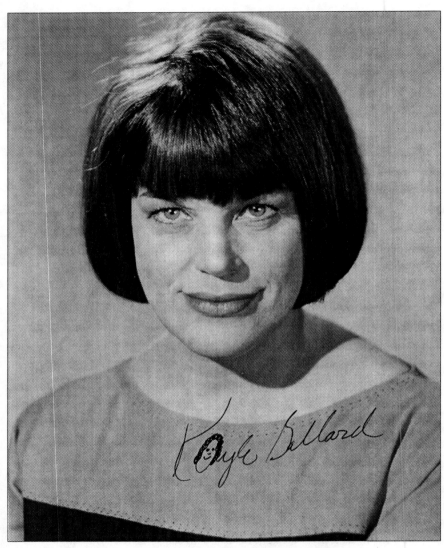

Ballard as "Kaye Buell" from *The Mothers-in-Law*, 1967.

What do you think about today's comedies?
The world seems to have lost its wit. Does that make sense to you?

Yes, it does.
When I was doing comedy, it was about *wit*. Not anything to do with genitalia. Nothing dirty or risqué and all that crap. Just *wit*. I just don't get the humor today. Some say it's alternative comedy. I say it's alternative to *funny*, that's what it is! They're just not funny!

(*Laughing*.) You're right. I also think that today, a lot of shows are too *joke*-oriented. You don't get a chance to know the characters well. It's just joke, joke, joke.
Oh, God. I can't watch 'em! There isn't one sitcom today that I say, "Oh! I've got to watch!"

What *were* some of your favorites?
I thought *Mary Hartman, Mary Hartman* with Louise Lasser was a *hilarious* show. That was the only fan letter I ever wrote. Now Louise Lasser is one of my closest friends. I just saw her. She is *so* funny. She said to me, "Kaye, let's meet in the couch department at Bloomingdales." I said, "Why? What's there?" She said, "Couches! We can sit, we can talk!" She's hilarious! I love her!

I also liked some of the *Seinfelds*. I thought *Maude* was brilliant. I enjoyed *Alice* [Ballard guest-starred in a 1977 episode, "The Hex"] and *The Golden Girls*. I would have *loved* to have been a guest on that show. And, of course, *Designing Women*. Now *that* was a funny show. For me, that was one of the last of the funny shows on television.

And your old chum Alice Ghostley played Bernice Clifton. What a great character!
Yes. And she is the most wonderful human being in the world...

I watched the *Cinderella* DVD [a 1957 live broadcast thought lost until recently discovered in the CBS vaults, starring a twenty-one-year-old Julie Andrews in the title role] where you and Alice played the stepsisters and sang "The Stepsisters Lament." You two were great fun to watch in that.

That was a good show also. And you know what's funny? Alice Ghostley and I made the least amount of money in that because we took a flat salary. (*She laughs.*)

Tell me about Eve Arden. What was she like?
Eve was the most wonderful ... (*She pauses trying to find the right words.*) There was never an unkind word between Eve Arden and myself.

It's nice to hear things like that.
Oh, it was a joy, a joy! The whole show was. The tragedy was when Roger C. Carmel insisted on a two-hundred-and-fifty-dollar raise. Then Desi said, "Well, I'll replace you."

Two-hundred-and-fifty dollars would be considered a *joke* today.
Yes! We were all supposed to get a two-hundred-fifty-dollar raise the second year, and suddenly Proctor and Gamble wouldn't do it. So Desi said, "Either you do it, or the show doesn't go on." And all this when we were still in the top ten! What was so funny was that Eve and I were telling him, "No! We *want* to do it!" (*Laughing.*)

It's fascinating the difference [in salaries] today. Eve and I didn't make that much money. Eve Arden, who was a *big* star then, made six-thousand a week, and I made two. When you compare that today to Ray Romano making one or two million dollars an episode!! It's crazy!

What are your memories of Roger C. Carmel?
Roger C. Carmel was the most wonderful actor. Perfect for that role.

Do you feel that it hurt the show when he was replaced by Richard Deacon?
Oh, I think it made a *big* difference. I know it made a big difference for *me*, because I loved working with him. It was like a perfect combination. And Richard Deacon was not Roger C. Carmel. He was a wonderful actor, but I had a chemistry with Roger C. and I could hit him, no matter how hard! But when I'd hit Richard, he'd go, "Owww!" Richard didn't really want to be there. He just did it because he wanted a job.

I never understood why they offered him the role. His personality was the complete opposite, not to mention the fact that he didn't look anything like the original Roger. There was just no comparison.
No. The real Roger was *it*... Oh, he was such a wonderful actor.

What about Herb Rudley?
Herb Rudley had a *terrific* sense of humor. He had a giant poodle, named Oliver, and he'd bring him to the set. Oliver used to escape every once in a while, and then I'd say, "Do you love Oliver?" And he'd say, "Well, if I had to choose between my wife and Oliver..." And then there would be this *long pause*, and we'd both laugh. Oliver was his *love*! And I was always in awe of Herb because he played Robert Alda's brother in the Gershwin Brothers Story [*Rhapsody in Blue*].

I didn't know that.
Oh yes. And he was quite a bit older than me, which I didn't know at the time. I spoke to him sometime last year and he said, "You know, Kaye, I'm ninety-three now," or something like that, and I was so shocked! Oh, he was great. *Everybody* in the cast was wonderful! Everybody in that show was a joy to work with! We all got along perfectly. As a matter of fact, we never even said goodbye because we were so sure that we were coming back for another season.

Who would get the most nervous before tapings?
Me! I'm always nervous. Always, always.

I remember that Joe Besser [Shemp Howard's replacement as the third stooge in *The Three Stooges*] was on a few episodes of the show ["Two on the Aisle," "The First Anniversary is the Hardest," and "How NOT to Manage a Rock Group"]. He was such a funny man!
He was the sweetest, dearest man. He's like all these people that I admired so much who at the end had nothing. Desi would hire him just to give him work. You know, it's so unfair that only a few get recognized. The people that devoted their lives to entertaining, they die without anyone noticing them, and that always hurt my heart. I always thought that's wrong.

It's not only wrong, it's sad. He was another *great* character actor. His reactions were priceless! I think my favorite was the episode called "How NOT to Manage a Rock Group," and he played a Salvation Army-type bandleader, and you four made a record with his band, and were dressed in this Salvation Army garb marching along and singing with the band.

Oh, I don't remember that one!

You need to watch that one again. It was *so* funny.

Yes. I've got to see them. I haven't seen any of them in years.

Was there anyone that broke up the most during rehearsals?

Well, Eve Arden and I had a lot of fun. I remember an episode we did with Joi Lansing ["Take Her, He's Mine"]. Oh, God. Eve and I couldn't get through it! Joi has the biggest *bazooms* in the world! As a matter of fact, when I sat down and looked up, I couldn't see her face! (*Laughing.*) Eve Arden and I just *screamed* with laughter. I just stopped in the middle of it and said, "How does that happen?! Cause when I get fat, I get fat *all over*!"

(*Laughing.*) Yes, I remember her.

God, it was hysterical! We laughed so ... We couldn't get through it!

Did you and Eve keep in touch over the years?

Oh yes! Right until the end.

And I know that Roger C. died years ago.

Roger OD'd, which *shocked* me! 'Cause I didn't even know he smoked *pot*!

I remember. He was only in his fifties! He was pretty young.

He was *very* young! ... He was just the most wonderful actor to work with. This macho thing between him and Desi [over the salary dispute] was so stupid! And then he would say to me, "Babe, it's not about the money. It's the principle of the thing." I'd say, "Oh, forget about the principle!" "Nah. It's the principle of the thing!" he'd say. It was just so stupid.

Do you think he regretted not coming back?

(*She pauses.*) I think so. Yes.

Do you have any of your old scripts?

I've got *all* the scripts. Some signed by Eve, and the different people that were on the show. And I don't know what to do with them! I should put them on eBay I guess. [Note: She did, and the author ended up winning one.]

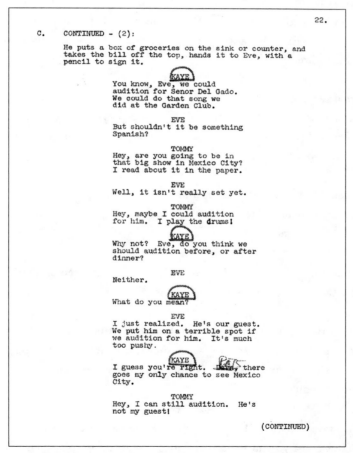

A page from Ballard's personal *Mothers-in-Law* script, "The Hombre Who Came to Dinner Pt. 2," written by *I Love Lucy* writers Bob Carroll Jr. and Madelyn Davis. In this episode, the role of grocery boy Tommy was played by Desi Arnaz, Jr.

Do people recognize you from *The Mothers-In-Law*?
It's amazing! I was at a book signing in Washington, and *everyone* would come up and say, "We love *The Mothers-In-Law*!" It's amazing that that show would have that kind of impact. We're talking 1967 to '68 to '69!

Did you stay in touch with the kids from the show? [Jerry Fogel and Deborah Walley]
Well, Jerry, my son, I do. He's happily married for the third time, and living in Kansas. And he's still a disc jockey. He was always a disc jockey, even before the show. And it's so funny because I was thirty-eight when I played his mother, and he was thirty-three!

I never realized that!
Yes. I was like seven or eight years older, but I was playing his *mother*. And Deborah Walley *died* [of esophageal cancer in 2001]! I couldn't get over it! *I* was shocked! She was so young! That was so sad.

Yes, it was... I hated hearing about that. Was she nice?
Very nice, and I believe she was dating a rock star at the time, and I think she married him eventually.

Do you know if and when *The Mothers-In-Law* will be released on DVD?
They were talking about it, but nothing is set.

That's unfortunate. It would be such a treat for all the people who remember and love that show. If it ever is released, they should let you do some *commentary* on some of the episodes. Fans would absolutely love that!
And I could! I could!

(*Smiling*) I know you could!! It's a delight to know that you were so happy playing Kaye Buell, and you have made countless others happy playing her so well.
Ah, thank you... It was a wonderful thing to be able to do. It was the happiest time of my life in show business!

KAYE BALLARD

Catherine Balotta; my favorite Italian.

[Kaye Ballard lives in the desert community of Rancho Mirage, California. Still performing, she continues to receive rave reviews for her work in the theatre. Ballard has co-authored a marvelously entertaining book with Jim Hesselman, chock full of anecdotes about her life in show business called *How I Lost 10 Pounds in 53 Years* from Backstage Books.]

Stan Livingston
My Three Sons: Chip Douglas 1960-1972

My *Three Sons* has the distinction of being the second longest running sitcom in the history of television (369 episodes!), second only to *Ozzie and Harriet*. It was also one of the first to showcase a single parent raising a family; in this case, widower Stephen Douglas, played by former movie star Fred MacMurray.

My Three Sons was unique in the fact that it contained an all-male household, opening the door to a lot of comic possibilities. From 1960 to 1972, MacMurray played father to four sons. Yes, four (I'll explain in a minute...); eighteen-year-old Mike (Tim Considine), fourteen-year-old Robbie (Don Grady), and seven-year old Chip (Stanley Livingston).

When son Mike gets married and moves away (i.e. leaves the show) the Douglas household adopts Chip's friend, Ernie (Stanley Livingston's real-life brother, Barry), when he becomes an orphan after his parents are killed in a car crash.

Even someone like Fred MacMurray had to have some help in raising three growing boys, so it came in the form of his father-in-law, Michael Francis "Bub" O'Casey, played by William Frawley. Frawley would stay with the household until 1965, when ill health forced him into retirement. Luckily Bub's brother, Uncle Charley (William Demarest), was able to move in and take over the household duties until the series went off the air in 1972.

Toward the end of the series, the Douglas household is no longer an all-male entity. Robbie marries pretty, blonde Katie Miller (Tina Cole, a member of the singing King Family) and they eventually become parents to triplets (three sons, of course.) Widower Steve meets Barbara Harper (Beverly Garland), who has a daughter named Dodie (Dawn Lyn), and they tie the knot. Then middle son Chip elopes and marries Polly Williams (Ronne Troup). With the addition of these pretty ladies to an already large household, a more fitting name change to the series might have been *Full House*.

Stan Livingston, now 57, described what it was like growing up as one of America's "Three Sons."

Tell me how you began in show business, Stan.
I got started because my mom was mortally afraid of me drowning. I had a cousin that drowned when I was young, so she took me to a swim school in Hollywood to take lessons. The lady that ran the pool used to put these little shows together called "The Water Babies." It was a ploy for her to get more publicity for her pool, so that she could get more parents to bring their kids in for lessons. It was right in the heart of Hollywood. In fact, it was right on Hollywood Boulevard. She was quite the PR person because she got several of the magazines of that era to come down and do articles and pictorials on us like *McCalls* and *Vogue*. She even got the TV show *You Asked for It* to come down and do a segment on it. So pretty soon she was getting a lot of Hollywood-type people bringing their kids so they could learn how to swim. There happened to be an agent there whose daughter was learning how to swim, and she kept noticing me. She talked to my mom and told her that she should send me out on something and try to get me into show business. So my mom finally agreed and I went out on a couple of things. I started out as an extra and got my feet wet, and I happened to be doing an *Ozzie and Harriet* as an extra, and low and behold, Ozzie, for whatever reason, gave me a line and that's how I got into the Screen Actors Guild and became a professional actor.

Wow!
Yeah! And the Nelsons had me back, so from 1956 to 1960, I did a few shows as a neighborhood kid. So that's how I got started. And once I got started, I

started getting into movies. I did *Please Don't Eat the Daisies* with Doris Day and David Niven. I did *Rally 'Round the Flag, Boys!* with Paul Newman and Joanne Woodward, and that's the movie that introduced Joan Collins. That was her first movie. [It was, actually, Collins' 20th film] In fact, my brother [Barry] got hired as my brother on that movie, but they fired him because they said his eyes crossed and Paul Newman wouldn't have a son with crossed eyes. (*Laughs*.) So by noon that day, my brother was at the eye doctor, and guess what? He got glasses, and because of the glasses he worked even more. He kind of pioneered the "nerd" look. He had glasses and buck teeth and he just looked adorable and kept going with that kind of look and that's how he got started.

I remember he was on a *Lucy Show* episode as Mr. Mooney's son. He was a new kid in the neighborhood and Lucy didn't realize who he was, and talked him into letting her try out her new barber clippers on him. And in typical Lucy fashion, he ended up going home almost completely bald and, of course, Mr. Mooney blew a gasket.
Oh yeah, yeah! That was a good show.

Did you get the opportunity to ever work together before *My Three Sons* came along?
Actually, yes. We worked together on an *Ozzie and Harriet* in 1959. In fact, it was the last *Ozzie and Harriet* I did because they knew I was going to do *My Three Sons* and wouldn't be able to come back to that show anymore, so they brought my brother in. After that, he kind of took over as the neighborhood kid.

Interesting story!
No nepotism in show business, huh?

(*Laughs*.) So what do you remember about Ozzie?
He was a really great guy, gentle, especially working with kids. I'd worked with some other directors and actors on other shows, and some of them were real screamers and they were really kind of uptight people and not very good with

kids, but Ozzie was. The whole set was a very relaxed atmosphere and very family-oriented. The crew was kind of like extended family and he had his real family working there, so he really knew what he was doing.

Where was that show filmed?
At a lot called General Service Studios. Then later it became known just as the Lot, and now I think it's called Producers Studio or something. It's right at Las Palmas and Santa Monica Boulevard right in the heart of Hollywood.

Another thing I remember about the show is a lot of times at the end of the episodes, Ricky would sing. And if you think about it, those are almost like the first MTV videos. In those days, that was huge! *Ozzie and Harriet* was network, and in those days there were just three. So when you went out, you're going out to fifty-sixty-million people at a pop. So it was a really strategic move on Ozzie's part to realize the power of TV in those days and to basically jump-start a career for Ricky. He had the voice and the look, and the songs were pretty good, so Ozzie was a pretty smart business man.

Did you audition for the role of Chip, or did they know your work from *Ozzie and Harriet*?
I did audition, but at that point in my career I had done a lot, and they were interested. And I was actually the first actor hired. They knew immediately they wanted me and the only other person hired at the time is the person who the show was built around, which was Fred MacMurray.

Did he have any input on casting?
Not really. I think he would have the input after they got going and did the pilot. For example, if he didn't like somebody or something wasn't working out, I'm sure he would have a say in that.

He was one of the first big movie stars to come to television in those days.
Right! When Fred MacMurray came to TV, movie stars just didn't do TV then. There was this big division between the two. But TV had been around a little bit by then, and had established itself. Fred had done a little TV, but when movie stars did

Livingston as a young Chip Douglas.

it, they mainly did it as guest stars, like he did on *The Lucy-Desi Comedy Hour* ("Lucy Hunts Uranium"). But at that time, they just never did a series. It was unheard of. At that time, Fred MacMurray was a huge, huge movie star who probably had eighty films under his belt. He had just been in *The Caine Mutiny,* and had this legacy of all these great comedies and suspense films. He starred with Claudette Colbert and Barbara Stanwyck. And what's unfortunate is some of the younger kids today don't really know who he was. They'll ask, "Who was Fred MacMurray?" And I'll say, "Look. To put this in perspective, it would be like Mel Gibson or Michael Douglas saying, 'Hey, you know what? I want to do a TV series.'"

Good comparison.
That's how huge it would be. It was just unheard of.

Fred had a very desirable working contract.
Well, that's how they enticed him into it. It was strange but not unheard of. To make it work for Fred, they brought him into it by saying, "If you do this, you'll work for about two or three months prior to the summer and then you'd have off." And we'd do all the scenes without Fred and then at the end of the year he would come back and pick up any scenes that he still needed to do and we would catch up with him again and finish off the shows.

So he came in, did all his scenes for all the shows, and then left.
Right.

So, most of the writing for the season had to be done before he came in. Then you all would come in and film around the scenes he had completed.
Exactly.

When you were working a typical week, would you be doing a lot of different shows at once?
Yeah, because they were shooting so far out of continuity. That's what they would do. We would be working almost everyday on two or three different

shows. Fortunately, they didn't totally shoot everything out of order. In other words, we'd rotate. We might do two or three scenes in the kitchen, but they would be out of different shows. Then we might move to the bedroom and do a couple of Chip and Ernie scenes in their room. So it was varied. We'd shoot approximately nine or ten pages a day.

Wow. I bet that was quite a job for the continuity person to keep track of how your hair looked and what clothes you were wearing in each show.
Yes. We had a continuity lady who was really kind of amazing. Her name was Pat Miller. She wrote the Bible for all the people who do the continuity stuff now. Originally, there was a lady named Jeannie Belcher who did it, and then she left about the third year, and then Pat came in for the rest of the time. She was amazing. Nothing would get by her! She'd know how many buttons you had buttoned, or if you had a hair sticking up, which way the cup was facing, if you were holding something in your left hand, that kind of stuff. She was a total hawk-eye! It's funny. I produced a movie a couple of years back. Actually, we're just finishing it right now for distribution, and the girl that we had who was our continuity person had studied with Pat Miller. She said, "I studied with this lady, Pat Miller." And I said, "You're not gonna believe this, but I know her! She was the continuity lady for *My Three Sons* for eight years." She couldn't believe it.

My Three Sons was originally shot at Desilu, correct?
Yes. Originally it was at Desilu, which was the old RKO studios in Hollywood. We did the first seven or so years there and then we moved to CBS Cinema Center in the San Fernando Valley, which was the old Four Star Republic studios. That's where they used to do all the old Westerns and stuff like that. They were doing a lot of movies and different TV series at that time.

What TV shows were there then?
They were shooting parts of *Gilligan's Island* and *Hawaii Five-O*, which mainly shot in Hawaii, but occasionally we'd see people from the show there doing pick-ups or something. And they also shot *The Wild Wild West* there, and *The Big Valley*.

Right. I talked to Peter Breck and he mentioned that *Gilligan's Island* shot there sometimes.
Yes. They had kind of a swamp on the back lot. (*Laughs.*) It wasn't even the size of a swimming pool. They used to call it the lagoon.

Did you ever meet Lucy or Desi?
Oh, sure! When we were at Desilu, Lucy used to shoot *The Lucy Show* right next door to us. They were on the next stage over, so a lot of the times I'd go over and we'd ride skateboards or bikes with the kids from her show, Ralph Hart, Jimmy Garrett and Candy Moore.

Tell me about William Frawley who played Bub. What do you remember about him?
Well, he was pretty much as you saw him on the show. He was kind of a can-tankerous old guy and I think he loved playing that part. He was pretty much a gentle soul, but he had cultivated this bark and gruff exterior that people expected him to have. He was a great guy to work with. In fact, I sort of became his surrogate grandson. We kind of bonded when the show began. I'd eat lunch with him almost everyday.

Was he still into baseball then like he was when he was doing *I Love Lucy*?
Yes, very much into baseball. I went to a couple of baseball games with him. He was very into sports. I'm sure he was probably into betting too, but that's another story. (*Laughs.*)

Was he cantankerous in a one-on-one setting?
Not really. He would just kind of do it in an entertaining way. Once you got to know the guy, you realized it was all for show, really.

Bill left the show in '65. Did he leave because of health issues?
Yeah, they just couldn't get him insured. The insurance guy said, "Hey, this guy should be dead by now. I don't know how he's alive, and I just can't sign off on him." So they basically decided to replace him and that's when they brought

My Three Sons: The "Bub" years. (Why so serious, guys?!) From left to right:
Don Grady (Robbie), Tim Considine (Mike), William Frawley (Bub),
Stanley Livingston (Chip), and, seated, Fred MacMurray.

William Demarest in. I think for Bill, unfortunately, that was the final nail in the coffin. He lived for the show and to have that taken away, was it. He ended up passing away about four months later.

How did they write him out?
You know, I don't really remember. I'd have to look at those shows again. I don't know if it was thinly veiled that he passed away, or that he had to leave to go some place or something. And then Uncle Charley shows up, who was supposed to be his brother. They were both cut from the same cloth, both being kind of crusty. So that worked out pretty well. To be perfectly honest, William Demarest was a much bigger star than William Frawley. Bill Frawley was basically known from *I Love Lucy* and had worked as a character actor, but Bill Demarest was *huge*. Probably the quintessential second banana. He was in huge, huge, films [*Mr. Smith Goes to Washington*, *The Devil and Miss Jones* and *The Jolson Story*, in which Demarest was nominated for an Oscar in the 1946.]

Was Demarest anything like the character of Uncle Charley?
He was pretty close to that. Kind of crusty. When I'd go to Palm Springs, I'd stop by his place and he was always cordial. He'd invite you in to have a beer and hang out for a while. He wasn't quite as profane as Bill Frawley was on the set. (*Laughs.*)

So Frawley didn't care if there were kids around on the set? He'd let loose, huh?
We'd be doing a scene and they'd say, "Bill, could we do it again?" And he'd say, "Go f--- yourself. I don't need this shit." (*Laughing.*) They'd just let him go, cause there was no stopping him.

It's funny picturing Fred Mertz saying that. (*Laughing.*)
And those were probably the kindest words you would ever get out of him! He was pretty handy as a wordsmith. (*Laughs.*)

What kind of schedule did you work?
For me, it was five days a week, probably nine hours a day, with an hour for lunch. It was a full day, and in that period of time, I'd have to find time for three hours of school too. That was mandatory by law.

I saw you on the A&E documentary that Tony and Lauren Dow produced, *Child Stars: Their Story*. You mentioned how your friends thought it was the coolest job in the world to be on a TV show, but you would tell them, "Okay, if you think it's so great, come spend a day and see how really boring it is."

Right. That's the whole story of Hollywood. Everybody sees what Hollywood wants you to see. It's all done with smoke and mirrors, as they say. There were a lot of magazines back then that made it out to be so much fun to be on a movie or TV set, and made it sound like the end all. And the reality is, you're there nine hours a day, and most of the time you're waiting for them to light the set, and it's pretty boring. I've heard war described as boredom punctuated by extreme terror ... War is the same way. You're doing nothing, and then all of a sudden, somebody is shooting at you, and for ten minutes or an hour it's intense, and then it goes right back to being boring again. And that's pretty much how moviemaking is. It's extremely interesting when you're up on your feet doing it, and in between you're just waiting for people to light and things.

Is that the time that you'd have to get school in?

Right. That's what I would do. If I wasn't in any scenes, a lot of times I could get my whole three hours in, or pretty good chunks of it, and then some days, I'd be in a lot of scenes and getting it in fifteen-minute increments all day long. You had to be in there for at least fifteen minutes, so it could be pretty crazy sometimes.

Most people have told me that it was pretty much just them and their teacher.

Right. That's how it was for me until my brother became a permanent member on the show. Then he was in the schoolroom with me. And unless they had other kids working with me, I was in that room with myself and the teacher and that was it. The good news is that you had a tutor all to yourself. But the downside is you don't have anybody to play with or talk to.

Did you have much homework?

Yes. Almost every night, once you get from junior high on. There's always reading in high school. And you only had three hours. And then when I was going to college, the teacher would say, "Have this book read by next week." And it'd be like *War and Peace* or something. (*Laughing.*) Then you'd have tests and all that too.

Any favorite subjects?

Not really. I was somebody that really didn't mind school. I've always been sort of a curious person, whether it was Math or English or Science, I was pretty much into it. I was a pretty good student all the way through it. I made mainly A's and some B's here and there if I didn't study hard enough, but it prepared me, because the last four years of the show, I was going to college at night.

Wow!

Yeah. From '68-'72, I had a little deal worked out with the producer that they would let me off at six o'clock so I could go to night school. I was going to a UCLA extension at night, and Los Angeles City College I picked up the various classes I needed. I was going four nights a week too. Plus, I was married and had a kid.

I read that you got married pretty young and had a little girl.

Yeah. My daughter was born in '69. I was nineteen when she was born, so I had a full plate going to school four nights a week, doing my homework, and doing the show nine months out of the year. I think about it now, and think, "How the hell did I find the energy to do that?" (*Laughs.*)

As far as salary was concerned, I understand the Coogan Law said your parents had to put back a certain percentage of what you made. Is that right?

Yes, there was a set amount, but it was very small. I think maybe five or ten percent. But my parents had thirty or forty percent of my money put away, so I had a pretty good chunk of money, but probably another thirty or forty percent of that went to taxes and an agent. My parents probably kept around ten percent. They were the ones that had to buy clothes, things like that, but it kind of improved the family living. But I would say, for the most part, a good majority of my money was there, and when I turned eighteen, I went down and got it and gave a good bit of it to my business manager who made some good investments for me. Thank God! I really lucked out on that.

Yes. I have heard where some people would just blow it.

Well, I've always been pretty conservative with money. I guess I hung around

Fred MacMurray too much. (*Laughs.*) It's not like I drove exotic sports cars. I don't think I ever had one. Just a regular old car was okay with me.

Did you keep anything from the show?
I have a few scripts, but I was never really much of a collector of memorabilia. And I was never really any good with the fan mail and all that.

How so?
Even though I was in showbiz, my life seemed pretty normal to me. I'd do the work, come home, go play with my friends, and do my homework and all that, and I just couldn't get into the fact that people saw me as a TV star. I thought my life was pretty boring or mundane. So the fact that somebody would be sending me fan mail thinking I'm living some kind of exciting life, I just couldn't relate to it. So I pretty much dumped my fan mail.

Did you really?!
Yeah. I didn't answer too much of it, but now I'm doing penance. Because I actually answer it now or I try to, anyway.

What kind of things do people say in their letters when they write now?
Well, kind of like, "I'm in jail. Could you write and send me money and a free picture?"

You're kidding.
No, I do get jail mail, but most of it's from regular people expressing their gratitude to the show and what it meant to them, or how it helped them grow up, and how they wish life could be more like that. And then the other part is from kids that have seen it on Nickelodeon or TV Land. It's kind of funny to get stuff from kids. They're looking at the show and seeing me ten or twelve years old and they think they're writing to a kid. It's kind of startling sometimes when you go do a gig and you have all these kids coming to meet Chip and here's some guy with a beard and slightly gray hair. It's like, "Who the hell is this?!" (*Laughs.*) But that's the one thing that TV has done. It's kind of preserved people in time, and that's kind of interesting.

What was Fred MacMurray like?

I hate to say it, but he was pretty much what you saw. He was just a very gentle, easy-going guy, and really concerned about the quality of the show. It wasn't past him to ask story questions, or we'd be rewriting something right on the set. I never saw him get mad at somebody. I never saw him yell. I'd even venture to say that he probably was the kind of person that if he had something to say, he wouldn't come and say it to you. He would tell the production manager, or the producer, and they'd be the one to take you aside and say, "Be careful of that," or whatever. You'd hear about him gently doing things like that sometimes. For the most part he was a really nice guy. He was very cordial to work with, and as an actor you really learned a lot from him. He was always warm and friendly, even when I'd run into him years and years after the show was over. But it would have been a much more interesting experience for me, had I been in my twenties when I worked with him. But when you're in your teens, you're thinking about guitars and girls and all of that. He was a one of a kind guy that you could talk to about acting and the craft. He was very approachable, and I'm sorry to say that I didn't get to know him better than I did.

Tim Considine, who played Mike, the oldest brother, got married on the show and left. How did that come about?

Tim wanted to leave the show. He just wanted to move on and do some other things, and by that point my brother was playing my friend, so they just replaced the third son with somebody that was right there under their nose. There's that nepotism again. (*Laughs.*)

Did you keep in touch with him?

Oh yeah. Tim and I are really good friends. We do a lot together. We actually went to Panama at the beginning of the year. In fact, we went with a bunch of other guys; Jon Provost, Paul Petersen, Billy Gray, so we kind of have a little club going. Tim's kind of responsible for the whole thing. And he's totally into the world of automotive racing. Even when we were doing *My Three Sons*, Tim was obsessed with cars. He writes for *Car and Driver, Motor Trend*, and all that. He's a highly respected automotive writer. He was the president of the Automotive Writers Association for a while. He's written a couple of books, one being a big coffee-table book about the history of auto racing in the United States. He's an interesting guy. He's kind of like an older brother to me. Tim would actually come and get us and we'd go to his parents' house to swim, or he'd take us to do things. He actually would make a cool older brother. I guess I always wanted one, so okay, Tim can be it. (*Laughs.*) He's a really cool guy in my book.

What are some of your favorite episodes?
Probably the one with the lion ["A Lion in the House"]. This circus lion gets loose in the Douglas household and we keep missing it when we're walking through the house.

There was another one where I think Don starts a birthday cake factory in the house ["Happy Birthday World"] and it kind of culminates with a slapstick pie and cake fight. That was fun to do. But I'd probably have to say that my favorite shows are not any particular show, but just the old black-and-white ones. There was a completely different feeling about those shows; the way they were shot. It really kind of evokes another era, even the style of what they were about and the way they were shot as opposed to the later years. I don't know, I just never really liked those later ones.

Are any of those out on DVD?
We don't have any out on DVD yet. I get asked that all the time. They were out on VHS for a while. Columbia House was marketing them, but that was probably about ten years ago now. I wish TV Land or Nickelodeon would show them again. They did start running them in '85 on Nick at Nite for a while, though.

I remember. And they showed the old black-and-white ones, and I don't remember ever seeing those before.
Well, they *weren't* seen. In fact, a lot of them weren't seen at all. Because in those days we shot thirty-nine shows so they would show thirty-nine, and then only thirteen more to finish out the year, and the other thirteen weren't seen. So when they finally got around to doing that in '85, they were really just being seen for the first time in twenty-five years. Those were kind of fascinating to see. And that introduced them to a whole new generation.

Were you anything like Chip?
Probably a little, but I was a real person and had real friends, so I was probably doing more stuff that I wasn't supposed to. (*Laughing.*) Fortunately, I never got caught. Don't get me wrong. It wasn't anything that anybody else didn't do. I wasn't out robbing banks. Maybe I was driving a little too fast, or maybe smoking something here and there, but that just wasn't done on TV.

Tell me about Don Grady (Robbie Douglas).
He's a good guy. He's an amazing musician and composer. Even back when we were doing the show, he was developing his music, played every instrument, and was always up there writing in his dressing room. In fact, his dressing room was right over our schoolroom so we'd hear him up there all day long working. And that's how he makes his living now. He's a composer, an arranger. He writes a lot of stuff for the Learning Channel, and the Discovery Channel. He has composed music for a lot of shows at Universal Studios, and he's done some eclectic stuff as well. I think he did the music for the 1996 Democratic Convention.

What was it like working with your brother?
Barry and I get along, so it was great. We actually shared a dressing room, and we'd ride to work and ride home together. We had a bedroom we shared at home. It was an extension of that. I don't remember us ever really fighting.

How much younger is he than you?
He's three years younger. He looked a lot younger than he was.

Are you guys still close?
Yep. Real close.

Why did the show go off the air in '72? Was it canceled, or did Fred want to stop?
We were actually pretty high in the ratings, but what happened was in 1972, the FCC changed a lot of the laws about ownership of shows and how they could be distributed. Our show was originally owned by Don Fedderson and Fred Mac-

Murray, who sold the show to the network in 1967, and continued to produce it under a license for the network. So the actual rights were transferred to CBS and they were the actual owner of the show. So then in '72, the FCC came up with laws that said the network was not allowed to produce shows anymore because they were considered a distributor. So the attorneys and the FCC worked out something where CBS could only keep one show, and they chose *Gunsmoke*. It was their flagship show. I think it had been on the air for almost twenty years. So they euthanized the other shows and we were one of 'em.

And you know all those laws I was just talking about? They've all been quietly undermined and the very same thing is going on now with these monopolies, and I think it has ruined TV. What they were worried about is vertical integration, which means the studio is not only producing it, but they're showing it, they're controlling total content. There's no free market, meaning producers on their own creating shows, so you have a depth and breadth and point of view coming to the network who could only buy them from the producer. That's just free enterprise. Our nation is based on that. But these greedy little piggys at the top decided "Why don't we own everything? We'll not only make the things, but we'll distribute them." And they quietly eroded all those laws away. And while they were at it, they said, "Hey! While we're making this, it'd also be good to own a movie studio, and a couple of cable companies." So now, it's like you have three or four companies running everything and you either work for one of those, or you don't work. You're either with the Viacom-CBS-Paramount conglomerate, or the Disney-ABC conglomerate, or the Channel 4-NBC conglomerate. I think it has just killed creativity and the free market in television. They've just hushed all voices, and if you're doing something controversial and they don't like it, it's never going to be seen! That's totalitarianism at its finest. They're in complete control of what you see and hear, and that's what the FCC was trying to stop in '72. Somebody got paid to look the other way, and now that's where we're at. The Screen Actors Guild is trying to address that at this point.

Oh, are they?
Yeah. There's a lot of things wrong with it from the actor's point of view. Say you're in a TV series, and you've done it, and now five years has gone by and they

want to syndicate it, which is where all the residual money is, so instead of selling it on the free market to whoever bids the highest, they just say, "Hmmm. We're CBS. Why don't we just sell it to Viacom? We already own that, and guess what? Instead of paying five hundred thousand dollars, why don't we pay a dollar? We'll give the actor his one percent, he now gets a penny. But if it sold for five hundred thousand dollars, now we have to give this guy fifty-thousand dollars."

Unbelievable.
Yeah. It's just totally insidious what's going on. It's all vertically integrated, so it keeps people from getting their rightful shares. It's just a legal way to cheat you out of all your money.

I see your point. I've never really given that much thought. It sure gives you something to think about.
Yeah, it's really bad.

How was it to have Tina Cole and Beverly Garland join the show?
I think it kind of rejuvenated it. Having the element of women in the show kind of took it away from what it originally was, an all-male household. It also kind of made it more interesting. The characters were growing and it just made sense. I thought it was a pretty good idea introducing women. Though it took the show in a different direction, it was a welcome relief. I think it helped in terms of where else to go with the show. I mean, how much more were they going to get out of us all being bachelors?

Tina was great. We had like a real sex symbol working on our show. She was part of the King family; the King Cousins, and that was a lot of fun. Beverly was nice too. I really like her.

Do you ever do any of the autograph shows at the Beverly Garland Hotel?
Yes. I see her all the time. Her hotel is right down the street from me and the documentary that I just produced we actually shot at Beverly's hotel. We used one of the big convention rooms there.

What's Dodi (Dawn Lyn) doing now?

I don't really know. I got an e-mail from her a while back. I know that she remarried and recently moved to Hawaii, but that's all I know about her.

So tell us what you've been up to recently.

Actually, I have two projects going on at the moment. I just got finished producing a movie called *Checkers* that hopefully will be released in '07. We're doing our distributor screenings right now.

What is *Checkers* about?

It's a black comedy. It's kind of the opposite of *My Three Sons*. It's about a father that comes to visit his four sons, and he's not well received. It has an edge for people that are baby boomers, because when you get to be our age, it's about your parents kind of circling back in the later part of your life and how they're received sometimes isn't too well 'cause some parents weren't the best parents in the world. And then a lot of times the kids don't want to take responsibility for them. It's kind of a timely theme. We screened it at a film festival last year, and it was really well received. We were shocked! Not that we didn't think it wasn't good, but you just don't have any idea until you get it in front of an audience. But they got the nuances of the black humor in it. It's pretty much about these sons passing the dad back and forth to each other. Then you find out some things about the dad that you didn't realize at first. The sons are all sort of damaged goods because of this guy. It's interesting how the story plays out and the bit of redemption that comes at the end. It's a timely story because a lot of us are starting to deal with, or have dealt with our parents. It's a pretty good little film. I'm really proud of it.

Sounds interesting. I'd like to see that. What's the other project about?

It's called *The Actor's Journey for Kids*. It's basically an informational program on DVD for parents who are interested in involving their children in the movie industry. In this day and age, it seems there are hundreds of thousands of parents that want to do this for whatever reason, and the information on the business

A grown up Chip.

side of the industry has not really been unavailable till now. It has nothing to do with craft, or learning how to act. It's totally about the mechanics of the business, and for some reason, that's just not taught anywhere! It's a way to let people know what over one hundred industry professionals and veterans really learned in their twenty or thirty years in the business. It makes better sense of the motion picture industry and a lot of the things that are not touched on by the entertainment channels. They basically show people walking down the red carpet, and that's not really what our industry is about. The industry professionals who participated in this project and are disseminating the information are highly credible. A lot of the people in it have won or have been nominated for Emmys, Oscars, and Cleos. The depth of the information you're getting is amazing. I've seen a few of these tapes done before about "How to Get into Show Business," and they usually only last about 20 or 30 minutes and say to get a picture and a resume, and try to get an agent and start working. Well, if it was that easy, everybody would be doing it. This project is four DVDs. It's five hours long, with thirty segments that really touch on all the really, really important topics. This thing took about five years to make, because we really wanted to cover everything from A to Z, because we're just tired of seeing people get damaged or ripped off. So once people avail themselves of the information here, they probably stand a pretty good chance to get in, because they'll know what they're doing. I'm hoping that this will revolutionize the way people get into the industry and what they know before they get involved, and give them the tools they need to do it.

That sounds like it's something that's long overdue. I think you should have a great response to that. Good luck with that.
Thanks.

Stan, I appreciate your time. I've enjoyed this immensely.
You're welcome. It's guys like you that keep us alive and in people's memories.

[Stan Livingston lives in L.A. and continues to work in the entertainment industry by directing and producing documentaries and films.]

Jon Walmsley
Jason Walton: 1972-1981

The Waltons first began visiting our homes on a weekly basis in the fall of 1972. The heartwarming drama of a large, loving family living in the rural mountains of Virginia during the Depression of the 1930s, struck a genuine chord with audiences all across America.

Surviving stiff competition from *The Mod Squad* and *The Flip Wilson Show*, it continued its climb into the top twenty, and into the hearts of viewers.

Engaging storylines and strong acting garnered the series several Emmys during its run, and the fond "Goodnight's" said at the end of each episode became the series most endearing trademark.

Jon Walmsley, now 50, portrayed red-headed Jason Walton, the third eldest of the brothers, and the family musician. As affable as the character he played, Walmsley enthusiastically shared his time on the series.

Jon, a lot of people are unaware that you had done a lot of television prior to playing the role of Jason.
Yes. I had been acting for a few years before that. I started acting when I was ten.

What was some of your previous work?
I had done several shows including *Combat, Daniel Boone, My Three Sons, The Bill Cosby Show, Adam-12, Nanny and the Professor*. I did a feature film for Disney called

The One and Only Genuine Original Family Band, and I had been the voice of Christopher Robin in the *Winnie the Pooh* cartoons for Disney.

So you had quite a resume before *The Waltons* came along.
Yes. So *The Waltons* was kind of just another audition for me. They wanted a boy with red hair and freckles who played the harmonica, and I did. So I got the part.

In the Christmas movie *The Homecoming,* Patricia Neal originally played the role of Olivia Walton. What was she like to work with?
She's just so wonderful. She is very warm, and very, very funny; exceptionally funny, and a fantastic actress. She's very candid. She'll tell you anything about her life and career. She's just a hoot!

Do you know if she was offered the role of Olivia Walton, when the series began, or were they looking for a different interpretation of the character at the time?
I think she would have wanted to do it, but they thought that she wouldn't be interested in doing a television series. So we were very lucky to get Michael Learned.

How long after the show began did you realize it was becoming so popular with the audience?
It actually took a little while to catch on. We had very stiff competition. There was actually a "Save the Waltons" campaign that was started. People said, "Hey, you've been asking for something family-oriented on TV, and now here it is, so you better watch it." And luckily they did. By the end of the first season it was number one and had won some Emmys, and was in the top twenty for a pretty long while after that.

What type of schedule were you on?
Early on, I was going to school on the set for three hours a day. That would be interspersed with shooting. We would do twenty minutes of school at a time

A first-season cast photo. Clockwise from bottom: Kami Colter (Elizabeth),
Mary McDonough (Erin), Ralph Waite (John), Michael Learned (Olivia),
Jon Walmsley (Jason), Will Geer (Grandpa), Ellen Corby (Grandma),
Judy Norton (Mary Ellen), Eric Scott (Ben), Richard Thomas (John-Boy)
and David Harper (Jim Bob).

while they were lighting the set. We'd get there early in the morning and do
make-up and wardrobe, then we'd go to school. Then when they were ready
to rehearse the first scene, we'd rehearse it, then we'd go back to school. Then
when they were ready to shoot it, we'd go back to the set to shoot, and then
we'd go back to school again. It was three hours of school, four hours of being
on the set, and an hour for lunch.

Where would you take classes?
We had a studio classroom, but sometimes it might actually be on the soundstage, or in a trailer outside. We had to be very close to the set at all times.

How long did it take to complete an episode?
It would take about six and a half days to do one show, and they were not shot in sequence. For example, we would spend entire days doing inside scenes, or entire days doing outside scenes. All of the kitchen scenes would be done at the same time, or all the scenes at the mill or the barn would be done at the same time for that particular episode.

Where was the exterior of the Waltons house?
It was on the back lot at Warner Brothers.

Talking about the exterior reminded me of one of my favorite episodes called "The Burnout." The Walton homestead catches fire and you all had to be separated while the house was rebuilt. Do you remember that episode?
Yes. I remember that well.

Was the exterior of the house actually destroyed for that particular episode?
No. It was all controlled. They had the part that looked like the inside of the house all rigged with gas jets, and they could turn them on and off. And, of course, they had a lot of fire people on hand to make sure that nothing got out of control. The house did eventually burn down, but it wasn't on that show.

What do you mean?
There was a fire on the lot later that actually did burn down the exterior of the house, but it was after the series was over, and the studio eventually rebuilt it for the reunion shows.

What is Michael Learned like when she isn't playing Olivia Walton?
Michael is much more worldly and sophisticated than Olivia Walton. She's a fantastic actress, and incredibly versatile. She's had tremendous stage training and experience and she has a wonderful sense of humor. She's very funny. We were just really lucky to have really talented people who were unique and fun to be with. We all just clicked personality wise.

The Waltons watch their burning home in a scene from "The Burnout."

And Ralph Waite?

Ralph, actually, was a minister before he became an actor. Ralph is a wonderful person and an incredible actor. Not long after Ralph began *The Waltons*, he went in Alcoholics Anonymous, and he became very active with that. I think he credits *The Waltons* for that; turning him around, because he said he really didn't feel that he could play this guy on television *and* be an alcoholic. And the thing was, we never knew! It never affected his work in anyway.

We had this crew member that was a big jokester, and one day Ralph came to work and this guy said, "Ralph, we never knew you were a drunk until you came in sober." (*Laughs.*) It was funny, but it was true. It never affected his performance. He just decided that it was the right time, and the right reason, and that's what he was going to do.

He's such a compassionate guy. He really likes to help people. At one point he made a movie called *On the Nickel*, which was about the bums on skid row. I think it's Fifth Street in L.A., where all the homeless people hang out, so that's why they called it *On the Nickel*, because Fifth Street was called the Nickel. He did that to try to bring attention to that and try to help people. Later, he did the same thing when he went into politics. He really was a champion for the under-dog, and it's a shame that he didn't get the chance to do more in office. But he still continues to do so in his private life and that's the important thing.

What are your memories of Will Geer?
Will was actually very much like his character on the show. His friends used to tease him about taking money for playing himself. He was tremendous. We would go on walks sometimes, and he was an expert on flowers and plants. He could tell you the Latin name and the common name of every plant that he would come across. He'd say, "You can eat this one. You can use this one to put on your skin." You know, all that kind of stuff. It was just amazing.

I used to perform with him sometimes away from the set where he would do these concerts and readings where he would do portrayals of Mark Twain, Walt Whitman, and Robert Frost. And he would also sing Woody Guthrie folk songs. He also started a theater that still exists, The Theatricum Botanicum, in Topanga Canyon.

And Ellen Corby?
Now Ellen was very different from her *Waltons* character. She was a world trav-eler, and she'd been to India and studied transcendental meditation under the Maharishi. She was very sophisticated. The Grandma character was very differ-ent from what she was like. She never had any grandchildren, and I never had any grandparents, so when the show started, we kind of adopted each other and became very close. She was always especially supportive of me and my music. We used to do a lot of things together. She wasn't married, so she would call me when she was going to something like the Emmy Awards, or the People's Choice Awards, or the CBS affiliates dinner, she would invite me to be her es-cort. So I'd put my tux on, and go pick her up, and be her date for the evening. So that was a lot of fun. Sometimes I'd just go to her house and hang out.

Will Geer passed away one summer while the show was on hiatus. Was that news unexpected?
Yes. Very! He hadn't been sick or anything like that.

How did you hear about it?
We all got a phone call.

And Ellen suffered a major stroke.
Yes.

What do you remember about that?
We were in production and she didn't show up for work that day, which was completely unlike her. Eventually someone went to her house and discovered her there. The amazing thing about all that for me was that she was able to recover and come back to the show. I think that's the only time that anyone that had suffered a stroke played a stroke victim on a series. I think that was to her credit and to the show's credit that it was dealt with that way. I thought that was terrific.

It sounds like she had a great attitude about getting back in there and working through it.
Yes. Yes, she did.

Tell me about Richard Thomas. What is he like?
Richard is extremely bright and really funny. He's a terrific actor. He could memorize lines instantly. It was just amazing. He was like my big brother. We would hang out together and do things away from the set. He was just a few years older. I couldn't drive early on, so he would drive me places and we'd go do things. We had a great time during those years.

Do you feel that it hurt the show when he and Michael left?
Yes, I think so. I think the show was the strongest when everyone was there, because the ensemble interaction was one of the best things about the show.

Were the other members of the cast aware that they were leaving? Had they talked about it, or was it more of a surprise?
Yes. We all pretty much knew.

Do you keep in touch with your Walton siblings?
Yes. As much as we can. Eric Scott [Ben] is a great guy and has a great family. Eric went through some rough spots. He lost his wife at the time that she gave birth to their daughter. Around the time that she was due to give birth, they discovered that she had leukemia. So they took the baby but they were not able to save her.

That's tragic. But later he remarried.
Yes, he did, and he's very, very happy now. He has a great wife, and they had two more kids together. He's doing great. He is the president of a courier company, and they're very successful. He started there years ago as a driver, and now it's his company.

Judy [Norton, eldest daughter Mary Ellen] recently moved back to the area. I have not seen her for a few months, but she's back in L.A., after living in Canada and Northern California. She seems to be very happy. She has a son that's around eleven. She's still doing a lot of acting and directing.

David [W. Harper, youngest brother Jim-Bob] is such a sweet guy. He was always kind of sensitive and artistic. He's doing great. He's lived in various places but he's back in L.A. now as well. He's gotten very interested in music, not so much as a career, but a hobby. He's very good at it. He writes songs, and sings, and has done some performing. He credits me with kind of getting him started by teaching him guitar, but I don't really remember that I showed him that much. I heard him play maybe a year or two ago and I was so impressed by how good he was and how good his songs were. I asked him, "When did you learn all this?" And he said, "You taught me!" And I don't remember that! Everything he did he did on his own. That's my perception of it.

I read that Kami Colter [youngest sister Elizabeth] became a teacher in Virginia.
Yes. In college her major was in educational studies for rural areas. That's how she came to be a teacher in Virginia. She was there for a few years and did well,

Jon and I meet at an autograph convention in Chicago, 1997.

and liked it very much, but then she decided to move back to California, to be near her family. Her parents are still out here. She's now headmaster for a school in West L.A.

Mary McDonough [Erin] is probably the one I see the most often because we only live about fifteen minutes from each other. It's funny because when I was in Sherman Oaks, we lived about ten minutes away, and now I live in Long Beach and she lives in Westminster. So we both moved about an hour south.

It's nice to hear that everyone still keeps in touch. Do you have any favorite episodes of the show?
There's one I like called "The Gift." Ron Howard was in it, and he played my best friend that was dying of leukemia. He was great to work with. That was a lot of fun.

Then there was one where Merle Haggard was the guest star, and we got to play some music together. That was a lot of fun for me.

One of my favorites was a later episode, "The Best Christmas," where Olivia wants everyone to be together one last time for the holidays. But a tree falls through the roof of the church, and you and your dad are called away to help get it repaired for Christmas services the next morning, Miss Fanny's car goes off the bridge into the icy water, and all kinds of things happen to take everyone away from home on Christmas Eve.

Yes. I remember that one. That was a good show.

John Ritter played the minister.

Yes. He was just incredible. He was exactly how you see him. He was funny all the time. None of the stuff that he did was a put-on. He was just naturally funny, but also very sincere. A lot of times, you feel that with comic actors, a lot of what they do is all put-on. John wasn't like that. That was just his personality. He was a very down to earth person.

Tell me about Earl Hamner.

Earl was the ultimate Southern gentleman. We still stay in touch. We're actually working together on a CD project right now. It's a spoken-word CD that he wrote, and I'm writing the music.

Music seems to have played an important part in your life. When did your interest in music begin?

I was always interested but I started to play the guitar when I was eight, and I started performing shortly after that. That's actually what got me into television. The first time I appeared on TV was a kind of amateur talent contest at a local station in L.A. I was seen by some producer and asked to audition for a film, and as a result of that, I got an agent and started auditioning for other shows.

What different kinds of instruments do you play?

I play a lot of different instruments, but my primary interest is the guitar. I also play a lot of bass, keyboards and drums, but when I do gigs, it's primarily on guitar and bass.

Did you take lessons, or did it come to you naturally?
I started by taking lessons, but after that, I also started playing by ear. When I was around twelve, in junior high, I started playing the cello in the orchestra, and the flute in marching band.

A few years ago, I bought a *Waltons* Christmas CD called *Together Again*. You produced that, didn't you?
Yes, I did. I also wrote some of the songs on it. A lot of the cast was on that.

I also have an old, old *Waltons* Christmas LP.
That's the one that none of us kids are on! (*Laughs.*)

Yes. Will Geer was the only cast member on it. And Earl Hamner did the narration, of course.
Yes. That's right.

As the show progressed, were you allowed to give any input into the storylines?
A little bit here and there. If we had a suggestion for our characters, we would offer those.

Did you have time to read any of the fan mail you received?
I tried to, but it was tough. I got a fair amount, and I was working and going to school. It was difficult.

What was it like when you went back to do the reunion shows?
It was a lot of fun. The funny thing was, it was like no time had passed. That was the weird thing. It was so funny and actually very lucky that we all clicked when we first met, and then after not having worked together for years, it was like not a day had gone by. It was pretty wild.

Did you like the way the characters turned out all those years later?
Yes. I think so. For my character, they kind of used my life as a prototype for how

A shot from a *Waltons* Reunion.

Jason turned out. At the time I was doing a lot of work in Nashville, and that's where they had Jason going. They borrowed a lot from my actual life.

You're more into the music end of the business now, aren't you?
Yes. I play music full time. I do a lot of live performing, and I work with a lot of different bands, and I do sessions for television shows. I also do some producing.

Do you have your own band?
I do, actually. I have a British Invasion band called The Ravers. We have our own website at www.theravers.org. You can actually hear some song samples on there. I also recently did a show in San Diego called *Primal Twang*. It was a musical about the history of the guitar. It featured a lot of amazing and famous guitar players each playing in various styles. Doc Watson was in it. Eric Johnson did the rock part of it. Albert Lee did the country side of it. And there was classical, and jazz, and flamenco. It had pretty much everything that you could imagine, covering the whole history of the guitar. They filmed it for release in DVD. It was unbelievable and a lot of fun. I can't wait to see it!

What kind of music do you enjoy playing the most?
I do a lot of different kinds of music. I play more rock than anything else, but I just like good music in general.

Well, on that note -- no musical pun intended ...
(*Laughs.*)

I have one last question for you.
Sure.

What are you most proud of about being a part of one of the most beloved shows in the history of television?
I think it would have to be the way that it has affected people. It meant something to them. It enriched their lives and in a lot of cases, helped them through hard times. I've heard a few stories about that that were really touching. We never even

thought about that when we were doing it. We just intended it to be entertainment, but I've heard some pretty amazing stories of particular episodes that had deep meaning for people and really helped them through things. It sometimes changed their lives. That part of it is pretty amazing and gratifying.

Jon, thank you for sharing your experiences on *The Waltons* with me. You've grown up to be a very nice and accommodating guy. John and Olivia would be right proud. (*Smiling.*)
(*Laughs.*) My pleasure.

[Jon Walmsley is an accomplished musician, composer, and producer. He enjoys making appearances with his band and meeting fans of the show. He lives in Long Beach, California.]

Ernest Thomas

What's Happening!! & What's Happening Now!!:
Roger Thomas 1976-1979; 1985-1988

What's Happening!! *was* a 1970s hip, black, urban ABC comedy, loosely based on the film *Cooley High*. The popular series originally debuted as a four-week mid-summer replacement in August 1976.

Centering on the relationships of three high school friends, Roger "Raj" Thomas (Ernest Thomas), Dwayne Nelson (Haywood Nelson), and Freddie "Rerun" Stubbs (Fred Berry), the show became an immediate hit, landing the initial four episodes in the top ten.

Shirley Hemphill played snappy, sassy waitress Shirley Wilson who worked at Rob's Place, a local soda shop hangout for the boys. On the home front was Roger's no-nonsense single mama played by Broadway veteran Mabel King, and impertinent younger sister Dee (Danielle Spencer), who was continuously zinging one-liners, and tattling to Mama about the trio's latest escapades.

I spoke with Ernest Thomas about his time on one of the funniest and first all-black shows of that era.

How did you get the role of Raj?
Actually, I auditioned for Bud Yorkin and Saul Turteltaub, and from there they took me to Tim Flack at ABC. Afterwards, there were still a lot of call-backs and screen tests. I was one out of two-hundred or so actors they were looking at. It was based on the film *Cooley High*, and everyone was trying to get that. There were not a lot of black shows on at the time, so every actor and his mother,

literally, were trying to get on it. How it really all began was I did an episode on *The Jeffersons* that was very well received.

How was that experience?
Oh, it was incredible. I was on cloud nine, and Sherman Hemsley actually told me, "You're good. You're gonna have your own show." And then Mary White, who was the agent for Isabel Sanford, told me, "They have this new series that you should audition for. You'd be perfect for it." At that time, it was called *Cooley High*. And that's how it all began.

Some of the characters on *What's Happening*!! had the same last names as the actors. You and Haywood Nelson used your last names, and Shirley Hemphill's first name on the show was Shirley. Whose idea was that?
Ours. We were given choices. We could choose our names because when they changed it to *What's Happening!!*, then it wasn't going to be totally like *Cooley High* anymore. They said they would give us a choice for names, so I decided on Roger, because I stayed at the Roger Williams Hotel in New York when I was studying acting, and then I chose Thomas for good luck.

So Shirley chose her character's first name.
Yes. Sometimes I wish I had done that. (*Laughing.*) Then I wouldn't be called "Raj" so much.

Does that bother you?
No. Not really. I graduated from The American Academy, and they send you out knowing that you have the ability to do an array of characters and emotions, so you aren't going to be pigeon-holed. It was part of the training. It's not like I was discovered off the street and that's all I ever knew. But then, you realize that people just love you. Muhammed Ali helped me with that. He said that people simply feel that they know you, and love you. And out of all the millions of people in America, God chose you to bring this kind of entertainment, and to make people happy when they're having a bad day. And he also pointed out that you should

never correct people and say, "Oh thanks, but my name isn't Raj. It's Ernest." 'Cause then they'll look at you and say, "Yeah, and your name's also Asshole!" (*Laughs.*) Even when we were doing *Malcolm X*, Denzel [Washington] was telling me to tell people that I wasn't Raj, because we would do locations, and people were going nuts, knocking on the dressing room door, things like that.

Really?

Oh, yeah! One time we were all in the make-up trailer and they knocked on the door, and started doing the [Raj] laugh and the dance. And Denzel said, "Man, you gotta tell them that you're not Raj. This is a serious movie." But James Mc-Daniel, who was later played the lead on *NYPD Blue*, said, "No. Why would he do that? That would be insulting to the people. They're just coming from their experience."

Well, I have to agree with that, because when you think about it, it really is a compliment; that someone would love your character that much.

Yes. Yes. And people are always happy! They're all giggly and everything. Even last night, I was at a party and this lady came up and she was telling me about her son who was ten years old, and how he has all three of the [*What's Happening!!*] DVDs. Then she called him while I was there, and I talked to him. I was just totally dumbfounded, 'cause he was telling me, "Yeah. I have all three DVDs, and I remember that one where you did this, and this...." Now we have a whole new generation of kids watching. Kids come up to me and they'll recite verbatim what I did, how I stood, what Rerun did ... It's almost surreal. This past August was our thirtieth anniversary. We debuted August 5, 1976. It's just amazing to me!

I read that it originally began as a four-episode summer replacement.

Yes. Four episodes, and all in the top-ten.

Are those four shows included in the first-season DVD?

(*Thinking a moment.*) Yes, they are.

Is there any particular episode that people mention the most?
Oh, the Doobie Brothers ["Doobie or Not Doobie, Pts. 1 & 2"]. I get a lot of
comments about that one with Michael McDonald and all those guys. We just
all got like brothers.

A nice group of guys?
Oh, my God, the best! You couldn't find better people on earth.

**That was a two-part episode. Because of their schedule, did you actually work
two weeks or was it all done in one?**
I think we got it all done in one week. That was a lot of fun. Janet Jackson even
came by that week to get autographs, because she was doing *Good Times*.

How would you describe the character of Raj?
Raj is everyman. He's everyman's best friend, every mother's favorite son, and
every teacher's favorite student.

(*Laughing*.) Right. Just ask Miss Collins.
Yes! (*Laughs*.) To me that's what it was. That's how I really see him. In *Cooley
High*, he was a little slicker. And Glynn Turman did an incredible job. I loved
Cooley High. It's still one of my favorite movies. But that wasn't me. I wasn't
"street." But that "every man" stuff was in me.

When did your interest in acting begin?
Actually, in college. I was a late bloomer. I went to Indiana State University, where
Larry Byrd later went, and I had my mind set on being a social worker. I was study-
ing sociology and psychology. But then I took an acting course, and a friend of mine
said, "Ernie, you are really good! You could do whatever those guys are doing on
TV."

What did you like best about "Raj"?
I liked that he represented hope. Everything was going to be all right. Even
though he got into a little mischief, you knew he was gonna do the right thing.

He was gonna somehow pull it all together. I liked the morals he was taught by his mother, you know, she's a no-nonsense mother. She's a good example. He got a lot of that from her, and I hear that from people all the time.

The "Raj laugh" is a classic trademark of the show. How did that come about?

We had great writers, but no matter how good the writers are, every show has lines that you know are just so-so. It just ain't workin'. You just can't get the laugh. So I'd say, "I just don't get it." And they'd say, "Well, you don't, but Raj thinks it's funny." You know what I mean? Raj has this corny sense of humor and to him it's funny as hell. Every time, if the joke was so-so, I'd go into that laugh, and people loved it! That's how it came about. I'd be out in the street and people would say, "Do that laugh for me." Sometimes, I'd have to say, "No. I just don't do that," because I was being asked *all* the time, and sometimes I just didn't have the energy!

Elizabeth Montgomery from *Bewitched* was said to be the same way about twitching her nose. She hated to be asked. Whenever she was out, everyone would say, "Twitch your nose! Twitch your nose!" And she would politely decline.

(*Laughing.*) Yes! I can relate! People from all walks of life know the Raj laugh and the Raj dance. People like Muhammad Ali, Sugar Ray Leonard, Tupac, rappers, to Southern whites and rednecks, to Asians, to Spanish Harlem, to gang members. It's just amazing.

Tell me about the set. Was it fun to work on?

Yeah, it really was. I tell people it was like heaven on earth. I prayed for that. I don't believe in luck. I know a lot of people do, and I don't knock that, but when you refer to me, no. I can't use that word. I literally prayed for it, and I got it. I believe in that. I was taught that. From the time that I was born, I was taught that if you have faith the size of a mustard seed, you can move mountains. I believed that. As a child, I bought into that. There was nothing that God couldn't do. But being human, you're still amazed! You're like, "God, you really did this!" So you're still in awe that it happened, and here you are on this set, doing something you love with these people you love. And it's real!

Was each show taped once or twice?
At that time, they had two audiences on the taping days. So you did two shows. One was a dress rehearsal, then the real show. But they used stuff from the dress rehearsal.

So they would take the best parts of each show and put them together.
Absolutely.

You and Mabel King had great chemistry. I was watching an episode last night where you and Rerun graduate ["The Apartment"]. There was such a nice feeling between Raj and his mom. In all the episodes, it came across that they were close; that he loved his mother, and she loved him.
Yes, and I have the greatest mother in the world in real life, and I'm a mama's boy, so that was easy to play with Mabel. She always called me her son. She was multi-talented. But at times we'd bump heads, because she was very strong-willed. She bumped heads with the producers, and wasn't on that last year.

That was one of my questions. Did they let her go, or did she just want out?
She wanted more control of the scripts. And, you know, they just don't do that! She didn't have that type of power. You have to be getting a hundred-thousand letters a week for that. So they let her go.

Do you think that she was surprised?
Well, they did try to reason with her. They gave her a counter offer. She wanted script approval, x amount of money, and they countered it. Then when she didn't want that and insisted on more, that's when they let her go.

So she had the chance to stay.
Oh yeah. She had the chance. They didn't *want* her to go. She just would not receive the revised offer.

Do you feel that it hurt the show when she left?

(*Long pause.*) Ah, it's hard to say. I really don't think so because the focus of the show really was the three guys and their relationship.

Do you think she later regretted her decision not to come back?

She probably wouldn't admit that, but I believe in her heart of hearts that she regretted it. She was a multi-talented lady. She could fluently speak French. She did theater in France. She wrote songs and scripts. She could sing her butt off. She was agile on her feet even with the weight. But it didn't mean anything to this industry, no matter how talented you are. You have to have the power, meaning that you can prove the numbers, and that you can make a dent with the dollar sign. And she couldn't.

Tell me about Shirley Hemphill.

Shirley was to me, and still is, one of the funniest people that I ever met. She's naturally funny. She knew she could get me laughing and I could not control it. She could say things that went right for the jugular. You wouldn't want to get into a "Yo Mama" war with her! (*Laughs.*)

Who did you have the closest working relationship with during the show?

Well, at various times it was different. Initially, Fred and I were close. He would come over a lot and tell me about his problems. Then Danielle got really attached, being she was nine. She wanted me to spend time with her. And Haywood was like my little brother. And I'd have to say with Haywood and Danielle, it has lasted.

That's nice to hear.

As I look back, they've always loved me as a big brother. Always came over and made fools of themselves, showing me what they could do in the pool, that kind of stuff, expressing themselves. And back then, I just wasn't hearing it. I didn't get it.

But, thank God, we're at the stage now when I can tell them how much I appreciate them, and not take them for granted, and thank them that they loved me all that time. Now I get it. I'm glad I could come to that. It's like, "Wow, Man.

Danielle Spencer (Dee), Shirley Hemphill (Shirley), and
Ernest Thomas (Raj) in a dream sequence from "Dwayne's Dream."

They really truly love me!" They've kept in contact even when the show was over.
They'd want me to meet a girlfriend or boyfriend if they were going with someone.
They wanted me to talk to that person. "What do you think of them?" And you
realize that's a big thing for them to value my opinion. Even today, they give me
that love, and I love them dearly. They're just like my brother and sister.

What are some of your favorite episodes?
Well, definitely the Doobie Brothers. Then I would have to say "No Roger, No
Rerun, No Rent." I like that one, and I love the one with the older woman where
I thought the landlady liked me ["The Landlady"]. That one was dramatic and
had the comedy. And I like the one where Fred and I compete about who's the
best lover. ["Making Out"]

Did they save any gag reels from the show?
You know, I hope they did.

That would have been enjoyable to watch on a DVD release, or if you all had done some commentary on the episodes. Did they ever talk about that?
You know, we really didn't get why they didn't do that. Even Haywood said, "I can't believe they're not doing commentary." People would've loved that. That surprised me.

Was there anyone in particular that was the hardest to get back into character if they blew a line or got tickled?
I think we *all* had our moments. If it wasn't your day, you'd just get so tickled. And we had our inside jokes. Even beyond what the audience knew. We'd all have our little inside things, and we loved to see the other suffer.

If you had a line that worked throughout rehearsal and the crew is laughing up a storm and now, you get in front of the audience and it bombs, it was a "cricket." A "cricket" we'd call it. You'd do a line, and then it's just silence, then someone under their breath would say, "Crickets." And we'd be all over the floor. They're laughing at your expense, but it was funny. Actually, I liked when we weren't perfect. It was more fun.

When you did the last show for season three, did you know at the time that it would indeed be the "last"?
No, I didn't know until I read it in the paper. It was in *The Hollywood Reporter* that we had been canceled.

Did you keep any of your scripts or mementos from the show?
You know, I don't think I have any of the *What's Happening!!* scripts. I wish I had. I have some *What's Happening Now!!* scripts. A lot of stuff got lost in moving around. I have one of those old cast pictures that everyone had signed. One of my friends in Ohio had that, and he gave it to me.

How did the idea for *What's Happening Now!!* come about?

What's Happening Now!! was really my idea. I had wanted to bring the show back, and they told me that would not be possible, that there was no audience for it. So I did what I always do, which is go against the grain, and tried to write something anyway. Then we got a letter writing campaign going but then I decided that was going to take too long. So I went ahead and presented the treatment to Herman Rush at Sony. He was very nice and sent me a note saying thank you, but there's no audience. So I thought, "Well, at least I tried." And that was it. And then months later my agent called and said, "Ernie, guess what? They're going to do another *What's Happening!!* series." They did some research and found out it was more popular in reruns than it was in prime time. And the rest is history.

How did the rest of the cast initially feel about it?

Even some of the cast said, "Ernie, it's over!" They loved my energy and enthusiasm, but they said, "We did that already. Let it go, babe." (*He laughs.*) But I didn't. And that's what I tell kids when I'm doing appearances: to never forget you have to move to the beat of the drum within you, and that if everyone else is out of sync, and say that you're crazy, if you believe in your heart of hearts that God is putting something on you, you have to keep going! Doing another *What's Happening!!* didn't make any sense to most people. It wasn't logical.

Well, it was unprecedented. I believe it was the first prime time show to ever be revived in syndication with most of the original cast reprising their roles.

Yes. Yes. That had never been done before.

And it paved the way for revivals of syndicated shows like *Mama's Family*, *Gidget*, and *The New Leave it to Beaver*.

Absolutely.

Why was Danielle Spencer only in a handful of episodes? Was she offered the chance, or did she not want to do it?

The producers just said they didn't see her doing a lot of them. I went to them and asked to put her on more. I just didn't get it.

Raj is about to meet his maker in this photo from an
episode of *What's Happening Now!!* ("The Challenge")

Did she want to do more episodes?
She wanted to, yeah. I even asked the entire cast to come with me to the producers. I remember that day. I said, "Look, we're gonna have to speak on her
behalf." And they [the producers] weren't mean at all, they just said they'd try
to fit her in, but I guess when she was young, it just fit better.

Did the cast go with you?
Yes, they did. Even with Mabel, I tried.

That was my next question. Was she asked to reprise the role of Mama?
I tried. I told her to come to the taping and I told the warm-up guy to make
sure and really make a big deal about her, because we were trying to get her on
the show. So maybe the producers will see how popular she is with the fans. I
thought Mabel could perhaps be prepared to sing or something.

So, was she for it?
Yes. She was all for it. I told the warm-up guy to ask her to sing during a break in the
taping and tell the crowd, "Oh, we have Mabel King who played Mama here tonight!
Mabel, you sang in *The Wiz*, and you were so great! Could you sing something for
us?" And she did. She had the people on their feet, and it still didn't do anything.

So she would have come back.
She *wanted* to come back. They just didn't want her back.

Had you known she was ill before she passed away?
Yes. She had been ill for years with diabetes.

I read where she lost her legs due to diabetic complications.
Yes, and I would go and see her sometimes. She was getting very depressed, understandably, a lady with so much talent. We had Muhammed Ali call her. And
the last time I saw her, we had a big birthday thing. I emceed it at Marla Gibbs'
club. Stephanie Mills said she couldn't make it, so I asked if she could videotape
herself with a birthday greeting, which she did. And that was a big surprise for

Mabel. She really loved that. She was very touched by that. But, understandably, it was a very sad time for her.

But there again, we all have to be careful of our health. Especially blacks with diabetes. Diabetes and high blood pressure is a big thing. It took Nell Carter and Fred Berry from us. You have to eat healthier. Because no matter how talented a person is, the body is the body. It doesn't care about you getting an Oscar. If you have heart problems, and you won the Oscar, you still have the heart problems. You have to take your medicine, and you better not party all night long, and just eat whatever.

Tell me about Shirley. She died very young.
Shirley was very close to her mother. She lived for her mother. She was motivated by her mother. Her mother was her be all, end all. Her father had left, so she was determined to make her mother happy. And she did that.

We were doing *The Vibe* show and she told me that her mother had passed. And when she told me that, I just had a chill go through my body because I knew Shirley would not be long. I just knew it.

So you had a feeling.
Yes.

Was *The Vibe* the last time you saw her?
Yes. We were catching up and she said, "We lost Mama." And I'll never forget that.

So you weren't totally surprised when you heard about Shirley.
Right. Not surprised. She had been dead for two days when they found her. The gardener actually found her. She kept changing her phone number. At *The Vibe* show, we knew she had the kidney problem, and we said, "We're gonna keep in touch. We're all we have left! We made history together, so we're gonna keep in touch."

But she kept changing her number. I think she was proof that someone can die of a broken heart. I think she just did not want to have the medicines, or have anyone to revive her, or call 911. I think she wanted to go out just like that. If she really wanted to live, she would have made provisions to live, you see.

I remember seeing her on a show shortly before her death, and she had lost a tremendous amount of weight, and I remember wondering if there was something wrong with her, because she just didn't look well.
Yes, she had the kidney thing.

I read that Fred had a stroke before he died.
He said he didn't, but I heard he did, from that diabetes thing. That's debatable.

Were you surprised when you heard about Fred?
Yeah. I was *really* surprised about Fred. That was definitely a surprise. We thought it might have been one of those things with people saying someone died. Haywood actually called me and said, "Did you hear that Fred had died?" And I said, "Oh man, they say that stuff about us all the time. We all died at some point in time." He said, "Well, should we call around?" So we finally got the roommate's number and he said, "Yeah, he died." And we were just stunned. I remember Haywood had to get off the phone. The guy kept talking and we were both just silent. So Haywood got off, then I said I had to get off too. We just couldn't deal with it. It just didn't make any sense.

How far into *What's Happening Now!!* did Fred begin making demands for more money? Do you think he thought that they would never really let him go?
I think he thought he *was* the show; with the fat jokes and all. Just like Mabel. Fred and Mabel were similar in that sense. They both thought that they were indispensable.

So it was basically the "I want more money, or I'm walking," kind of thing?
Yes. They tried to reason with him like they did with Mabel, but he felt he was indispensable.

But the show continued, and it was funny as hell.
Yeah. And that paved the way for Martin Lawrence.

Do you think Fred regretted his decision?
Oh sure. He probably wouldn't say it, but when people have this fake self-esteem, that sometimes happens.

And being a celebrity, don't you find that there are always people around telling you how wonderful you are, pumping up your ego, telling you that you are indispensable, so that you actually begin to believe all the hype?
Absolutely. And Fred had people in his ear doing just that. Each time he did that, he had a guy telling him that he basically was the Messiah, and without him there was no show. And the cast knows that too. So don't try to go in with them, because they're part of the problem too. Fred would tell you, "I am the show. Without the fat jokes, there's no show."

When was the last time you saw him?
It was actually with another friend of mine who's a fraternity brother. He and Fred became very close. They were like best buddies. So that friend called me one day and said, "Let's all get together." So we did. And Fred was listening to Greg and I talk about our college days because that was new to him. He enjoyed listening to our stories.

Anne-Marie Johnson played your wife on the show. She was very attractive, and a very good actress. What is she doing now?
I see her in a lot of stuff. She worked for a homeless foundation, feeding people, and things like that. She was always very much into charity.

You said you and Haywood are still close. What is he like?
To me, Haywood is a Renaissance man. People don't get it. He's not Dwayne by any means. He's a philosopher. He can debate on any issue. He's very well read. He's a licensed pilot. He has a degree in Engineering. He mountain climbs. He's a computer whiz. He's actually a great writer.

What kind of things does he write?
He can write anything. Dramas. Comedy. Again, he's not Dwayne.

Would you call him a nice guy?
Definitely. He's definitely one of my favorite people. He's my brother, no doubt about it.

You told me that you're writing a book which details your life coming from Gary, Indiana. What is it called?
From Raj to Riches. It's kind of a motivational biography. Anyone that reads it will definitely know that if I made it, they can!

[Ernest Thomas lives in Los Angeles and is an actor, writer, producer, and manager. He currently has a recurring role as the funeral director on the popular CW sitcom *Everybody Hates Chris*. One of his great passions in life is connecting with young people and fans when he travels throughout the country as a motivational speaker.]

Haywood Nelson

What's Happening!! & What's Happening Now!!:
Dwayne Nelson 1976-1979; 1985-1988

E rnest Thomas was right about his co-star. The real Haywood Nelson is about
as far as you can get from the naive and gullible character Dwayne Nelson,
whom he portrayed from 1976-1979. Nelson would later reprise the role in *What's
Happening Now!!,* an unprecedented eighties revival of the original series.

Articulate and interesting doesn't begin to describe this dynamo, who, to most,
is best remembered for uttering the trademark catch-phrase, "Hey, hey, hey!"

Haywood, when did you become interested in acting?
When I was five, my godmother worked with a man whose family member was a
manager, and she was gathering a roster of children. So when my mom got a call
from my Godmother about whether I'd be interested, she asked me if I'd like to do
commercials. So I said, "Sure. Okay." So I went down and met the manager, had
a really good time, did a photo shoot, and began going on auditions and booking
commercials right away. So, I don't know if I can say there was a certain moment.
I was just asked if I'd like to and from there, we just went for it.

How did you land the role on *What's Happening!!?*
I was on a show called *Grady* with Whitman Mayo [A spin-off of *Sanford and Son*].
When it was canceled, Whitman Mayo, who played Grady, came to me and said
he had something else he wanted me to check out. He thought it would be really
good for me, and wanted me to get back to New York right away. So my mom and

I went back to New York, went to the audition, and at that time, it was called *Cooley High*. When I walked in, Danielle Spencer was there auditioning, and Mabel King was on stage, and I went up and auditioned and I got it! It was, at that time, for the role of Pooter in *Cooley High*. Then they brought me back out the very next week, so I was only home in New York for one week before I had to come back to California. Then we began reading for *Cooley High*, and began rehearsals. That's where I met Ernest, Fred Berry, Shirley Hemphill, and *officially* met Danielle Spencer and Mabel King. Then I came to realize that the production team was the same production team from *Grady*, Saul Turteltaub, Bernie Orenstein, and Bud Yorkin. TOY Productions. Then, in their little battle with Eric Monte, who wrote it, they switched it from *Cooley High*. They asked all of us what we should call it. They said, "What's a popular term?" And I was like, "What's happenin'?" And they all said, "Yeah!" So they went with that name, and then they had us each name our characters, and I named mine after somebody I grew up with, and pretty much based the character Dwayne after somebody we called Smiley in my neighborhood. (*Laughs*.)

And you chose your real last name.
Yes.

How would you describe Dwayne?
I think that Dwayne was a very naive, young, adolescent. He was someone who was somewhat insecure, but instinctually sure of himself, if that's possible. He had his insecurities big time, but the things that told him yes and no, he was very, very adamant about. Thus the words, "Uh-Uhhh!" (*Laughing*.) I took a lot of guff for saying "Uh-Uhhh!" at first, because people were saying that I was allowing myself to portray Dwayne as somebody who was uneducated and dumb, and it wasn't reflecting very well on youth, and not encouraging them to speak proper English. I remember addressing that on a panel once. I said, "Look, first of all, it's a situation comedy. It's not reality. Secondly, he's a young teenager. He's not supposed to be a rocket scientist." That kind of pissed me off. So I kind of got on 'em in that panel. (*Laughs*.) Dwayne wasn't a dummy. He knew when he wasn't interested. He was also a cool guy, and liked the ladies.

Do people try to get you to do the "Hey,hey,hey!" thing all the time?
Everyday of my life.

Do you ever get tired of it?
I don't get tired of it; I just don't think it's always appropriate. And I don't let other people pick and choose. I do.

Ernest said the same thing about the Raj laugh. Sometimes he says he just doesn't have the energy.
I can understand. I *never* feel like doing "Hey, hey, hey." Especially because it's not something that I would just say arbitrarily. It's something I would say if I was entering the room. I used it as an entrance on the show, and if I'm not entering, it's not appropriate. But I have said it for people, because it makes people smile, and really that's what it's about.

In the theme song during the first couple of seasons, there's a clip where you ride out of the driveway on a skateboard and as you begin to turn onto the sidewalk, you fall off. Was that planned, or did the camera just happen to catch it?
(*Laughing.*) I was actually supposed to turn the corner and go down the street. I was a very good skateboarder, but not that particular day.

(*Laughing.*) Well, it made a good clip.
It was an excellent clip, but it didn't make for a good behind! I felt that! (*Laughs.*)

Where was the show taped?
In Los Angeles. We started off at KTTV, and then we switched to KTLA.

So it wasn't at a studio like Warner Bros.
No. We were at independent studio lots. Channel 11, and then we went to Channel 5. Even though it was coming on ABC, we shot at their different studios.

What was a typical work week like for the cast?

We worked a five-day week. We were in there about nine or ten o'clock in the morning on a Monday. We'd do a reading for the entire executives of the network and the producers, and we would read it cold. We had never seen the script before. So we'd sit down at the table to a cold reading, and read it for the first time as the characters. Then the writers would get a feel for what worked and didn't work, and they'd go back to the drawing board and start rewriting.

We would then go out on the stage with Mark Warren, our director, and begin the process of blocking, or walking through the very rough choreography of the staging; the entrances, the exits, and where we crossed to, what camera and all that. Then we'd pretty much end the day early.

Tuesday we'd come back early and start blocking again, doing the foot choreography all day long, and starting to learn the lines, and starting to put the book down. We'd put down the script. Then we would get changes. They'd give us those before Wednesday, because Wednesday night we'd have to do a big dress rehearsal for all the producers. No book in hand. No wardrobe. Just walking through the entire show on Wednesday night, like it's a real show. And you pretty much had to know it.

Then come Thursday, we would go for the first time on camera. We would rehearse it so the camera could learn what was going on. All the lighting, the sound effects, and everything would be rehearsed. Then at the end of the day we had a full dress rehearsal, with full make-up and wardrobe, not only for producers, but also the executives at ABC. And we would do the whole show from top to bottom. The whole thing.

Then they would go and write all their changes and revisions so that when we came back in on Friday, we would start walking through it again with all the new pages and all the new changes. We basically had to relearn the whole script. Then once we relearned it, then we would block it, and rehearse, and rehearse, and rehearse. It was hot with the lights but we'd go over, and over, and over it again, until they'd say, "Just one more time. We had a little bit of trouble here with the camera." And we'd do it again. That was all day long until the near end of the day. Then we would go get into full make-up and wardrobe. All the extras would come, and all the atmosphere actors, and then we would go out and do the show in front of a live audience. They would introduce us, and we'd do the show once. Then, we'd go and eat dinner, get into wardrobe and make-up again, and come back out for the real big show. We did it in front of a big audience again, but this time, with all the energy and all the changes.

After that, the audience would leave and we'd stay and do pickups. They'd repair whatever didn't work right or whatever they missed, like sound effects, any kind of voice-overs, things like that. And then we could go.

So Friday was a very long day.
Yes. Friday was a rough day. But you know, Thursday was the harder day to me. Friday was a great day because you had the audience. They'd pump you up. Thursday was tough because you were on your feet all day long, and you couldn't move. I remember my feet would get very uncomfortable. You had to stand in place and rehearse, and get your light right. Sometimes they would bring in our stand-ins, but for the most part it was just us standing there in those hot lights.

Are you a quick study with your lines?
(*Laughing.*) I used to be. I guess I pretty much am.

What works for you in helping you memorize your lines?
For me, it's all about getting it and walking with it in my hand, and getting a feel for the room, and where I think I should be by what line. And then after I do that a few times, I start to improv a little bit. Saying my own lines.

They didn't mind you doing that?
Yeah. They hated it! (*Laughs.*) But I did it anyway. I would say my own lines, and use my own improv. I'd improv the whole thing as I walked through it. I'd say lines that had the same likeness of what is supposed to be, and from there I could get my natural feel. Then I would go back and commit to their words, and try to get their words as close as possible with a little bit of improvisation of my own thrown in.

What are your memories of Mabel King? What was she like off-screen?
Off-screen? Very different from on-screen. Mabel was a black Mae West.

(*Laughing.*) Really?
Yeah. She'd say, (*imitating her*) "Hey baby. Come here, baby. Why don'tcha come over here and give Mama a hug. And then go to the store for me."

(*We laugh.*) That is funny.
And that's just how she was.

Tell me about Shirley. How would you describe her?
A very sensitive genius. She was so sharp. I'm in awe of all stand-up comediennes; every single one. And please print that because it means everything to me. They are the epitome to me.

Shirley started out in stand-up, didn't she?
Sure, and remained so throughout the entire duration of the series and afterwards. Like her peers, she was so intelligent, so quick. Their wit, the comebacks, the thinking on their feet, the lines. Even though she was tough-talking in her routine and in her role portrayal, she was one of the most sensitive people that I've ever met in my life. Oh, my gosh. You'd say one thing wrong and she'd start welling up with tears. We had to be very careful with Shirley. She was very sensitive. But that's what you loved about her, you know?

A sweetheart, huh?
Very. Completely. That's why she was always hurting. People would act like jerks, and they would hurt her. The tough-talking character she played wasn't like she really was. It was very interesting for me to watch that dynamic.

She was also a very practical person. I liked that about Shirley. She was very frugal with her money. Very smart. She invested in real estate. She drove a Volvo. She was very, very practical. Unlike myself. (*Laughs.*) The first thing I had to do was go get me a Toyota Celica, then I had to rush and get me a 280 Z Datsun. That's my head.

How old were you when you started the show?
I was fifteen.

What are your memories of when the Doobie Brothers were on?
That was the first time I was ever on a rock tour in my life because we got to actually be with them. That was an amazing process to me. Listening to the sound checks, watching Michael McDonald sit up there and start vocalizing a capella. To get with Jeff Baxter and his guitar and watchin' him just rippin' off some licks. It was just hot!

And they did this "mini-concert" right in the middle of the show! That had to be a first.
Yeah! It took us two weeks to shoot. We did a week with them, and I remember they came back in, and did a couple more pieces. We did our full week, but it wasn't our normal week, like the week I described to you earlier. It wasn't that kind of week at all. We had the aspects of it that were typical, but then there was the concert part of it. That was a big, big venue. Then afterwards, I remember us doing some pickups. Not the first Friday night, but the next.

When you were doing the show, who do you feel you became closest to?
I would have to say Danielle and Ernest together. There was a real camaraderie between Danielle, Ernest, and myself. It was a lot of fun some of the things we did together. Whenever we had scenes with just the three of us, we bonded. It was just so unique. We were completely out of our minds. We couldn't even say our lines. We'd laugh constantly.

Then there were these times when I felt like not so much an outsider, but I had come from Broadway, and had already done *Grady* at that point, so I felt like I had to be the serious one, and do some "serious acting." Not knowing at the time that Ernest had done so much theater and how talented he really was.

What did you do on Broadway?
I was in *Thieves* with Richard Mulligan. Ultimately, we started off with Valerie Harper, but ended up with Marlo Thomas. It was an incredible cast when I

think about it now. Professor Irwin Corey, Pierre Epstein, Sudie Bond. All phenomenal actors!

What were Valerie and Marlo like to work with?
Incredible! Valerie, first of all, is to die for. Oh my god. Working with Valerie Harper? Are you kidding me? She's such the professional. She's so good in theater! She was just so trained and loving, but tough at the same time. I really, really enjoyed her. I learned a lot by watching her and listening to her. But with Marlo, it took a while for me to get adjusted to her.

Why was that?
She was more of a TV star than a theater actress. I didn't get that same gritty feel that I would get from Valerie or any of the other women in the cast. I had to get accustomed to her. But, oddly enough, that alienation thing that I felt with her is what helped with my character. But I had some tough times on Broadway with Marlo. If I flubbed a line, she was not very fast to feed me the next line. That's just something you do in Broadway, and something you do in acting class. You learn how to just stay in the moment and work with whatever is comin' at ya. No matter what, you never stop the performance.

So she took a little longer to help you get back on track?
No. Not longer. She'd be totally stumped! I forgot my lines repeatedly for one week at the very same place. And she didn't know how to help me get by that hurdle I was having. And as a result, it put a real stop in the show.

Did she get upset with you?
I think everybody did. I was mad with myself, because the bottom line was, as soon as the scene was over I could go and do the whole scene from memory. But I couldn't understand why I was having this glitch at this same point every single time. Eventually, they put up my understudy and they weren't happy with what he was doing, so they asked me to get back up, and when I went back up, it was fine.

What do you think changed for you?

I really think it was because I was tired. I was a fourteen-year-old who was going to public school every day, then rushing into the city and doing my homework on the subway, then getting into make-up and doing a show, and staying there for notes until twelve o'clock at night. Then getting into the car with my mom and dad, and driving back to Long Island, and falling asleep in the car, and then getting to bed, and then up, and then to school again by 7:30. So after doing that for two years, I think it caught up with me.

I imagine that might have something to do with it. (*Laughing*.)

Yeah. I just needed a break. I got about four days of a break and then I was fine.

When you were doing *What's Happening!!* were you going to public school as well, or were you being tutored?

I was being tutored on the set. But I was still attending public school. They were sending my work to my tutor.

Did you ever watch any reruns of the show?

Well, I know them all. I have occasionally gone through them to see if I could use any of it on my acting reel, or if a particular show wanted to do a segment on me, and they'd need some footage, I would go and look at different episodes to pick something where my character was featured.

I've caught it on TV Land a couple of times when I was flipping the channels, and I left it on, and ended up laughing my head off. I'd remember the scene. I enjoyed *What's Happening!!* It was a funny show!

What are some of your favorite episodes?

I think one of my favorites is the one where they had to try and sell what they had purchased at the auction at the church, and they had the moped, and they needed to sell the moped. And Dwayne outbid everybody, and they ended up buying their own moped back. [He could be referring to the episode "Black and

White Blues," where they break a TV set meant for a church auction.] And, of course, the Doobie Brothers episodes ["Doobie or Not Doobie, Pts. 1 & 2"]. Then I'd have to say the one where everyone is betting on football games based on Dwayne's hunches, and come to find out, he's basing all his hunches on the color of the team's football helmets ["Give Me Odds"].

Recently, I caught the one where Dwayne gets a job selling peanuts, and he's wearing this big old peanut on top of his head ["Dwayne's Dream"].
Yes. I remember that one. That was *not* one of my favorites. (*Laughing.*)

What's Happening!! ran for three seasons. When you did the last show of season three, did you think you were coming back for another one?
Absolutely. I had just bought a home for the first time. I held off for three years and then bought a house, and bought a Porsche. I was livin', you know? And then I get this phone call in March that we were canceled, and it disrupted my entire life.

Did they explain why?
There's a lot of opinions out on it. But to the best of my recollection, there was a little bit of something going on. This is my conspiracy theory. I believe because *What's Happening!!* was successful, there was an anxiousness to begin the business process of syndication, of which we were a test-bed for.

They say that's where the money is.
That's right. That's where the money would be for the producers, who I felt were a little disgruntled and sick of the whole thing, because Ernest Thomas and Fred Berry had made it a living hell for them. Ernest and Fred were a handful. They were rough. They were in their twenties. They were partying every night, having parties out at Ernest's house in Malibu. And they had walked off the show.

I have heard that.
You wanna know a funny thing? I was on the internet one day, and some website said that *I* had walked off the show. They claimed that *I* walked off the show because I felt I deserved more money; that I was better than everybody else. I

was sixteen years old! If I had walked off the show, my mother would've clocked me in the head with a shoe! There's no way! *They* walked off the show. We were out of work for like four to six weeks while we waited for them to try and negotiate a better contract. If I remember correctly, they didn't get a better contract, so they came back to work.

I see.
I had a meeting with Bud Yorkin, Saul Turteltaub, and Bernie Orenstein and they let me know that they were very tired of what had been going on. They were very, very upset with it all. So I believe they made a choice to syndicate it, which means they could still make good money, but they wouldn't have to deal with all the nonsense. So they canceled us in a very suspicious way.

Are you saying that this is what actually happened?
This is what I saw happen. This is Haywood's view of what he saw occur. And since there were only three seasons of the show, they decided to bring us back as *What's Happening Now!!* so there could be more episodes included for syndication. That's my take on it. I wasn't happy about it. It disrupted my acting career. It pissed me off enough to say, "F--- it! I'm going to college!" And I broke away and went to school. I went to school for architecture, and from there to electrical engineering. I left engineering to do *What's Happening Now!!,* and then when it was over, I went right into camera and cinematography for feature films. I began as a loader, then a second assistant cameraman, then I started pulling some focus, and then operating.

Tell me what a focus puller is.
A focus puller is somebody who sits on the camera with the camera operator, and maintains all the distances in a particular set. He knows where each actor is and how far he is from the camera and he can rack, they call it racking or pulling the focus, and turn the dial to make sure that the lens is always focused to whatever is the subject at the moment. It's a very important job.

Operating has always been a goal of mine. After acting, and loving my acting, which is my first passion in life, to be cut off so abruptly like I was, I got disgruntled and said, "Now, wait a minute. You can't do that to me. From now on, I'm gonna find a way to control my future and destiny a little better than that." And I sought out to do that, and I'm still on my pursuit today.

Tell me about the fan mail you received during the show.
We got tons of it. And being the teenager, I was in *Tiger Beat Magazine, Right On Magazine,* and all that. I couldn't answer it all! I couldn't, man, and I felt so bad about that. That's the one thing that I have some regret about. It was too much for me. I had a fan club and they started answering some of it with generic letters. They'd say on behalf of me, yada, yada, yada. But for a while there, I was trying to answer them all myself but it was way, way too much. I couldn't do it, and do the show at the same time. Plus, I was going to school.

So the studio doesn't help with that?
They would collect it and made sure they delivered it to me at the studio.

But, I meant, didn't they supply you with photos to send to fans?
No. Not at all.

Did you keep any of your scripts?
All of them. Every last one. Not just one, I kept every *version*. Remember, I said like on Monday we'd get one with white pages, then they'd start rewriting, then we got the pink pages, then we got the blue pages, then we got the green pages. I kept a copy of each of the revisions of every script as well as all the ones on *What's Happening Now!!* also.

When you were on the show, did anyone ever stop by and visit the set that you were especially excited about meeting?
Yes. Only one.

And who was that?
Muhammad Ali. Ernest brought him by. Oh man, that was the biggest treat to me in the whole world. I didn't know what to think or say. I was just so happy to meet him. He was awesome.

The show was incredibly popular, and I know there are tons of perks, but what are the down sides to being so famous that most people don't realize?

It's not being able to do what I want to do in public. Friends or family would say, "Let's go here. Let's go there." And I felt that hesitation because I felt like I couldn't go. But I'd go anyway, and then I'd get mobbed. It's rough. My family all understood, but where it became difficult was I was not able to go to amusement parks. One of my favorite things to do in the world is to ride roller-coasters. I love them! Always have, always will, and I couldn't do it. There was no way. Even now, I'm having problems. While people look at my face and they go, "I think I know him from somewhere," the moment I open my mouth and they hear my voice, I'm done! I'm toast! (*Laughs.*)

Did you enjoy reprising your role of Dwayne Nelson on *What's Happening Now!!?*

Well, at the time, I was trying to finish two degrees. I had finished architectural school, then I jumped into engineering, and I wasn't able to finish it. My agent called me up and said they were bringing the show back, and they wanted me to consider the contract. So I read the contract and went ahead and went with it. I was a little disgruntled by the fact that I think the contract stunk.

Really?

Yeah. And I wasn't smart enough to listen to my attorney who told me not to sign it, and I signed it anyway. I don't think it was a great contract at all.

Did you feel that you wouldn't be a team player if you had not signed?

I felt very much pressured to sign it. Like I told you earlier about what I read about myself on the internet holding out for more money, then that would have been true. It would look as if I'm trying to act like I'm better than them, and I don't feel like that *ever*! So, I signed it, thinking it was a favored nation's contract, meaning what one gets, all get, only to find that wasn't the case. Others had negotiated better contracts for themselves, so I was pretty upset by that. Then beyond that, it bothered me that the new producers not only seemed to have less knowledge about the original cast and the original characters of the show, they didn't seem to have an interest, either. They wanted to do something *new*. And I don't think you can do something new. It bothered me because *What's Happening Now!!* did not have the same essence of *What's Happening*!! It really upset me.

What I was happy about was that Ernest was being given a chance to really do his thing. I enjoyed his acting so much that I enjoyed that part of it. But I did not enjoy the fact that they were stifling Dwayne, maybe not on purpose, but by the fact that now it was focused on Raj and his wife. There was less to be done with the three guys, and I understand that, but it just bothered me because it didn't give me much to do. So by the end of it, I felt like I was just walking through the whole thing. And acting is not that for me. I could have stayed in school.

Did you have any input into Dwayne's character?
No, and when I tried to write some scripts, they turned me down. They said that they already had all the scripts they needed. I tried to direct and they turned me down again, saying that it had already been promised to other people who had come before me.

You're kidding!
No! And I asked them how they could possibly promise other people to direct before considering the actual, original cast of the show.

That's exactly what I was thinking.
But they told me there was nothing they could do. So at that point, I realized that the producers were not committed to the same quality that the public expected and that the rest of the cast wanted to deliver. It very quickly became just a check. It's like let's just walk through this, let's get it done, get paid, and move on.

Has there been any talk of releasing *What's Happening Now!!* on DVD?
I haven't heard anything. I think what they would probably do is put it out on TV Land first, and then release the DVD.

A headshot from *What's Happening Now!!*

How did you feel about Fred walking off of the show?
I was really pissed off with him, because it was the same old thing that was going on back in the seventies when he and Ernest did it. But at least this time, Ernie was sticking close. I was really upset with Fred for doing that because had he held his position, they were going to spin Dwayne and Rerun off into a series of our own.

That's interesting. I've never heard that until now.

That's when Rerun got his apartment and then Dwayne moves in and they became roommates. We were becoming a new "Odd Couple" and he blew that! It was totally going our way. But everyone has to make their own choices. I'm not trying to make him wrong. It's just that strategically it was not a very good move. But he did it for his own reasons, and you have to respect a person for doing what they believe.

Did you ever talk to him about it afterwards?

Sure. Fred and I were really close. There was a time when Fred and I even shared a house together. We were roommates. And even during the original show, I used to go up to San Francisco with him and his wife and we would hang out for the whole weekend and go to jazz concerts, ride horses on the beach together … We were very close.

But I know that in the end he regretted it, because it became very difficult for him to do anything. That's when he got stuck in the whole thing of being Rerun, and changed his name to Rerun and *became* Rerun. I have to be honest, though. Rerun was not part of *Cooley High*. Rerun is Fred Berry and what he brought to the part. The name Rerun was something that we all kind of named him, because he had been repeating the twelfth grade so many times.

So that's where the name came from.

Right. He had been in the twelfth grade for three years in a row.

(*Laughing.*) Right!

Thus the name Rerun.

Do you think it hurt the show when Fred left?

Yes.

When did he leave?

It was the second season. He did the first season. He didn't do the second or the third.

When was the last time you saw him?

The last time I saw Fred was at the premiere of *Dickie Roberts: Former Child Star*, the movie. Then we went to the after party at the roller-skating rink, and he was just sitting by himself. I guess he was really going through it. He had had a slight stroke, so he was walking with a cane, and I guess on the red carpet that kind of blew him out 'cause everyone was like, "Rerun didn't have a cane. Rerun dances and flips in the air!" That made it a hard pill to swallow.

I was trying to comfort him at the after party, especially because the character in *Dickie Roberts* was somewhat like what Fred had become: somebody who lost his own identity, and became the identity that he was known for. It was almost like it was a spoof on him. I don't think it was written maliciously like that, but it came across like it was a spoof. Ernest and I talked about it the night of the premiere. We watched him before the movie. He was all pumped up, and after the movie he was all deflated. Then we saw him at the wrap party and he just sat by himself. He wouldn't engage. They wanted to interview him but he wouldn't interview. I was trying to get him to come and hang out, but he wouldn't, and that really upset me. It bothered me, so after that I called him a lot, just trying to talk to him on the phone and see if he was okay. Then a few weeks passed, then a month, and I hadn't talked to him because I was traveling back and forth to New York. Then I got the phone call that he had passed away when I was back in New York.

Were you surprised when you heard the news?

I was completely shocked. *Shocked*. My cousin, who is a bass player in New York, had become very good friends with him. He called me and said that he had heard that Fred had passed. I went, "WHAT?! No! I know nothing about this. I'll call you right back." So I hung up and called Ernest and he said the same thing. But Ernest knew the name of his roommate, so we called him. He three-wayed me in, and the roommate told us that Fred had died the day before. That was devastating.

Ernest told me that at first he thought it was one of those rumors where they say one of you had died.

Oh, my God! You wouldn't believe it! I've been dead, I've been gay, I've been a Martian! (*We laugh*.) All kinds of stuff. That kind of stuff was happening constantly.

Did you keep in touch with Shirley?
Yeah, but you know, Shirley was a hard one to stay in touch with. She was tough. She changed her phone number all the time. But toward the end, I started calling her and spending Thanksgiving with her, 'cause she was by herself when her mom passed away, so I would drive out to West Covina and go have Thanksgiving dinner with her.

We spent two Thanksgivings together, and then I was planning to come back and spend the third one with her, but my dad was ill. He had cancer. So I spent it with my mom and dad. And I was trying to reach her, and when I called, her number was changed, and it was shortly after that that I found out that she had passed away.

Was that a shock to you as well?
Yes. Shocked. I knew she had been sick but I didn't think she was gonna die. I thought that she might have a long life of having to deal with the illness, but in a way, I'm glad she didn't have to deal with that. (*A pause*.) I still miss her.

Is there anything that people don't know about you that you wish they did?
Probably that I'm an avid adventurer. I am "Mr. Adventure." (*Laughing*.) I'm a motorcycle nut. I'm really into motorcross. One of the big things that I was into during the years when I was doing the show was motorcross racing in New York. I spent many years motorcrossing from the time I was eleven right up to the time I did the show. I was quite a veteran at that point. Broken legs, broken arm, the whole bit. Then, from there, I went into racing motorcycles from the track. I enjoy that.

What other types of adventures do you enjoy?
I mountain climb. I'm a general aviation pilot. I enjoy flying. I love boats. I'm a sailor. I'm a powerboat guy. I'm also a scuba diver. I love scuba diving and

shooting underwater cinematography. That's one of the hot things I love. But I don't think any of the passions are as strong as the motorcycling one on the track.

What are you most proud of about the show?
That it made people happy. It's so important that that's what it ended up being to me. It far exceeded my expectations. It permeated every culture, every generational group, and every gender. Everybody got something out of it, and it made them laugh and smile. It has never *once* been a negative thing for me. When people come up to me and talk about Dwayne, or the show, they always have something *positive* to say. They don't approach me as a fan; it's more like a member of the family. And that is a blessing.

[Haywood Nelson, an accomplished writer and producer, lives in California. He recently founded Igriot TV, an internet protocol television network. A form of new media, Igriot promotes everything from consumer-generated programming, to any research available on the many different types of cultures around the world and is available on demand from the internet, WiFi, and digital cable.]

Index

BearManorMedia

Can you resist looking at these great titles from Bearmanor Media?

   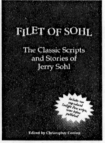

  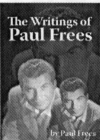 

We didn't think so.

To get details on these, and nearly a hundred more titles—visit
www.bearmanormedia.com

You'll be sorry!

...if you miss out.   P.S. Don't be sorry.

Printed in the United States
94412LV00003B/20/A

9 781593 931209